To Your Posts!

To Your Posts!

Fort Meigs in the War of 1812 through the Voices of Those Who Fought There

Larry L. Nelson

MICHIGAN STATE UNIVERSITY PRESS | *East Lansing*

Michigan State University Press
East Lansing, Michigan 48823-5245

Library of Congress Cataloging-in-Publication Data
Names: Nelson, Larry L. (Larry Lee), 1950– author.
Title: To your posts! : Fort Meigs in the War of 1812 through the voices of those who fought there / Larry L. Nelson.
Other titles: Fort Meigs in the War of 1812 through the voices of those who fought there
Description: East Lansing : Michigan State University Press, [2025] | Includes bibliographical references and index.
Identifiers: LCCN 2024056247 | ISBN 9781611865455 (cloth) | ISBN 9781611865462 (paperback) |
ISBN 9781609177911 (pdf) | ISBN 9781628955545 (epub)
Subjects: LCSH: Fort Meigs (Ohio)—Siege, 1813—Sources. | Fort Meigs (Ohio)—Siege,
1813—Personal narratives. | Harrison, William Henry, 1773-1841.
Classification: LCC E356.M5 N45 2025 | DDC 973.5/2092—dc23/eng/20250203
LC record available at https://lccn.loc.gov/2024056247

Cover and book design by Anastasia Wraight
Cover art is *Siege of Fort Meigs*, c. 1845, D. W. Kellogg & Co., Brown University Library Special Collections

---

Visit Michigan State University Press at www.msupress.org

DEDICATION

For Linsfield Bicknell, b. c.1782–d. 1862, private in Leslie Combs's Company of Spies, Kentucky Militia, April 17, 1813–June 3, 1813.

"On July 17, 1834, in Madison County Kentucky, Linsfield Bicknell, a resident of Estill County Kentucky, made application for an increase of pension, and further stated that he was a private in Captain Combs's Company of Militia in Colonel Dudley's Regiment and was placed on the pension roll on account of having received a wound in the shoulder with a tomahawk splitting the gap of the shoulder; and on account of it, the shoulder often slips out of place and is always in danger of being dislocated by labor; that he received said injury while in line of duty in said service on May 5, 1813 in Dudley's Defeat at a place called the Rapids of the Miami of the Lake opposite Fort Meigs in Ohio, and is still disabled in consequence of the injury."

"Leslie Combs, late captain of the spies of the Kentucky volunteers attached to Col. Wm. Dudley's Regiment, made oath on May 17th, 1819 that Linsfield Bicknell belonged to his company and was wounded as he stated on the 5th of May 1813, and with this deponent, was taken prisoner by the enemy."

"Linsfield Bicknell," Old War File 6647, Kentucky Militia,
Kentucky Historical Society

Contents

Preface

Fort Meigs was a U.S. military garrison built on the outermost reaches of Ohio's northwestern frontier during the War of 1812. This book recounts the history of Fort Meigs through the voices of those who lived and served at the post during the conflict. When we study the history of Fort Meigs and those who served there, that history, like all history, is a complex mixture of objective description, subjective recollection, cultural conventions, social or political exigencies, and an articulation of both individual and collective memory. This book relies upon what historians refer to as "primary" accounts to tell the story of Fort Meigs. Primary materials are those created by participants who either had firsthand experience in the events that they are describing, or were in a position at the time to have legitimate insight into those events. Historians understand that primary documents can sometimes be problematic—that they may lack perspective or context, often include portrayals that are incomplete or frustratingly vague, and are at times shaped by personal biases that can deeply inform both what was recorded and what was omitted when the account was first created. But the best primary sources are also unmatched in the detailed descriptions they provide for their creator's circumstances, in the emotional intensity with which they saturate past events, and in creating a strong sense of personal intimacy with the people and occurrences that they reveal.

Fort Meigs is fortunate to have a large and diverse collection of primary materials chronicling its past. The pages that follow rely upon diaries, journals, later reminiscences and memoirs, personal letters, official correspondence, routine paperwork, and other materials created by Britons, Canadians, Native Americans, and Americans who were both officers and enlisted men serving in the regular army, state militias, and volunteer corps. Hopefully, these materials will illuminate the lives of those who lived and served at the post during this moment of great peril.

Historians labor under the knowledge that their understandings of the past will always be imperfect. Despite its diversity, depth, and richness, the documentary record for Fort Meigs is exasperatingly incomplete. Women were at Fort Meigs in significant numbers. During the War of 1812, it was common for wives of noncommissioned officers to accompany their husbands into the field, where they were paid to serve with their husbands' companies as laundresses. Native women accompanying bands who had allied themselves with and lived among the Americans must have been seen in camp frequently. Further, the garrison was also home to American and "Interior French" refugees (French-speaking civilians who lived in the countryside far from Detroit) from the River Raisin and lower Maumee regions. These refugees included wives, widows, unmarried women, and children of both sexes. Yet women are mentioned only once in the numerous surviving sources: a single sentence in the general orders issued on August 1, 1813, noting that any married woman "who has or shall abandon her husband and shall be found strolling about the camp or lodging in the tents of other men shall be drum'd from camp."[1]

Likewise, African Americans were clearly at the post, but their presence is also diminished and, to a degree, obscured in the surviving documentation. Slavery was illegal in Ohio in 1813. But while African Americans at Fort Meigs are usually described as personal "servants" or "waiters" accompanying commissioned officers, their actual status is difficult to ascertain. Captain Daniel Cushing of the Second Regiment of U.S. Artillery noted that on January 1, 1813, while on the march to Fort Meigs, he had "sent all the officers and men to two houses in the neighborhood except two wagoners, my black boy Ferguson, and four soldiers who stayed with me." Cushing also reported that on March 29, 1813, Major George Tod of the 19th Regiment of Infantry "sent his young man out after his horse a short distance down the river this evening in company with some others; they all returned but his waiter, who is missing." The following day, Cushing noted that Tod "sent an ensign and a party of men this morning after his waiter; they returned, reported they could not find him."[2]

Perhaps the most telling episode illustrating the status of Black individuals traveling with the army was recorded by Lieutenant Joseph Larwill, Cushing's immediate subordinate in the Second Regiment of Artillery. Larwill related that while he and some of his men were on detached duty at Fort Stephenson at Lower Sandusky (present-day Fremont), "my Black boy Lewis was tomahawked by a private in Lieut. Maddes' company while he was engaged transacting his business at one of the sleds. Some misunderstanding took place between them which occasioned words between them. The private, named Patrick, struck him on the side of the head with the tomahawk which cut him considerable. Lieut. Maddes corrected Patrick for the offense. The boy was much hurt." Women and Blacks, therefore, along with others such as British deserters and prisoners of war, civilian contractors, and sutlers (civilian vendors licensed by the post commander to sell food and other items to the soldiers stationed there), await the discovery of further documentation before their stories can be completely known.[3]

This history differs from previous studies of Fort Meigs in several ways. First, the first siege of Fort Meigs centered on an action known as "Dudley's Defeat." In this engagement, Native forces fighting for the British destroyed an eight-hundred -man column of reinforcements from Kentucky led by Col. William Dudley. Previous histories have attributed the blame for the defeat squarely to Dudley and his undisciplined troops. This examination assigns an equal responsibility for the loss to General Harrison, who knowingly presented an overly complicated plan to soldiers having neither the self-control, training, or experience to accomplish his goals. Second, the British campaign against the fort in July 1813 has usually been characterized as an inadequately planned and ineptly executed prelude that foreshadowed a decisive and far more influential American victory at Fort Stephenson in the days following. This study argues that the British assault, while ultimately unsuccessful, was nonetheless a carefully considered and deftly prosecuted action.

Third, Fort Meigs was constructed originally as a supply depot and staging area to allow Harrison to amass the troops and supplies that would permit him to undertake an invasion of Canada. The post was extremely large, enclosing nearly ten acres. Following Perry's naval victory on Lake Erie, Harrison undertook his planned campaign to Canada, and the troops and materials housed at Fort Meigs were redeployed to take part in the Canadian invasion. The large, ten-acre post was demolished and replaced by a smaller, "second" fort that remained in service until just after the end of the war. Previous histories make virtually no mention of the fort following its reduction. This book's examination of the smaller fort's construction and occupation until the end of the conflict constitutes an important advancement to our understanding of the site and its continuing contribution to the war effort.

Fourth, the survival of Native oral histories describing their speaker's participation in the War of 1812 is quite rare. This study contains two Native accounts. The first, an extended memoir dictated by the Sauk war captain Black Hawk, has been known and used by scholars for many years. But the second, the translated and transcribed speech of four Shawnee "chiefs" to American authorities detailing their experiences while fighting alongside the Americans at Dudley's Defeat, has never been published. This document is an important addition to our understanding of Native participation within the conflict as American allies.

Lastly, this book's final chapter recreates a diary kept by Capt. Daniel Cushing from October 1812 through July 1813. Cushing served with Cushing's Company of the Second Regiment of U.S. Artillery at Fort Meigs, and his diary is the most extensive and detailed surviving account of the events surrounding the post during the war. Unfortunately, the diary suffers from a large omission where it appears that several pages have been removed from the original document. Those pages were transcribed in 1813 by another soldier serving at Fort Meigs and copied into his personal letter book. The version of Cushing's diary presented here, using the entries preserved in 1813, restores for the first time the full text of the original diary.

In the chapters that follow, the next ten relate the story of Fort Meigs in chronological order, beginning with its siting and construction at the foot of the Maumee Rapids in February 1813, and continuing through its abandonment after the war's conclusion in May 1815. The book's final chapter recreates Cushing's diary.

I have edited the following documents lightly, only so that they conform to modern spelling and punctuation. The commander of British forces in the Detroit Theater during the War of 1812 was Henry Procter. His name appears as "Proctor" in many of the early-nineteenth-century source materials. I have used the modern spelling throughout all of the documents that follow. Lastly, during the War of 1812 era, the name of the Maumee River had not yet been formalized. The historic sources refer to it variously as the Maumee, the Miami, the Miamis, the Miamies, or the Miami of the Lakes. In all cases, I have retained the designation found in the original document.

It's a truism that authors amass debts, and I'm no exception. This book is the beneficiary of many contributions from friends and colleagues. Furthermore, as we grow older, we all become increasingly aware of the indirect but lasting influence of others on our professional and personal lives that extends well beyond any particular project or work-in-progress. In 2022 we lost Randy Buchman. Randy enjoyed a nearly fifty-year-long career as a professor of history, archaeology, and museum studies at Defiance College in Defiance, Ohio. Randy's academic interest in Fort Meigs extended back many decades. His archaeological investigation of the site in the 1970s remains the only sustained, rigorous, and research-model-driven archaeological investigation ever undertaken at this important National Historic Landmark site. Moreover, throughout his distinguished tenure, his infectious enthusiasm instilled a love of history into generations of students. His wisdom, advice, and counsel informed the pathways of many who have gone on to prominent careers as public and academic historians and archaeologists. Randy exemplified what it meant to be an educator, mentor, and friend.

We also lost John (Jack) Ahern in 2022. Jack was a professor in the Department of Education at the University of Toledo. Jack based much of his career around a curriculum that emphasized local heritage and culture coupled with the use of local history, museums, and other community institutions to foster a deep appreciation of place and cultural identity. Numbers of Jack's University of Toledo students have gone on to long and meaningful careers as educators and administrators. Jack always had a story, always had a joke, always could make you laugh, always could make you forget your troubles and get on with the task at hand. He was a brilliant, engaged professor who was generous with his time, his insights, his humor, and his willingness to help. Every word in the pages that follow has been shaped in some measure by Randy Buchman and Jack Ahern.

Dave Skaggs, whom I studied under at Bowling Green State University, remains a trusted friend and advisor. My goal in this book has been to try to meet the high standards for scholarship and exposition set by Dave for his students.

Frank Melhorn, a Toledo attorney, has pursued an avid interest in Fort Meigs for many years. When Fort Meigs State Memorial moved from the direct administrative oversight of the Ohio Historical Society (now the Ohio History Connection) to a locally appointed and funded administrative model, Frank was particularly generous with his time, talents, and resources to ensure that the historic site was placed on a firm and sustainable operational footing. This book grew out of a conversation that Frank and I had several years ago where we both agreed that there was a need for a concise history of the fort that also introduced readers to the broad range of pertinent historic sources available to historians and other researchers.

Bill Pickard, a now-retired archaeologist with the Ohio History Connection who spent many a summer day at Fort Meigs investigating various aspects of the site's past; Ashley Phlipot, the current executive director at Fort Meigs Historic Site; Bruce Bowlus, my former Ohio Historical Society colleague and now happily retired from the history faculty at Tiffin University; and John Trowbridge, the former command historian for the Kentucky National Guard and former director of the Kentucky Military Museum in Frankfort, were kind enough to read early drafts of this book. In so doing, they focused my thinking, clarified my prose, and prevented me from making numerous errors of fact and interpretation.

John Trowbridge has devoted much of his career to understanding the history of Kentucky soldiers who served in the Maumee Valley during the late eighteenth and early nineteenth centuries. Because our research interests overlap, I had met John occasionally at conferences or presentations and had communicated with him about various matters over the years. After I retired, I became interested in genealogy and learned that I am a direct descendent of Linsfield Bicknell, a member of the Kentucky Militia during the War of 1812 who was wounded and captured during the first siege of Fort Meigs in May 1813. I am Bicknell's four-greats grandson. John is also a four-greats grandson of Linsfield Bicknell. After much reflection, I'm still not sure what to make of the fact that some 210 years after the battles at Fort Meigs, two heirs, widely separated but with mutual interests articulated within similar professions and career paths, would collaborate on a project that attempts to put some sense to what must have been the most unthinkably chaotic, excruciating, and terrifying moment in our common ancestor's life. Some things, I believe, simply reside beyond our ability to fully calculate.

I was aided immeasurably by the prompt attention of numerous archivists and librarians as I assembled the materials for this volume. Among the many staffs who assisted me in my research were those at the Burton Historical Collection at the Detroit Public Library; the Center for Archival Collections at

Fort Meigs and the Detroit Theater, 1812–1814.

the Jerome Library, Bowling Green State University; the Clements Library at the University of Michigan; the Filson Historical Society; the Genealogy and Local History Collection of the Toledo–Lucas County Public Library; and the Ohio History Connection. Many others responded anonymously to online requests for digitized materials held at other repositories.

Stephanie M. Lang, the editor for *The Register of the Kentucky Historical Society*; Donna M. DeBlasio, the editor of *Ohio History*; and Mary D. Young, the managing editor, and Kat Saunders, the assistant editor, for the Kent State University Press all graciously allowed me to present material here that had appeared earlier in their respective publications.

Lastly, Jackie, my wife of more than fifty years, our children, and our grandchildren have sustained my efforts with patience, enthusiasm, and good humor throughout my entire career.

This book has been materially strengthened through the hard work of many others. My debt to those who helped is enormous. To each, please allow me to say "Thank you." Any errors that follow are mine alone.

Introduction

The American War of 1812 grew out of the Napoleonic Wars, fought by France against a series of opponents consisting of Great Britain and her allies from 1799 to 1815. Asserting its rights as a free and sovereign nation and hoping to benefit economically from the conflict, the young United States declared neutrality in the contest and attempted to maintain trade and commercial relations with both belligerents. Both combatants protested America's willingness to trade with its enemy, but only Great Britain, commanding the largest and most capable navy in the world at the time, had the means to effectively impact America's trans-Atlantic commerce with France.[1]

Great Britain employed a full range of oppressive measures against U.S. shipping, including armed blockades; the forced search of American vessels and confiscation of American cargos; and impressment, the illegal seizure of American seamen off American ships to serve in the British Navy. British tactics became so aggressive that in 1807 the British ship HMS *Leopard* fired upon, disabled, and boarded the U.S. frigate *Chesapeake* off the coast of Norfolk, Virginia, in a blatantly belligerent search for contraband.

The incident raised already strained tensions between the two nations. Diplomacy cooled passions and, for the moment, preserved the peace, but

England refused to disavow the action. A series of economic measures, including an embargo against British goods initiated by the Americans and non-intercourse policies adopted by both European combatants, failed to quell the animosity, and American resentment remained high.

Maritime issues were not the only ones fueling the ill will between Great Britain and the United States. Violence between Native peoples and Euro-American settlers had declined significantly in Ohio following the 1795 Treaty of Greenville, which had removed Native peoples from eastern and southern Ohio and relocated them to the northwest corner of the state. Indeed, with the exception of those lands abutting Native territory, by the early 1800s such violence was virtually nonexistent throughout much of the state. In north-central and northwest Ohio, only sporadic aggression still occurred with any degree of frequency. But while rare in Ohio, such violence remained much more common in the territories adjacent to the state, particularly in Indiana.[2]

The vehemence demonstrated by Native peoples in the Indiana Territory was driven in large measure by the ambitious land acquisition policies of the territory's governor, William Henry Harrison. Taking office in 1800, Harrison had aggressively acquired title to millions of acres of land previously owned by the region's indigenous nations. Harrison's tactics were perceived to be so rapacious that in 1805, the charismatic Shawnee mystic Tenskwatawa (The Prophet, or Open Door) began to urge a religious and cultural revival among the region's Native peoples, calling for the restoration of traditional Native practices and opposition to the further cession of Indian lands. By 1808, Tenskwatawa was joined by his brother, Tecumseh (Panther, or Shooting Star), who fully endorsed his brother's vision but who also began to change the movement into one advocating strident political opposition and armed resistance. As the Indian crusade gained momentum and the region experienced an increase in the occurrence of Native violence, many of the territory's European settlers believed that Native warriors were being armed, provisioned, and equipped by British authorities across the river from Detroit. Native resentment was both genuine and deep-seated, to be sure, but did not require British involvement to be acted upon. Nonetheless, belief that the Indian violence was facilitated by British intrigue remained persistent and widespread.[3]

By 1811, Harrison believed that he could break Indian resistance by attacking Tenskwatawa and his followers at Prophet's Town, located at the confluence of the Wabash and Tippecanoe Rivers near present-day Lafayette, Indiana. In November, Harrison, at the head of one thousand troops, moved against the settlement. Tenskwatawa attacked the American force as it camped near his village, but Harrison was able to overcome the onslaught, defeat the village's defenders, and scatter the remainder. Most of the survivors made their way to northwestern Ohio and southeastern Michigan, where they could utilize easy access to British authorities near Detroit. The Battle of Tippecanoe, as it became known, had little lasting military impact. But it did harden Native resolve and pushed them closer to an open alliance with the British.[4]

Continued harassment on the high seas and the widely held perception that British authorities were colluding with Native peoples to foment violence on the nation's frontiers led the United States to declare war on Great Britain in June 1812. By doing so, America opened a conflict with one of the most potent militaries in the history of the globe. American military planners understood that they could never achieve victory by confronting Great Britain directly on the world's oceans, but believed that Britain's North American possessions were vulnerable. Accordingly, they devised a strategy that called for American forces to invade and acquire Canada, not to take the colony as a conquest, but to use it as a hostage to secure concessions from the mother country. Federal authorities proposed a powerful thrust into enemy territory by way of Lake Champlain, and then along the St. Lawrence River for a direct assault against Montreal. But Canada also seemed susceptible from the west, at Detroit. American leaders also planned for United States forces to occupy Detroit and then move eastward across Upper Canada (present-day Ontario) while other, smaller garrisons throughout the West would pacify the region's Native peoples. From the war's beginning, therefore, Detroit would constitute an important, albeit secondary, theater in the conflict's prosecution. In July 1812, William Hull, a brigadier general and the territorial governor of Michigan, set the American plan into motion by leading an American army from Detroit into Canada. But an unexpectedly vigorous resistance from British defenders forced the Americans back to Detroit by the end of the month.[5]

The construction of Fort Meigs was a response to Hull's failure and a distressing series of other American reverses in the West. In July 1812, British forces captured Mackinac Island in northern Michigan. On August 15, American troops abandoned Fort Dearborn (present-day Chicago) and were attacked and destroyed as they retreated. The following day, Hull surrendered his army, his post at Detroit, and the remainder of the Michigan Territory to the British. Throughout the remainder of the year, British and Native forces from Detroit made deep incursions into the Maumee Valley, menacing military and civilian resources all the way from Lake Erie's Western Basin to Fort Wayne. On January 22, 1813, British and Native forces at French Town (on the River Raisin at present-day Monroe, Michigan) destroyed a second American army led by Brig. Gen. James Winchester, created to repatriate Detroit and carry the war into Canada.[6]

William Henry Harrison, now a federally commissioned major general and the commander of American forces in the Maumee Valley, had been following Winchester with supplies and additional troops. Only a few days earlier, George Brown, a sergeant serving in the Ohio Militia, had met Harrison for the first time near Lower Sandusky (present-day Fremont, Ohio). "I was greatly disappointed in his appearance," claimed Brown. "I had formed the idea that our commanding general, the hero of Tippecanoe, must be a man of vast proportions, a real giant in his whole frame-work. But how I was surprised and disappointed when I saw him—a mere hoop-pole in a military costume! But he looked as tough as a hickory withe, and his dark, keen, intelligent eye and his care-worn and thoughtful look immediately impressed us all with the belief that we had an able, trustworthy commander—the right man in the right place."[7]

Harrison learned of the French Town defeat from retreating survivors late in the afternoon on January 22. The American general understood that Winchester's defeat was complete and that he could not render any assistance. Therefore, he withdrew to the Portage River, near present-day Pemberville, Ohio, and consolidated his forces. On February 1, the American army advanced to the foot of the Maumee River Rapids, the site of present-day Perrysburg in Wood County. The following day, Harrison began to construct Fort Meigs. When completed, the fort was an expansive stronghold, one of the largest military posts in the country at the time, constructed to be a supply depot and staging area designed to accumulate and house the men, equipment, and stores necessary for Harrison to continue the push into Canada once his circumstances permitted. The post would successfully withstand two determined sieges by allied British, Canadian, and Native forces later that year.

In late April, a force led by Brigadier General Henry Procter consisting of British regulars with siege artillery and howitzers, Canadian militia, and a large force of Native auxiliaries laid siege to the American outpost. The Americans survived the ten-day attack, but suffered heavy casualties. Procter undertook a second attack against Fort Meigs during the third week of July 1813, returning to the Maumee Rapids with only 350 regulars but more than 3,500 Native allies, one of the largest forces of Native warriors ever brought against a U.S. military post in American history. Like the first siege, this invasion ended with the attackers unable to compel an American surrender. These victories, resulting in the garrison's continued American occupation throughout 1815, contributed significantly to a series of U.S. victories in the Detroit Theater late in the conflict and an eventual American supremacy in that sector at the war's conclusion.[8]

Fort Meigs endured no further attacks throughout the remainder of the war. In September, when momentum in the war shifted to the Americans following Commodore Oliver Hazard Perry's victory on Lake Erie, most of the troops stationed at the post, along with the provisions and supplies stored there, were redeployed in support of the long-anticipated invasion of Upper Canada. Harrison reduced the size of the large fort drastically, and only a steadily decreasing garrison of Ohio Militia remained at Fort Meigs until after the end of the war in December 1814. The last detachment marched from the fort in May 1815, when the military abandoned the post.

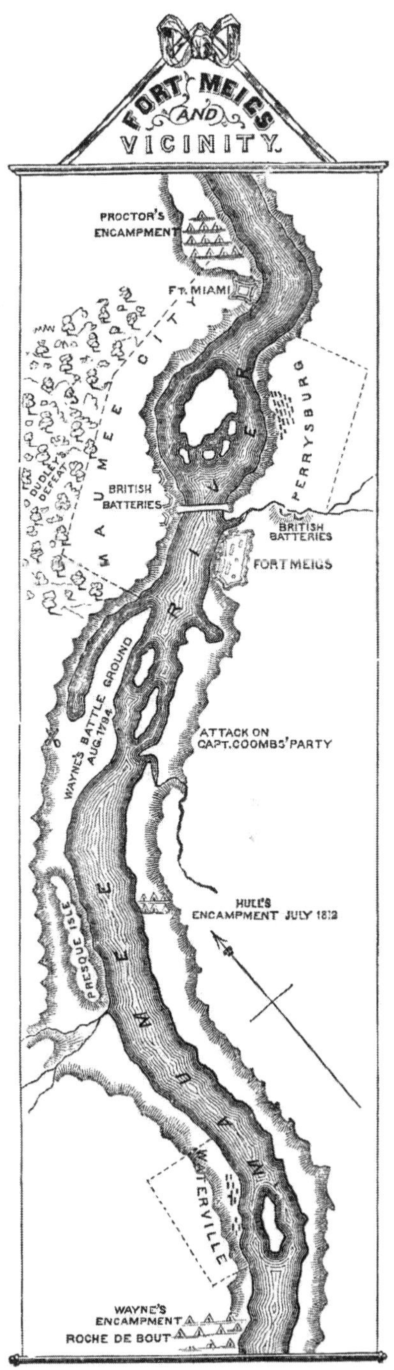

Fort Meigs and the Maumee Valley. Benson Lossing, *Pictorial Field Book of the War of 1812* [New York: Harper & Brothers, 1868].

Although fought on a remote frontier far from the seats of national power, the battles at Fort Meigs brought together Britons, Anglo-Canadians, French-Canadians, members from many Great Lakes Indian nations, and American soldiers from Ohio, the Michigan Territory, Pennsylvania, Kentucky, and Virginia. Among the British forces, the participants included some of the most distinguished Native leaders of their generation, including the Sauk war captain Black Hawk (Ma-ka-tai-me-she-kia-kiak, or Black Sparrow Hawk), the Wyandot leader Roundhead (Stayeghtha, or Bark Carrier), the Shawnee warrior Tecumseh, and his brother Tenskwatawa, The Prophet. Fighting alongside his Native allies was John Richardson, a young Canadian cadet serving with the British army who, following his military service, wrote novels based loosely upon his wartime experiences, thus becoming one of the foundational figures in Canadian literature. Among the Americans were William Henry Harrison, a future president; Richard M. Johnson, a future vice president; former territorial officials including Amos Stoddard, military commander for the Louisiana Territory; future state governors including Duncan McArthur in Ohio and John Miller in Missouri; and others who over the remainder of their lives likewise contributed significantly to their communities and their nations.

The occupation of Fort Meigs represents an important moment when the intertwined futures of both Ohio and the nation hung in the balance. The battles fought at Fort Meigs, and the men and women who occupied the post during them, sustained the nation's efforts within the region and contributed to the United States' eventual success in the Detroit Theater at the war's conclusion.

~ CHAPTER 1 ~

The Foot of the Maumee Rapids

The Rapids of the Miami may justly be termed the "garden spot" of the territory. No one can visit this place and not be charmed with its appearance and the local advantages of its situation.

—Samuel Williams

Major General William Henry Harrison sited Fort Meigs on the southeast bank of the Maumee River slightly above the foot of the Maumee Rapids. The foot of the Maumee River Rapids, located at present-day Perrysburg and Maumee, Ohio, was the head of navigation on the Maumee, and one of the most strategically significant locations in Ohio. It is no coincidence that the Battle of Fallen Timbers, fought in August 1794, took place only a short distance from the future site of Fort Meigs.

In the early nineteenth century, the Maumee River and its tributaries represented an important passageway for materials and individuals moving throughout the region. Water provided the only dependable means of transportation over long distances at that time. The Maumee, and the streams entering it, furnished reliable access to northwestern Ohio, southern Michigan, and northern Indiana. Travelers who journeyed along the river upstream to its headwaters at Fort Wayne could then proceed over a short portage to the Wabash River, and then travel that stream to the Ohio and Mississippi rivers. The Maumee River, therefore, was a significant portion of a generally unobstructed water transportation corridor capable of conveying goods and people across Lake Erie from western New York and Pennsylvania all the way to the Gulf of Mexico.

The Maumee Rapids, a series of shallow rapids extending for fourteen miles from present-day Grand Rapids, Ohio, to Perrysburg and Maumee, represented one of the few significant impediments encountered by travelers moving along the river. Large vessels carrying heavy cargoes that sailed upstream from Lake Erie's Western Basin could advance only as far as the foot of the rapids. There, passengers and cargoes would have to disembark, continue overland to the head of the rapids, and then reinitiate their journey by ship.

Because of the shallowness of the water at the rapids, invading armies, either from the United States moving northward into Michigan and Canada, or British forces moving from Canada to Michigan and then Ohio, had to cross either to the north or to the south along this section of the Maumee. By occupying the intersection of vital land and water transportation routes found at the foot of the rapids, Harrison could defend Ohio from invasion, protect the overland route that he hoped to use when he was ready to advance against Detroit, interdict the movement of British troops and supplies into Ohio, southeastern Michigan, and Indiana, and control the flow of reinforcements, provisions, and supplies to his own army.

When Fort Meigs was built, few Americans, and indeed, few Ohioans, knew very much about the Maumee Valley. Travelers traversed the area only infrequently. Northwestern Ohio was home to the Great Black Swamp, widely believed to be a forbidding, nearly impenetrable morass 140 miles wide and forty miles across. Because the area was regarded as uninhabitable, the federal government had ceded it to the northwestern Indian nations in the 1795 Treaty of Greenville. Other than the Native peoples who lived there, then, few had a reason to either visit or travel through the region.

The War of 1812 had propelled northwestern Ohio and the territory south of Detroit into the nation's consciousness. Americans followed the news of Hull's surrender, the Battle of French Town, and the first and second sieges of Fort Meigs intently. Samuel Williams of Chillicothe, Ohio, published an essay describing northwestern Ohio, the Maumee Valley, and particularly the foot of the Maumee River Rapids in *The Weekly Register* on July 7, 1813. He wrote this essay to inform general readers about the district's geographic character and strategic importance.

Williams was singularly well qualified to acquaint readers about the Maumee Valley. Born in 1786 in Carlisle, Pennsylvania, he moved to Chillicothe in 1807, remaining there for twenty years. In 1827, he moved to Cincinnati, where he resided until his death in 1859. Williams traveled through the Maumee Valley in 1812, when he served with a company of Ohio Militia commanded by Captain Henry Brush, assigned to deliver supplies to General William Hull, who then occupied Detroit. Following the war, Williams worked under Edward Tiffin, Ohio's first governor and a former U.S. senator who, at the time, was the Surveyor General of the Northwest Territory. Williams served as the chief clerk in Tiffin's Chillicothe office.[1]

Williams was a frequent contributor to the *Weekly Register.* The paper, founded by Hezekiah Niles in 1811 and published under a variety of similar titles until 1849, was one of the leading news outlets of its day, known for its comprehensive and accurate coverage of national and world events. This essay constitutes one of the earliest authoritative and widely read depictions of the Maumee Valley and the surrounding region.[2]

Interesting Topography of Ohio, June 9, 1813

TO THE EDITOR OF THE *WEEKLY REGISTER*

Sir—At your request, I have drawn up a sketch of the N.W. part of this state, which is herewith sent you. I have accompanied it with a small map of the *Rapids of the Miami* which shows the situation of *Fort Meigs* and other places worthy of notice in its vicinity, embracing about five miles of the river. From this map, a tolerable idea may be formed of the position of the enemy's batteries at the late siege of that post. The main battery was erected on the opposite side of the river from the fort near the site of "Hull's garrison," which was on a considerable eminence immediately above the ruins of a small village laid down in the map. It was this battery which was spiked by the *Kentucky* Militia. The plain to which they should have retreated lies between the village and the river. Here, they would have been perfectly secured under cover of the guns of the fort. The batteries which were stormed and carried by a sortie from the fort under *Col. Miller* lay on the same side with *Fort Meigs.*

The ground on which *Gen. Wayne* defeated the Indians on the 20th of August 1794 is also included in the map. The Indians were formed in ambuscade expecting to surprise the army; but *Gen. Wayne*, aware of their situation and intentions, marched across the river into the plain while a detachment which was sent round to fall in upon their rear had turned the right wing of the Indian line, outflanked and nearly surrounded them before they discovered their danger.

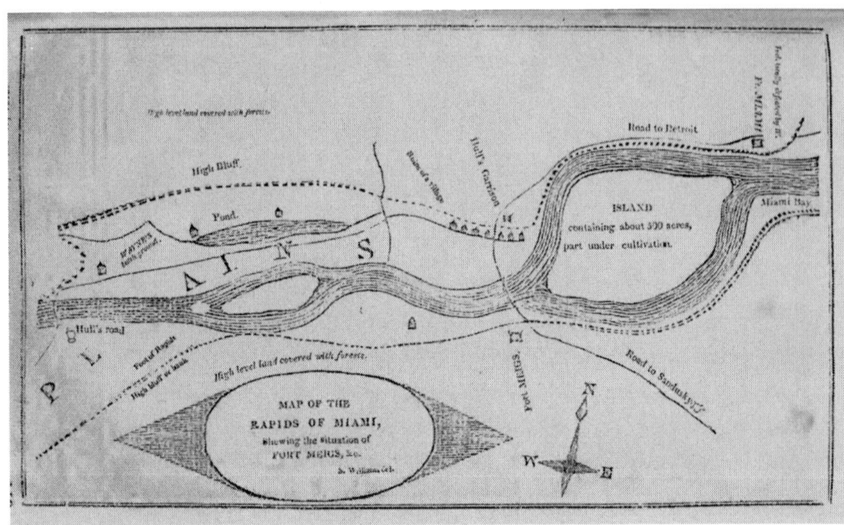

This map, published with Williams's article in 1813, is the first to show Fort Meigs and its situation at the Maumee Rapids. The map indicates the location of the 1794 Battle of Fallen Timbers ("Wayne's Battleground"), the route taken by Gen. William Hull and the site of a temporary post constructed by his army while on the march to Detroit the previous year, and the location of Port Miami, a small community established at the rapids in 1805 but abandoned early in the war.

The Indians immediately fled in disorder down the river about four or five miles to *Fort Miami* which was then occupied by the *British*,[3] from whom they sought refuge; but the *British* commander, fearing the consequence, refused them admittance; and being closely pursued and dreadfully harassed, they fled round the fort to a plain which commences at the foot of the eminence on which the fort stood, and many, in attempting to swim across the bay, were drowned or cut off by a detachment of our cavalry on the opposite shore. The rest were either killed, taken, or dispersed, and the defeat was complete.

The map is laid down upon a scale of 200 poles to the inch.[4]

A SUBSCRIBER
Chillicothe, (Ohio) June 9, 1813

A geographical description of the north-western section of the state of Ohio; or that part to which the Indian title has not yet been extinquished; accompanied by a map of the rapids of the Miami River, showing the situation of Fort Meigs other places of note.

Before the commencement of the present war with Great Britain, that part of the State of *Ohio* which lies north of the Indian boundary line and south and west of *Lake Erie* was not much known to the people of the United States. But the continual marching of troops and transporting of provisions and military stores through various parts of it since that time has thrown much light upon the geography of this section of the western country. As there is a great probability, from the present state of our relations with the Indian tribes, that their right to the soil will be forfeited to the United States or will otherwise pass into the hands of the government, and as its local and general advantages over most other parts of the western country destines it to become one day one of the finest settlements in the world, a brief geographical sketch may, in degrees, be interesting.

This beautiful tract of country is situated between the 40th and 42nd degrees of north latitudes and the 7th and 10th of longitude west from Philadelphia. Its greatest length from east to west is about 150 or 160 miles and its mean breadth from north to south 100 miles. It is bounded south by the Indian boundary line which separates it from the settlements of the state; west by Indiana Territory, north by an east and west line drawn from the most southerly point of *Lake Michigan* to *Lake Erie*, which divides it from Michigan Territory, north-east by *Lake Erie* and east by the *Cuyahoga River* and the *Tuscarawas* branch of the *Muskingum*.

The face of the country, in general, is perfectly level. There are, however, some parts a little variegated with low hills, or rather gentle eminences, which would present no obstruction whatever to the plow; and there is, probably, not an acre of land in this territory but may be cultivated to advantage. It would be a natural conclusion that the hilly parts would be situated in that quarter which is the source of the rivers; but the contrary is the fact. They are generally to be found contiguous to the lake. The southern part, stretching along the Indian boundary line and embracing the sources of a number of rivers flowing both into the *Ohio* and *Lake Erie*, is very flat and contains many small lakes or ponds which are not infrequently the sources of rivers. Towards the lake, the country abounds with beautiful plains, some of them many miles in extent and apparently as level as the surface of the water. These plains in the spring and summer seasons are covered with grass which in many of them, grows to the height of six or eight feet and a rich variety of fragrant flowers. Most of these plains are adorned with a few shrubby oaks growing sometimes in small groves of six or eight or more together, which adds much to their beauty.

After traveling some scores of miles through a thick and continued forest and suddenly emerging from it into one of those extensive plains, the sensations produced upon the mind are delightful beyond description. The traveler is almost ready to imagine himself suddenly transported into the *Elysium* of the ancients. Let the reader figure to himself a beautiful plain extending many miles, even until the distant horizon terminates his view. Let this plain be covered with the richest verdure and the finest tints of nature in its greatest exuberance and variegated with distant clusters of trees, and he will have some faint idea of the grounds here described. Indeed, the philosophic mind will rarely enjoy a richer feast than nature here presents him.

The swamps of this country have lately been much spoken of on account of the difficulties they present to the march of our troops and the transportation of heavy artillery and military stores. The "Black Swamp" which lies between *Fort Findlay* and the *Portage River* has been particularly noticed. The face of the country is so flat that there is little or no descent to carry off the water which, during the rainy seasons, accumulates in these swamps and renders them at times impassible. Yet there are few of this description that would present any serious obstruction to tillage, for there is no doubt if the country was well opened by settlement, that the greater part of these swamps would be dried up, and such as would not could be easily drained into some of the contiguous branches. When this is done, the ground may be cultivated to advantage.

The soil generally, but especially from the southern boundary line till within a few miles of the lake, is of the richest quality, well adapted to the production of grain and crops of almost every kind raised in the United States. A person may travel many miles through this part of the state and not find a hill, or a stone, or any other kind of land but such as is of the best quality. That part which lies more contiguous to the lake and embraces those extensive plains which have been described is somewhat inferior in quality, yet is too good to be ranked as second rate. There is a small portion of hilly or uneven land which is generally covered with a few small trees and whortleberry and other shrubbery common to thin land which may be classed as third rate.

The timber is the same that is plentifully found through the western country in the richest land. The most common is hickory, white, black, and red oak, white and black walnut, beech, ash, cherry, mulberry, locust, and sugar maple. Of the last, there are a great number of the most beautiful groves planted by the hand of nature seemingly for the use of man. Such groves are numerous also in the settled parts of the state, and many of our farmers have their "sugar camps" of three or four acres enclosed like their orchards. The borders of the lake abound with shrubbery of various kinds not known in other parts of the western country. The cranberry, particularly, grows in great plenty on the *Sandusky*, from which place many wagon-loads are annually brought into the settlements. They are sold at two dollars per bushel at this place . . .

The *Miami-of-the-Lake* is formed by the junction of the *St. Marys* and the *St. Josephs* (a small river which rises in Indiana Territory) at *Fort Wayne*; and winding its course through a rich, level tract of country to *Fort Winchester*, late *Fort Defiance*, it receives the *Au-Glaize*. At the distance of about 40 miles below *Fort Winchester*, the waters of this river are precipitated over a descent which forms the celebrated "*Rapids*;" and after passing at a short distance below *Fort Meigs* on the right and the ruins of a small village opposite on the east bank, and embracing a large island, it falls into a bay of the same name opposite the site of the old British *Fort Miami* about eighteen miles from the lake. Its general course is north-east; its width is about 150 yards.

The *Miami* is a handsome stream. Its banks are regular—not abrupt, but sloping gradually to the water's edge and covered in the summer season with verdure. This river is adorned with a great many plains along its margin which, though above high-water mark, are considerably lower than the adjacent country. The celebrated *Rapids* of this river terminate about three miles above the head of the bay. The channel of the river is here composed of limestone rock formed into regular strata by parallel fissures which sink perpendicularly into the rock and run transversely across the river. The face of the bank for several feet above the water is also composed of solid rock; and from its appearance it is evident that the current has worn the channel many feet deeper than it was in former ages. Few streams afford more eligible situations for water works than may be found at the *Rapids* . . .

The *Sandusky* has its source in the same plain with the principal branch of the *Scioto River* and winding its course through a rich, flat country and passing the post of *Upper-Sandusky, Fort Stephenson* (late *Lower-Sandusky*) and some Indian villages, falls into *Sandusky Bay*. The Sandusky is somewhat smaller than the *Miami*, but like it is adorned with beautiful and extensive plains which seem bounded only by the distant horizon. The rapids of this river, situated a few miles above its mouth, are erroneously placed in our maps very high up the stream. There is a portage of a few miles between the navigable parts of this river and the *Scioto* . . .

As the *River Raisin*, though probably not included in the bounds of the State of Ohio, has become familiar to everyone on account of the inhuman butcheries thereat committed by our barbarous enemy, some notice of it may not be unacceptable. This river rises in *Michigan Territory* and passing through a populous settlement of about fifteen miles in length, falls into *Lake Erie* about eighteen miles south of *Fort Malden* in Canada.[5] The *Raisin* is smaller than the *Miami* and its banks are equally handsome with those of that river; but towards the lake much lower, the adjacent country being only a few feet elevated above the water. The land is generally of an inferior quality producing whortleberry and other shrubbery indicating thin soil in great plenty.

The plantations have a very narrow front on the river but extend back some distance; and the houses being all built on the bank of the river gives it something of the appearance of the street of a town. From this cause, probably, the lower part of this settlement, which was the most populous, is known by the name of "French Town." The inhabitants are mostly French Canadians, some few natives of France and a few emigrants from the eastern parts of the United States. The Canadian settlers differ materially in their manners and habits from the American settlers and it may be reasonably expected that they did not at first relish very well our republican institutions and government, differing so greatly from that which they had formerly lived under. The militia of this settlement were formed into a regiment consisting of nearly 400 men, and when the territory was surrendered to the enemy last summer, the whole regiment was in the service of the United States for the defense of the settlement and the garrison established there.

The late garrison on this river was situated about three miles from the lake in that part of the settlement called "French Town." It consisted of two blockhouses with about an acre of ground enclosed by pickets at the distance of seventy or eighty yards from the margin of the river. The site had been very injudiciously selected for defense. It had no elevation whatever above the surrounding plain and the ground having a considerable descent from the garrison toward the rear, the greater part of the parade ground inside the picketing could have been easily and effectually annoyed over the tops of the rear line of pickets from a thick forest about a furlong in the rear. After the territory fell into the hands of the enemy and this post was abandoned, the Indians burnt the blockhouses; and when *Gen. Winchester* advanced to the river in January last, he found nothing but a few pickets sufficient to defend only a part of his camp . . .

All those rivers flowing into the lake abound with fish of almost every variety. Among those not known in the eastern states is the *White Bass*, a fish resembling the herring but considerably larger. They are taken in great plenty in most, or all, of these waters and are frequently brought by wagon loads into the settlements for sale, being much esteemed. The quantity of fish at the rapids of these rivers is almost incredible. So numerous are they at the *Rapids of the Miami* that a gig may be thrown into the water at random and it will rarely miss killing one! Some hundreds have been taken in the river at *Fort Meigs* in this way during the last spring. The writer saw last summer nearly half a barrel of them killed in less than an hour on the rapids with clubs and stones by three or four persons; and a letter which he has just received from *Fort Meigs* dated June 2nd inst. from a gentleman of undoubted veracity says "the quantity of fish taken at this place is most surprising. Some days there are not less than 1,000 or 1,500 taken with the hook within three hundred yards of the fort, of an excellent kind."

The great superiority and advantages which that section of the western country here described possesses over most other parts must be obvious to everyone. During the last twelve months, some thousands of the citizens of this state, obeying the call of their country, have visited or passed through this territory. With many of these, the writer has conversed since their return, respecting it. By all he was assured that they gave it the most decided preference to every other part of the United States they had seen. The *Rapids of the Miami* may justly be termed the "garden spot" of the territory. No one can visit this place and not be charmed with its appearance and the local advantages of its situation. The whole length of the rapids appears destined by nature to be lined with mills and other manufactories which the adjacent country might furnish ample employment for. The *Miami Bay*, commencing at the foot of the rapids, is navigable for small vessels and opens a communication with a vast tract of country stretching northward along the Great Lakes through an extent of some thousands of miles. This place affords a beautiful site for a town; and there is little doubt but that in a very few years it will boast as fine an inland town as any in the union. The country around is a wealthy, populous, and flourishing settlement. Such is the tide of popular opinion in favor of the lake side of this state that there is every reason to believe if, at the close of the war, these lands should fall into the hands of our government and be offered for sale, that the country will be settled with a rapidity unparalleled in the history of the Western world.[6]

~ CHAPTER 2 ~

Fortifying the Rapids, Building Fort Meigs

To complete this picketing, to put up eight block-houses of double timber, to elevate four large batteries, to build all the store houses and magazines required for the supplies of the army . . . was an undertaking of no small magnitude. So we fell to work to bury ourselves as fast as possible, and heard nothing of the enemy.

—Eleazer Derby Wood

Harrison arrived at the foot of the Maumee rapids on February 1, 1813, and began to construct Fort Meigs, named in honor of Ohio's governor, Return Jonathan Meigs, the following day. The site for the post was selected by Capt. Charles Gratiot, a West Point-trained officer and engineer. The most advantageous site for a fortification on the Maumee is on the north side of the river, somewhat downstream from the foot of the rapids and adjacent to the deep river channel that runs from present-day Maumee and Perrysburg to Lake Erie. Great Britain's naval squadron on Lake Erie denied Harrison this position. British naval control of Lake Erie was unchallenged until Perry's victory in September 1813, when a small American naval squadron swept British vessels from the lake. Had Fort Meigs been built below the rapids, it would have been possible for British ships to approach the post from Lake Erie and, while staying beyond the range of American artillery, bombard the fort into submission with their heavier caliber and longer range cannon. Gratiot and Harrison's decision to place Fort Meigs above the foot of the rapids reflected the American commander's concerns about the defensive posture of the post. Harrison's choice allowed Fort Meigs to carry out its essentially offensive mission as a staging area and supply depot while protecting it against direct British naval assault.[1]

Because Gratiot was suffering at the time from a persistent illness, the actual construction of the fort was supervised by Gratiot's immediate subordinate, Capt. Eleazer Derby Wood. The task before Wood was formidable. Frigid temperatures, inclement weather, a fragile and uncertain supply chain, and expiring terms of enlistment for many of the army's militia units conspired to impede the Americans' progress. Nonetheless, the Americans persevered. The troops encamped at the rapids were deployed in a "hollow square," a four-sided defensive alignment in which soldiers manning an outward facing perimeter defended their tents, supplies, and other equipment located in the center of the formation. On February 1, these soldiers were ordered to raise around their camp temporary defensive works consisting of an earthen and log embankment, or breastwork that surrounded the encampment, protected by an outer layer of abatis, an entanglement of branches and brush that acted much like modern-day barbed wire.

Field fortification manuals of the era directed that breastworks be constructed approximately four feet in height. Greenbury Keen, a private serving in the Pennsylvania Militia, noted that his orders were to "put up breastworks and fortify the camp, which was done in the following manner—a breastwork formed with logs about five feet high and an abatis formed with brush about three paces in front of the breast work. The butts were stuck in the ground next the breastwork and the tops sharpened." Within a week, this temporary work was completed and Capt. Daniel Cushing noted that it was then further strengthened by the addition of a "small redoubt [a detached earthwork] for the purpose of planting one six-pounder."[2]

While construction for this initial enclosure was underway, the army also began to lay out and erect a more substantial, permanent fortification. On February 2, Lt. Joseph Larwill assisted Capt. Gratiot in surveying the encampment and planning the next phase of construction. On the fourth, Lt. Alexander Meek wrote that "we have fortified this camp & are now employed in building blockhouses, magazines, and etc." Later in the week, Meek described to a friend that "We are building a handsome fort here called Fort Meigs for our governor, 120 feet square calculated to mount twelve twelve-pounders and garrison 200 men." On February 7, Cushing reported that his "troops are employed in building blockhouses, fortifications and stockading the camp."[3]

Despite the amount of work already completed, plans for the fort seem to have been ad hoc, fluid, and in a constant state of flux. On February 12, Cushing related that the engineers had spent the day "laying out the encampment in a smaller compass," and three days later noted "new orders this day to build a battery on the front of the hill sixty or eighty feet long to plant our eighteen-pounders." Nonetheless, Wood and the Americans pushed ahead.

When completed in early spring, Fort Meigs was an imposing and sprawling facility built atop a nearly forty-foot embankment overlooking the Maumee and enclosing nearly ten acres. An earth-and-log stockade augmented with seven blockhouses protected numerous storage and work buildings within the garrison. Two underground powder magazines supplied powder and ball to five artillery batteries along the post's perimeter. Just beyond the stockade, Harrison's men also constructed a bakery, raised artificer yards for the army's workmen, erected a facility for butchering beef cattle and hogs and processing animal hides, and fabricated a boat dock and landing area on the river immediately below the fort for the shallow-draft river vessels transporting supplies and materials to the garrison from upriver.[4]

The description that follows is taken from a diary kept by Capt. Wood. Eleazer Derby Wood was born in Massachusetts in 1783 and graduated from the U.S. Military Academy at West Point in 1806. Rising quickly to the rank of captain, Wood was assigned as an engineer to Harrison's army at the outbreak of the War of 1812. In 1813, he supervised the construction of Fort Meigs and the redesign and strengthening of Fort Stephenson at Lower Sandusky.

Wood served with distinction during the first siege of Fort Meigs, and Harrison's official account of the battle is effusive in its praise for the young officer. Brevetted to major, Wood continued to serve under Harrison as the Northwestern Army's chief engineer until following the Battle of the Thames in October 1813, after which he was reassigned to the Niagara frontier, where he was again brevetted to lieutenant colonel. Wood led a successful expedition against the British post Fort Erie, in Canada on the Niagara River directly across from Buffalo, New York, in the fall of 1814. He died after being wounded during a British counterattack against the post on September 17, 1814.

Wood was a skilled observer and insightful (if at times caustic) commentator. Highly trained, competent, and professional in his conduct and expectations, Wood's low opinion of the militia troops with whom he served is evident throughout his narrative. Wood's journal and the materials created by Daniel Cushing are indispensable sources for an understanding of Fort Meigs.

The manuscript for Wood's journal is held by the State Historical Society of Wisconsin in Madison. The journal has been published twice before, first in 1879 in George Cullum's *Campaigns of the War of 1812–15, against Great Britain, Sketched and Criticized; With Brief Biographies of the American Engineers.* A second version, edited by Defiance College professors Robert Boehm and Randall Buchman, was published in 1975 to mark the opening of the reconstructed fort and new museum at Fort Meigs State Memorial the same year. The text that follows is taken from Cullum's *Campaigns of the War of 1812–15.*[5]

Eleazer Derby Wood's Journal of the Northwestern Campaign, 1812–1813

General Harrison was unable to get farther than the Miami Rapids before he had the pain and mortification to meet the fugitives flying from the tragical scenes of the River Raisin. General Harrison immediately fell back upon the Portage River, a distance of fifteen miles, as well for the purpose of covering the artillery then in the swamp as to meet the reinforcements which were already far advanced from Upper Sandusky on their way to the rapids. This position was taken about the 24th of January and maintained till the 1st of February when the artillery and re-enforcements having arrived, the army again returned to the Miami and was encamped upon a beautiful ridge near the foot of the rapids on the right bank of the river, and about 150 yards distant from it. The camp was situated two and a half miles above old Fort Miami and directly opposite the ground on which old Anthony Wayne gave the Indians such a drubbing in '94. It was judiciously chosen by General Harrison and Captain C. Gratiot of the engineers, and afterwards fortified with blockhouses, batteries and palisadoes in such a manner as to stand the test of British artillery for five days, closely applied. . . .

Here the army lay with its rear to the river, being covered by a considerable ravine in front which extended round and communicated with another very deep and wide one, which passed the left and entirely secured it.

It was shortly afterwards directed by the general that a camp for 2,000 men should be laid out and strongly fortified; and that this work might be in a state of progression, the lines of the camp were immediately designated and a large portion of labor assigned among every corps or regiment in the army. Each brigade or regiment commenced that particular portion of work which was assigned it with great vigor and spirit.

The camp was about 2,500 yards in circumference, which distance, with the exception of several small intervals left for block-houses and batteries, was every foot to be picketed with timber 15 feet long, from 10 to 12 inches in diameter, and set 3 feet in the ground. Such were the instructions of the engineer. To complete this picketing, to put up eight block-houses (the number required) of double timber, to elevate four large batteries, to build all the store houses and magazines required for the supplies of the army, together with the ordinary fatigues of the camp was an undertaking of no small magnitude. Besides, an immense deal of labor was to be performed in excavating ditches, making abatis, and clearing away the wood about camp; and all this to be done too, at a time when the weather was extremely severe and the ground so hard frozen that it was almost impossible to open it with a spade and pick-axe. But in the use of the axe, mattock, and spade consisted all the military knowledge of the army. So we fell to work to bury ourselves as fast as possible, and heard nothing of the enemy. . . .

The weather being severe and the ground in many places where the men had to work extremely wet and bad, the lines of defense naturally progressed but slowly. No event of any importance occurred for some time. . . .

On the 4th [of March, 1813], Captain E. D. Wood of the Engineers was sent by way of the lake to Lower Sandusky with directions to assume the command of the garrison and to spend ten or fifteen days in constructing such additional works as in his opinions might be found necessary for the security of the post, and to save it from falling an easy prey should the enemy think its reduction an object worthy of his notice, then return to the rapids.

As the presence of General Harrison was no longer particularly required, he gave the necessary instructions to General Leftwich relative to the importance of a vigorous prosecution of the lines of defense and, on the 6th, left camp for Chillicothe.[6]

[In late March] the conduct of General Leftwich on this occasion was highly reprehensible indeed, for notwithstanding he had received express directions to prosecute the lines of defense with all possible vigor and to place the camp in the best possible situation to sustain a siege, which it was almost certain sooner or later it would have to undergo, and evidence of which became more apparent every day, yet this phlegmatic, stupid old granny, so soon as General Harrison left camp, stopped the progress of the works entirely, assigning as a reason that he couldn't make the militia do anything and, therefore, they might as well be in their tents as to be kept out in the mud and water, and accordingly were gratified. So, far from improving the works, they were permitted to burn the timber which had been brought into camp with an immense deal of labor for pickets and block-houses; not only did they burn this timber, but on the 20th of March, when Captain Wood returned from Lower Sandusky, he had the pain and mortification to find several of the men actually employed in pulling the pickets out of the ground and conveying them off for fuel. On asking them who gave permission for that matter, he was informed that nobody gave permission, but that it was a common thing for each mess to take what they wanted and nothing was said about it. Was not this most perplexing and vexatious indeed to an officer the least acquainted with our situation, and particularly to one intrusted with the important duty of planning and fortifying the camp, and on the success of which, in the event of a siege, his honor and reputation entirely depended?

Captains Croghan, Bradford, and Langham of the 17th and 19th regulars remonstrated in the strongest terms against such an abominable and wanton destruction of work which had been erected with so much labor and trouble; and on which, they foresaw, depended in a great measure the future salvation of the army, but all to no purpose. Captain Wood found great difficulty in stopping the militia from destroying works, but much greater in getting them to repair the breaches and depredations already made and committed on the lines. . . . .

On the 8th, Lieut.-Colonel Ball, with about 200 dragoons arrived at the rapids,[7] and in fine time to afford assistance, which was very much wanted in the completion of [the] works. A short time afterwards General Harrison arrived with a small corps of regulars and militia. . . .

Our blockhouses, batteries, magazines and connecting lines of defense were now generally completed and the appearance of the camp in every direction was such as to inspire confidence in the minds of those whose duty it had become either to defend, or with it throw themselves into the hands of an English savage.[8]

~ CHAPTER 3 ~

A Raid against the Indians

The companies marched in very compact order; each man being partially sustained by his comrades. These circumstances, together with the uniform and monotonous tread of the troops, acting on men so enervated, induced an unconquerable drowsiness. Numbers slept as they marched along. Some platoons thus dozing so far diverged from their course as to lose their companies and mix with strange columns. I not only slept myself, but had short, distinct dreams. In this way we marched all night.

—Alfred M. Lorrain

On February 8, a detachment of American scouts, or "spies" as they were then called, returned to the fort reporting that they believed a large, hostile force made up of perhaps as many as two hundred Native warriors was down river approximately fifteen miles from the post. Harrison immediately organized and deployed a detachment of six hundred men, including one piece of artillery and its crew, to discover and then engage the enemy. Unfortunately, the enemy force had withdrawn before the Americans' arrival, and the expedition was forced to return without taking any significant action.

The first document in this chapter was written by Alfred M. Lorrain. Lorrain was born in Maryland in 1791, but his family moved to Petersburg, Virginia, soon after his birth. At thirteen he went to sea as a cabin boy and sailed for the next seven years. At the outbreak of the War of 1812, Lorrain enlisted as a private in the Petersburg Volunteers, one of three companies eventually making up a battalion of twelve-month volunteer riflemen and infantry recruited to serve in the Northwest in the immediate aftermath of Hull's surrender in August 1812. Lorrain and the Petersburg Volunteers served at Fort Meigs from February through August 1813, and were present during the post's construction and throughout the first and second sieges.[1]

Following the war, Lorrain converted to Methodism, became an ordained minister, and spent the remainder of his life as a clergyman in Ohio. Lorrain wrote about his wartime experiences often, and in 1861, when he was seventy, the Springfield (Ohio) Conference encouraged him to pen his memoirs, hoping that sales from the autobiography would supplement his meager income as a retired pastor. The result was *The Helm, the Sword, and the Cross: A Life Narrative*, published in 1862.[2]

Lorrain created his memoir many years after the events that it purports to describe. Although the small details contained within it are at times at odds with those found in more contemporaneous accounts, his narrative is vivid, crisply drawn, insightful, and usually focused on the physical, emotional, and spiritual toll the war exacted on those compelled to fight it.

The second account is found in a journal kept by Joseph H. Larwill. Larwill served as a second lieutenant in Cushing's Company of the 2nd Regiment of Artillery, and commanded the expedition's lone piece of artillery. Prior to the war, Larwill, a trained surveyor and mapmaker, was instrumental (along with his two brothers) in the founding of Wooster, Ohio. Following the conflict, he remained active in Wayne County civic affairs for many years.[3]

Larwill kept his diary from April 5, 1812, through September 22, 1813. His account is focused, direct, and revealing. Moreover, the material found in his journal significantly overlaps the materials created by Daniel Cushing. The survival of two detailed accounts created so closely together by individuals so intimately associated is a rare historical occurrence. Larwill's journal, therefore, provides a unique degree of perspective and context for the events related within Cushing's diary.

Larwill's journal remains unpublished. The manuscript is held in the Burton Historical Collection of the Detroit Public Library. Henry Howe published a description of this expedition based upon a much-abridged version of the Larwill diary in his 1848 *Howe's Historical Collections*, and retained this version of events in subsequent editions of his volume.[4]

Alfred M. Lorrain, *The Helm, the Sword, and the Cross: A Life Narrative*

At one time our spies brought intelligence that a party of about seven hundred Indians were diverting themselves with a war-dance on the ice near the mouth of the river. In the dusk of the evening General Harrison, at the head of fifteen hundred troops, started for the party, although not particularly invited. At a late hour in the night the blazing fires of the enemy appeared on the bank of the river. We were now wide awake. The day of battle, about which so much had been said, was now right before us. The detachment, thrown into a crescent with the artillery in the center, cautiously approached. We found the fires burning bright with recent fuel; but the Indians had fled. This disappointment was probably owing to our imprudence in marching on the river. It is said that an Indian, by laying his ear flat on the ice, can discover the approach of a large force five miles distant.

It was now announced that those who were sick or exhausted might tarry by the fires till morning. Some were so completely worn out that they not only accepted the boon, but threw themselves down by the fires and, without a sentinel to guard the camp, fell into a profound sleep. For my own part, I felt that my strength was almost gone; but some very forcible questions presented themselves to my mind; such as, how far had the wily enemy retreated? Might they not now be lurking in the dark forest before us watching all our movements? Again, I rubbed the crown of my head and concluded to value my scalp at a higher price of suffering than had yet been realized. It also occurred that I was not made of softer clay than my fellows, and that there was a point of endurance beyond which none could go, a point at which the officers themselves must succumb. So I would not report myself among either the sick, the lame, or the lazy.

The general, being disappointed in the matter of the dance, concluded to proceed on to the River Raisin and to bury our dead who had been inhumanly left on the field and were now "bleaching in the northern blast." He therefore sent back to Meigs for sleds, pickaxes, spades, etc., and the main body moved on.

The frozen face of the river was an unbroken level. It had been put into excellent order by a previous sprinkle of snow. There was no impediment in our way to call for vigilance. The companies marched in very compact order; each man being partially sustained by his comrades. These circumstances, together with the uniform and monotonous tread of the troops, acting on men so enervated, induced an unconquerable drowsiness. Numbers slept as they marched along. Some platoons thus dozing so far diverged from their course as to lose their companies and mix with strange columns. I not only slept myself, but had short, distinct dreams. In this way we marched all night.

About day-break we began to approach the lake. The ice had evidently become softer. We pressed on till our way became quite sloppy. We persevered, however, till the wheels of our six-pounder broke through the ice. The expedition was then abandoned.

The troops were marched to a projecting point of land where we had a short intermission. About thirty minutes were spent in dozing or eating, as drowsiness or hunger prevailed, when we were again beat to arms and marched back to our fort where we arrived late in the evening, having marched sixty-four miles in twenty-two consecutive hours. The detachment was so prostrated that it was exonerated from all military duty for several days.[5]

Journal of Joseph H. Larwill Relating to Occurrences Transpired in the Service of the U States Commencing April 5, 1812

Sunday [February] 7th Spies was sent from camp to make discoveries. They returned on Tuesday the 9th. On the 10th, Wednesday after dark, 600 or thereabouts was ready to march down the bay as the spies brought the information that about 18 or 20 miles down the bay a body of Indians was encamped, computed to be 600. Not knowing whether they was a decoy with a reinforcement of British and Indians in the rear, we took the force before stated (600) and 1 piece of artillery, a six pounder which I commanded with fourteen men; we proceeded over on the ice. Marched in order, the main body in front, the artillery about 100 yds. in the rear, then Maj. G. Tod in the rear of the artillery with Capt Langham's and McCray's companies. Genl. Harrison was in front with his aides and staff and Genl. Perkins with his detachment.

About eighteen or twenty miles down, we discovered some fires on the north side of the river. We passed on until opposite, then turned left (that is every person faced to the left on the ground which we stood on) and went to shore. There we found the Indians had fled the day previous. We waited here one-half hour. The main body, the rear, and myself was not there more than ten minutes. We was then ordered to parade (the men had not warmed themselves). We was then informed that we was to proceed to River Raisin and all those that was unwell or fatigued too much might stay and follow after in the morning. While we was marching to the fires we had a reinforcement of 500 men come up to us which made our force 1,100 strong (they started about 1 hour after the first 600).

We delayed but a few moments at the fires; orders was given to parade and we marched in the same order as before. Had not proceeded more than one-and-one half miles when the horses and cannon broke through the ice, distant from the shore about one half mile. The moon was now nearly down, being about a quarter past two in the morning. In endeavoring to extricate the horses, I had released the off-hind horse from the traces. I came on the near side and was in the act of releasing the rear horse when I fell in with two of my men with me, Robt. Pearson and Jos. Lewis. With some difficulty we got out (the water was about five feet deep).

The army halted. Genl. Harrison ordered the army to proceed leaving me with men and ordering a comp[any] of militia to assist me to get out the cannon, and when I got it out, was to proceed after him with all possible dispatch. I found it attended with great difficulty in getting the horses out, which I accomplished, then sent four or five hands to the shore to cut handspikes and then took the cannon off the carriage and unlimbered the carriage, then got all out. After it was out I had the cannon mounted. We was much fatigued. Several of my men returned to fires with Sergt. Kelly. The militia that was left with me, excepting three or four, offered no assistance. By the time the cannon was mounted, it was daybreak.

I then proceeded after the army, overtook them by the sun one hour high. On an island at the mouth of the bay some of my men was much fatigued, particularly Pearson, who was very useful in assisting me. As we was going ashore on the island, where was the Genl. and army, the spies was then arriving. They had been to the River Raisin and brought one prisoner with them, a Frenchman who gave the intelligence that the Indians had gone to Malden and took the cattle with them; only a few was at the River Raisin. Genl. Harrison then thought it best to return as no opportunity offered us of carrying up with the Indians and our strength was insufficient to make a stand at the River Raisin [and] proceed to Malden. We had, when we marched, only one day's provisions with us, which was now exhausted. I was on this island about one half hour. We was ordered to return and reverse the line of march.

On our return, on the left side of the bay about five miles from the island there was some houses. We tarried there a short time. Found the inhabitants had fled and left some of their property. We took some of the corn and then proceeded on our march. By the time we arrived opposite the old English fort two and one half miles from our encampment, I took very sick, vomiting and headache. I found myself unable to proceed any further. I took my blanket and laid on the ground, sent the cannon to camp. I then got a horse to take me to camp. On my way, met Lieut. Meeks who came to my assistance; he procured a sleigh for me to ride. I arrived in camp just as the evening gun was firing. Numbers of men was yet behind. Sleds and horses was sent to bring them into camp. When I arrived in my quarters, I had some coffee made, which refreshed me much.[6]

~ CHAPTER 4 ~

An Expedition against the *Queen Charlotte*

The party proceeded to Put-in-Bay where they discovered that the lake was quite open between them and Amherstburg and that it was utterly impossible for the object of the expedition to be accomplished; so, after being absent several days, they steered for the mouth of the Miami and arrived at camp on the 5th of March. Thus did the coquettish Queen disappoint an ardent and sincere lover, reserving her smiles and charms for the more fortunate and gallant Perry.

—Eleazer Derby Wood

In late February, Harrison learned that the British warship *Queen Charlotte* was moored and held fast in the ice near the British post Fort Malden in Upper Canada (present-day Ontario), opposite Amherstburg. Disappointed that his earlier mission against the Indians had faltered and eager to reestablish any type of American momentum in the aftermath of the French Town defeat, Harrison immediately put forth a plan to send a force across the ice then covering Lake Erie and, using incendiary explosives, to destroy the ship as it lay at anchor.

Queen Charlotte was a tempting target of opportunity. The three-masted sloop was, without question, one of the most potent British military assets on the Detroit frontier and a fearsome engine of war. It was the most heavily armed ship in the British squadron patrolling Lake Erie's Western Basin. At ninety-two feet in length, the vessel boasted an armament of fourteen twenty-four-pound carronades (powerful, short range artillery pieces that were particularly effective against other ships or personnel on land or sea) and three long-range twelve-pound cannon. In contrast, Fort Meigs at the time was protected by only two five-and-a-half-inch howitzers, four eighteen-pound cannon, five twelve-pounders (four iron and one brass), and four six-pounders.[1]

But if the mission's potential reward was substantial, its risks were enormous. The march to Fort Malden across Lake Erie's frozen surface would be treacherous and physically exhausting, and to approach the British post undetected, even after dark, would be exceedingly unlikely. Moreover, even if the firebombing was successful, the assault would certainly prompt a ferocious counterattack from the infantry and artillery manning the enemy garrison. Retreat would be nearly impossible.

On February 24, Harrison revealed his plan to his senior officers, who agreed that the scheme was viable despite the peril. On February 26, the expedition, made up entirely of volunteers and commanded by Capt. Angus Langham of the 19th U.S. Infantry, set out. The route taken by the Americans was circuitous and designed to disguise the force's ultimate destination. Langham led his men overland to the southeast to Lower Sandusky and the site of Fort Stephenson. From there, the Americans followed the Sandusky River to Lake Erie and from there across Marblehead Peninsula to South Bass Island and Put-in-Bay, where they hoped to launch the final push against the British stronghold. But as with the previous expedition against the Indians, unseasonably warm weather had softened Lake Erie's ice, making passage to Malden impossible. The expedition, therefore, was forced to withdraw without taking any action against the British. The following two accounts were created by Eleazer Derby Wood and Joseph Larwill.

Eleazer Derby Wood's Journal of the Northwestern Campaign, 1812–1813

A plan was now set afoot for the burning of the *Queen Charlotte*, a British vessel then lying by the wharf at Amherstburg, *immediately under the guns of Malden.* But *that made no difference—she was to be burnt.* To carry this enterprise into execution, Captain Langham, a very gallant officer, was selected with one hundred men; Major Stoddard of the artillery and Captain Wood of the Engineers were directed to prepare suitable combustibles for the destruction of the unfortunate **Queen;** to prevent distortion of features and to preserve her beauty to the last moment, it was determined not to administer this inflammable dose by her head, but by her tail—or stern.

Everything preparatory to the enterprise having been reported ready, the forlorn hope (if there ever was one) was paraded; the general made a few observations to them, setting forth the dauntless courage of their commander and the important national advantages which must certainly result from the destruction of this Lady of the Lake; when, having finished, Captain L[angham] put himself at the head of his party and moved off by the way of Lower Sandusky for Malden.

Sleighs were got at Lower Sandusky in which the party proceeded to Put-in-Bay where they discovered that the lake was quite open between them and Amherstburg and that it was utterly impossible for the object of the expedition to be accomplished; so, after being absent several days, they steered for the mouth of the Miami and arrived at camp on the 5th of March. Thus did the coquettish **Queen** disappoint an *ardent and sincere* lover, reserving her *smiles* and *charms* for the more fortunate and gallant Perry.[2]

Journal of Joseph H. Larwill Relating to Occurrences Transpired in the Service of the U States Commencing April 5, 1812

[February] 24th, Wednesday Morning. While at breakfast Genl. Harrison came to the marquee and told Mr. Maddes and myself that he wanted to speak to us after breakfast.[3] Accordingly we attended the Genl., when he told us he had an expedition afoot wherein we might be engaged. The Genl. thought us proper persons to go, but no one should go but went agreeable to their approbations. We agreed to go. The Genl. stated the object was to burn or destroy the *Queen Charlotte*, the British vessel that was within 100 yds. of Malden. He intended to send 100 men Capt. Langham will command and 100 as a reserve. He stated he would give us more information hereafter. . . .

26th February After parade in the morning, Capt. Angus L. Langham marched to the parade with about sixty-eight regulars from the different companies in camp. Capt. Moore of Penna. Militia . . . was on the parade. Capt. Burns has about eighty men, Lieut. Wells thirty-two or thereabouts. . . .

Genl. Harrison stated to the officers and soldiers that they would have to be under the command of Capt. Langham and it was expected to be a voluntary act of those who went. They would have to be under the most rigid disciple, not even utter a single word when silence was found necessary. They would be made acquainted with the object in view before they had to act, time enough to return, and if at that time anyone should be timid or even think the undertaking too hazardous, they then might decline going; but if after that time they consented, they must expect to proceed. The undertaking would be a very hazardous one, required perfect silence and privations. He made a short speech promising to those who behaved themselves to be rewarded and their name forwarded to the gen[eral], government, & etc. & etc. They was then ordered to be marched off. Capt. Moore took command, Capt. Langham and self remained until after. We then marched off. . . . Mr. Maddes remained behind to prepare material for the expedition. This day we encamped about six miles from here on the road to Lower Sandusky.

27th Make an early start. This day was moist and disagreeable traveling. We leave our slides to overtake us in the evening. This day we marched twenty-five miles, was overtaken by Capt. Hukill, aide to the Genl. and acting as Qr. Master. Also Mr. Johnson, volunteer aide. He intended going with us on the expedition. They went on to a blockhouse dist[ant] from us one mile. We encamped upon a hard over-rise of ground on the so[uth] side of the road. On the so[uth]west of us was a swamp. After placing out the guards we supped and laid down on the bed of nature to repose ourselves having but a small portion of covering with us. The men had neither a watch coat nor extra blanket. The land this day much as yesterday. We crossed a stream about forty yards wide, Portage River, which is distant from Fort Meigs twenty miles.

28 This day much as yesterday. The land is more inclining to oak, and when we arrived at the Sandusky River, which was about one-and-a-half mile from where we encamped, the land is dry: oak pr[airie] and inclining to plains. We kept over the river to the fort, a blockhouse dist[ant] from where we are camped six miles. The river is about 100 yds. wide, a lip in places, rapid current some places, falls of one, two, three feet. Fine mills may be erected here as the banks and bottom of the stream is lime stone rock and sufficient height (the banks) for erecting dams. About the fort and blockhouse is some fine low lands, prairies which have been cultivated.

Apparently, for a number of years this post is occupied by the militia of Ohio—two companies, Latter of Jefferson County, Rupel of Connecticut Reserve. This day Lieut. Maddes came up with us. His party consisted of thirty-two strong, principle part was Canadians. Our watch force here was sixty-eight regulars from different companies comm'd by Capt. Langham; Penn. and Virg. Militia 120, Maddes thirty-two, Indians under two chiefs viz. Capt. John (Shawnee), Capt. Smith, Seneca twenty-two, making a total of 242 men besides drivers of sleds which was twenty-four, with several pilots or guides, the principal ones was Mr. Green of Connecticut Reserve, George Pease, and Mr. Rupel. We encamped on the north side of the blockhouse across a ravine on a high piece of land.

We now had to prepare to get necessaries to prosecute our journey. This evening I prepared wood to burn coal. The smiths being out, had it burned and the smiths set to work shoeing our horses. Had bread baking for us and meat cooking for six days' provisions. This night it rained; we procured tents to cover us.

March 1st Wet morning. We are busy preparing to start. Send men in different directions to get horses and sleighs together with gear. Our Indians are rather troublesome, having had too much liquor. It is impossible to keep them in due bounds when liquor is to be obtained. Some of the men was rather in a state of intoxication. I forgot to mention that yesterday my Black boy Lewis was tomahawked by a private in Lieut. Maddes' company while he was engaged transacting his business at one of the sleds. Some misunderstanding took place between them which occasioned words between them. The private, named Patrick, struck him on the side of the head with the tomahawk which cut him considerable. Lieut. Maddes corrected Patrick for the offense. The boy was much hurt. The blacksmiths and bakers was engaged the principal part of the night performing their duties. This evening cleared up and got quite cold.

2nd March 1813 All things being ready, we prepared to move having got our provisions packed up. A march was ordered. About 10 AM the slides moved down the hill. I marched in front, the other companies following. When we got over the river about one half mile; a halt was called. Capt. Langham then addressed the men. Made the object of the expedition known and those that had any objections to participate in the expedition, about twelve or fourteen, stayed behind at the encampment and six turned out here not desirous of going, thinking the enterprise too dangerous; also five or six Indians.

Capt. Langham made it known that the most strict and rigid discipline must be observed. We then marched, passing the place where the widow Whittican lived. The Indians have destroyed the building which was considerable. Here is fine small orchard. The land rather thinnish and off the river is wet. After traveling three and one-half miles, we took the river on the ice, which was tolerable firm. We proceeded with rapidity, arriving in the bay. It presents a very handsome appearance. On each side is considerable of marshy lands as well as on the river. The bay is about from two to four miles wide. Several islands in the bay. It bears north-easterly. We passed down the bay say three or four miles. We then took the land on w[est] side of the bay. We then passed through what is called the peninsula, which was where we crossed—about three miles. Principle part of the dist[ance] is low, marshy land, some few points of timber. The water and ice was about one foot deep considerable proportion of the distance. We crossed at the bay of Carrying River, where one of our sleighs broke in. It was taken out as well as the horses. No loss excepting a musket which was on the slide. This is in sight of the lake and about one-quarter miles dist[ant]. When we arrived near the lake an Indian was discovered which caused several of the men to give him chase. The Indian slipped; we found him to be one of our party. Some of our men was being near shooting him in mistake. Here we had a very handsome view of the lake and adjacent islands. Walked out some distance on the lake. Thought we saw a body of [men] moving towards us, we afterwards found it was the reflecting rays of the sun on the ice that was thrown up in ridges. We encamped behind the bank thrown up by the wash of the lake, and on the south was a pond, or rather slush land. After the guards was stationed, we supped. All hands retired to rest.

When a gun was fired by one of our men by accident, we thought it was an alarm. Every man immediately was at his post, ready for action as soon as possible. The detachment was mortified that it was an accidental shot. Capt. Langham was considerably in doubt whether he would not have the man that fired the gun shot for the false alarm as at this time it became particularly necessary to use all precautions. The man pledged his honor that it was accidental, and being the first offence, he was permitted to pass unpunished. I went to the Indians and stated to them that they must send out two parties to patrol, one up, the down the lake and continue out for three or four hours.

We now retired without any tents to cover us. The night was a very disagreeable one to pass over. It rained the fore-part of the night, then snowed.

In the morning, March 3rd, 1813, had the slide arranged to each part of the detachment in a proportional part. We proceeded to move on to the area of the Bass Islands, sometimes called Edwards or Put-In-Bay on account of the harbor that is situated on the NW part of the island being the best harbor for shipping on the lake. The course to the island was N2E, dist[ance] to the no[rth] side seventeen or eighteen miles passing by an island on the left called Snake Island. It is a small one, dist[ant] from Edwards two-and-a-half miles. During our progress to the island the day was stormy, blowing and snowing under foot. Quite slippery in places. We arrived at the NW side of the island by 1 PM. It now cleared off a little. In the afternoon it got more moderate. Sent out a small party to the no[rth] to another island. They went about four miles endeavoring to discover, if possible, any persons.

On our way to this place from the shore we discovered two slide tracks going in the direction of Malden. This we presumed to be two Frenchmen that started the day we did from Sandusky. There they stated they was going to the River Huron which was the contrary direction. We felt fully satisfied they was on to our designs and had gone to give the British notice of our intentions.

I went to the east side of the island. We encamped on Edwards after Capt. Langham, Moore, and others had been there and informed me the lake had broke up. Went and found the lake open about one-quarter miles from shore. Then walked to the no[rth] round the island. Several accompanied me. Found that the ice on the no[rth] side was not of sufficient strength to bare a man and had the marks of being broke up as far as we could see to the north. Walked around the point. While at a ledge of rock, I heard distinctly the evening gun that was fired at Fort Meigs. The gun fired for evening was an 18-pounder. This distance in a direct line is about fifty-five miles. The wind was favorable to hear, being then a gentle one from the SW.

After I returned, Capt. Langham inquired of the guides as to the practicability of our proceeding. They stated that it was impossible to go to Malden, that the river at Detroit was no doubt broke up and the lake from the Middle Sister to Detroit River; that there was a possibility of us getting as far north as the Middle Sister, but as the residue to the Detroit River—a distance of eighteen miles—had to be performed after night, they could not attempt going, being fully satisfied that they could not arrive at the point of destination; and as the weather was and had been soft, that should there be a southerly wind blow up, the lake would immediately break up and might catch us on it or one of the islands. They stated they had gone as far as they thought either safe or prudent and would not take the responsibility on them any further.

Capt. Langham then called all the officers and guides together. After the guides gave their opinion as to the possibility of us going on and the captain stating to us his instruction to be governed as to the guides so far as not to proceed without the guides should think it safe, we was called upon to give our opinion as to the propriety or impropriety of our proceeding. It was unanimously decided that it was improper for us to proceed and that we should retrograde our march.

March 4th, 1813 The morning still continuing unfavorable. However, the weather has changed in the night and become more cold, but was quite sloppy. The capt[ain] held a council of the officers and guides. They was still of the same opinion as the evening before. The capt[ain] then called the men and stated to them the opinion of the officers and guides, and the importance of our expedition to the government should we succeed. At the same, should our lives be lost in the lake in thus rendering this service to our country, that in that case it would be a loss considering this force was the prime of the army and etc. He wished to get their opinion whether they was of the opinion of going on or returning.

From all the statements made, they answered that they was willing and ready to go any place where the officers took them and expressed a desire of going forward should it be practical. They considered the officers the most capable of judging for them (excepting a few that thought that they would say go on although they felt fully satisfied that it was impossible). However, it was but a few and they, I believe, did not properly understand the question.

It was now decided that we should return. The sleighs was ordered to proceed, I had the van. Crossed the point of the island and took on the back track until we arrived at a large seam in the ice thrown up and occasioned by the breaking of the ice to the northward. This is within three miles of the shore. Here the principal part of the guides and some of the sleighs kept on the route to Sandusky Blockhouse.

We bore a westerly course to Locust Point, so called from the timber on the point of land that projects into the lake. The distance from where we took off is about fourteen miles. Large quantities of wild geese present themselves to our view. Lighting on the ice, they are very [ ]. Our men fired upon them a number of times, one of them killed while on the flight. From Locust Point we can see Cedar Point, distance fourteen miles. This point projects out considerable in the lake. It is a narrow strip of land, in the rear is a large marsh. The timber on the point is principally willow.

On our way there an express arrived direct from Genl. Harrison informing us that should our guides not think there was complete safety on the ice, to return immediately by the way of Presque Isle (this is in the upper end of Miami Bay) and as the weather had been very unfavorable since our departure to prosecute our expedition, he thought the ice was unsafe. That if any of our guides had any doubts as to the safety of the ice in going to the place of destination as well as making a safe retreat, that we must return. We was much pleased to hear this intelligence in as much as it corresponded with our conduct.

We encamped this night eight or ten miles this side of the point before mentioned. Had a very uncomfortable place to encamp. I forgot to mention that the morning that we left the lake's southern shore to proceed to the island that an ensign and thirteen or fourteen men from the Pennsylvania line deserted us as well as Capt. Smith of the Indians with several of his men.

March 5, 1813 Make an early march. Reached the point, start out across the point of land, the slide keeping round on the ice. Then they arrived at the point found the lake open. The Western Sister (an island so named) lies immediately opposite this point, dis[tance] appears to be about ten miles, course about N10 E from this point. We can see the coast on the so[uth]west side of the lake passing River Raisin. If the day was clearer, we could see the island at Malden, the distance in a direct line would be about thirty-six or forty miles.

We now incline more southerly up the bay. March about eight miles. We arrive at Presque Isle which has some French settlements. As I have before described this place in my former tour thus, I should defer noticing it any further. There, the land round the bay on the east side is marshy. Where timbered, it is chiefly of that quality that grows in scaled lands, swamp oak and etc. We rested here a short time.

When Genl. Harrison and suite arrived in about one-half hour afterwards, Major Alexander's Volunteer Battl. arrived composed of the Pittsburgh Blues, Petersburg Va. Vols., and etc., Greensburg Rifle Vols. Some short delay was made. Genl. Harrison, enquiring of the French that was with us as to the state of the dead at the River Raisin and whether they was in a state that would admit of their being buried, also whether the tools necessary to bury them could be obtained at the river. The Genl. finding it impossible to procure tools and etc., and if procured they was not in a state that would admit of us to deposit them in the earth as the hogs had chiefly destroyed them, we progressed up the river. The Genl. and suite returned to camp. Dr. Pendergrast and a guide with him proceeded on towards Huron. The Dr. was on his way to City of Washington.

We marched up the river about nine miles and was then going on the western shore to encamp when one of the sleighs broke in. I assisted getting it out by the time the troops had encamped. After the necessary arrangements: placing guards, making fires, and etc., we supped and took a hearty drink of grog, the volunteers having brought some with them, ours having run aground. I can fully state that it was quite refreshing to me. This night was cold & clear.

March 6 Being somewhat fatigued with my tour—being indisposed when I started which added to the fatigues undergone—I was induced to ride in a sleigh this morning to camp. It being cold I pulled off my shoes to set at ease. I pulled off my sword and set them by my side, placing my feet in a blanket. Having arrived within three miles of Ft. Meigs, the slide I was in broke through with the horses. I immediately shoved myself out on the ice and paid attention to have the horses extricated from the difficulties they was in. They was got out by great exertions but not without hurting them considerably. They must have been in the water struggling to get out nearly one hour.

The sword was one I borrowed of Adjutant Bettle Harrison to go on this expedition and laid by my side in the slide. When the slide broke through my mind was engaged in relieving the horses and taking care of the slide. After the horses was relieved I seen that the property in the slide, *viz.* guns of the men that rode and their blankets, together with my shoes, blanket (forgetting the sword) was in a dangerous situation. The guns belonged to the Petersburg Volunteers. They was afraid to approach the slide and, indeed, they afforded no assistance to extricate the horses, or slide, or property from the deep, but as soon as they had their property secured to them, they took French leave of us, leaving Mr. Jones the wagon master—the person that drove the slide—the 1st Sergt. of Capt. Jarvis Butler's company, and myself to attend to the fatigues. Having got the guns, blankets, and my shoes from the slide I then endeavored to get the slide out. All this time I was in my stocking feet without my shoes. After the slide was out I searched for my sword, but could not find it.

Repaired to camp; arrived there by dinner time. Found that Lieut. Alex Meek had gone home to Cincinnati, started this morning. He had been very unwell, and was so when he left camp. Genl. Harrison and suite left the encampment this morning. He intended going to Cincinnati where is his family.[4]

~ CHAPTER 5 ~

Life in Camp, Spring 1813

Officers and men all mingle together. We visit each other's tents of an evening, sing, tell stories, play music, and drink grog when we can get it, which by-the-bye is not often the case.

—A Member of the Petersburg Volunteers

Life at Fort Meigs was always difficult. During the winter, frigid temperatures posed a serious threat to those who lived at the post. Fort Meigs, in spite of its name, was in fact a large, stockaded camp. Those housed at the garrison, from Harrison on down, lived in tents whose thin canvas walls provided only minimal protection from the elements. The hazards associated with the intense cold were heightened by the lack of basic supplies such as adequate clothing. In January, while on the march to the rapids, Greenbury Keen, serving with the Pennsylvania Militia, noted that "the scarcity of clothing and severity of the climate subjects us to many hardships and difficulties." "Now is the time that tries the patience and fortitude of our troops," he observed, "many of them shirtless and coatless are obliged to turn out and stand on parade from before the break-of-day until daylight."[1]

As temperatures moderated in the spring of 1813, seasonal rains turned the post, built on the northern edge of Ohio's Great Black Swamp, into a quagmire. As early as March 11, Joseph Larwill complained that the "weather is soft," making the garrison "very unpleasant." Mud and water, he claimed, were "over shoe mouth deep" in every part of the encampment. On March 14, Captain

Cushing noted that high water had swept away a house that stood opposite the fort, along with a number of hogs, horses, and cattle. Later, Larwill commented that "It is observed by all the officers that I have had any conversation with who have been a long time in the service, some of them in the Revolutionary War, that this is the most disagreeable encampment they every saw. It is impossible to pass from one tent to another without being over shoe-mouth in mud, much less to keep in the streets of the encampment where it is one half-leg deep. I am much surprised that the troops keep as healthy as they do, having to suffer on account of fuel being difficult to obtain and nothing to lay on but the ground, which is not only damp, but wet."[2]

On March 18 Cushing continued to write about the deteriorating conditions, noting that

> The whole country is inundated with water and broken ice. Our camp is overwhelmed with mud and water; my eyes never saw such a place for mankind to live in—not a marquee or tent in the whole encampment but what has more or less mud and water in it, and what makes it much worse is for the want of wood. The timber is all cut off for a long distance from camp . . . Our men are very sickly; no wonder, lying in mud and water and without fire; not less than two or three men die every day, and I expect the deaths to increase unless the weather changes very soon.

The challenges presented by inclement weather were exacerbated by the extraordinary physical demands of waging a wilderness campaign. The heavily forested site for the garrison needed to be cleared of trees, the stumps removed, and the timber fabricated into materials for seven blockhouses, artillery platforms, magazines, numerous storage buildings and work areas, and a stockade enclosing nearly ten acres. Using only spades, shovels, and other hand tools, the soldiers dug wells, excavated trenches, and created earthen defenses within and without the palisade.[3]

Guards manning watch towers erected within the post and spaced along the stockade wall called out "All's clear!" every fifteen minutes, while sentries posted in a perimeter away from the garrison stayed on alert, both to protect the fort from its enemies and to prevent Americans from deserting the post. The sentinels knew that deserters could carry intelligence to the British, and also understood that the British were sending their own spies to gather information about the

Americans. All of these hardships were amplified by the ever-present danger of enemy attack, by the prevalence of disease, and by the vagaries of an unstable and unpredictable line of supply.[4]

Those living at Fort Meigs formed a large and surprisingly diverse community. Soldiers serving in the regular army worked side-by-side with volunteer and militia units from Ohio, Pennsylvania, Kentucky, Virginia, and the Michigan Territory. Some who served at the post from Michigan spoke only French. Harrison placed these men under the supervision of Capt. Charles Gratiot; "not exactly my command," Gratiot remembered many years later, "but because I spoke the French language, they were under [my] care."[5]

Many of the soldiers at the post had never traveled more than a few miles from the place where they were born and, as a result, were unprepared for the unexpected variety of people encountered within the American camp. "We were astonished at the mixed multitude," claimed Alfred M. Lorrain. "Some were from the north; others from the east and south. They were diversified in their habits, costume, [and] language. Bitter railleries sometimes passed. The Yankees laughed at the Tuckahoes; and they, in turn, at the Yankees and their odd proverbialisms. Indeed, their military phrases were not identical. One would cry out in the old Revolutionary style, 'Shoulder hoo!' another according to modern tactics 'Shoulder arms!' And I thought we were in a poor condition to breast the enemy."[6]

Some officers, including Daniel Cushing, Joseph Larwill, and Eleazer Wood, went on campaign accompanied by their African American servants. Some noncommissioned officers traveled with their wives, who were paid to act as laundresses in their husbands' companies. Civilian support personnel, including artillery conductors, livestock drovers, and wagon masters, helped maintain the post's logistical support. Sutlers, civilian vendors approved by the military to sell a variety of foodstuffs and personal supplies at the post, traveled to the fort frequently. Civilian refugees, including both English- and French-speaking inhabitants from the River Raisin and lower Maumee regions, and including women and children, sought safety within the garrison. Native allies played an integral role in Harrison's campaign, and Native peoples lived among their Euro-American counterparts, were in daily contact with American soldiers, and accompanied virtually every scouting and escort detail that issued from the post.[7]

Soldiers' lives were regulated by unchanging routine. Awakened before first light, the army assembled at dawn, the roll was called, and soldiers received their instructions for the day. Nearly everyone prior to the first siege was employed in building the stockade, earthworks, blockhouses, magazines, and storage buildings that made up the fort. At other times the men might be assigned to guard duty. Others worked on general fatigue (or work) parties, cutting firewood, bringing water, digging latrines, or policing the camp. Some went on patrol or escorted supplies and personnel to and from the garrison. When not assigned to work details, the men drilled to increase their proficiency in maneuver and marksmanship. The work and training were unrelenting, unceasing, physically demanding, and emotionally draining.

Soldiers camped with their companies, and each company was responsible for its own cooking, laundry, and the care of its sick and wounded. Rations, a company's daily allocation of food and other supplies, were sparse, basic, and monotonously repetitive. The allotment consisted of "eighteen ounces of flour, twenty ounces of beef or pork (three quarters of a pound if salted), and one gill [about four ounces] of whiskey per day," claimed Garret Wall, serving with the Pennsylvania Militia, with the addition of "one pound and a half of candles, four pounds of soap, a half gallon of salt, and a half gallon of vinegar per hundred rations."[8]

Opportunities for leisure and relaxation were rare, but not nonexistent. Captain Cushing enjoyed reading in his spare moments, and set out a garden. Adam Walker served at Fort Meigs in Capt. Theophilus Simonton's Company of Ohio Militia. Walker remembered that after his company had left the post to return home after their enlistment had expired and camped at Fort Findlay some miles south of the Maumee Rapids, "playing ball and running foot races, together with other small games passed away the evening." Following evening parade, the final formation of the day, his men continued to enjoy themselves by "drawing by the neck [i.e., standing side-by-side with their arms around one another's shoulders and necks] and singing songs till tattoo."[9]

Many enjoyed fishing in the Maumee River below the camp, and musicians frequently entertained their companions with familiar tunes when off duty. While at Fort Findlay, Adam Walker recalled that Samuel Coburn, who served with Walker in his company, "as has been his custom since we came here, gave a few melodious strains on the violin, and the day closed with cheerfulness."[10]

The selections that follow are taken from a variety of materials, including two company orderly books. General orders, the instructions issued to every soldier at the garrison from the camp's commanding officer, were hand copied into orderly books kept by the executive officer of every company within the garrison. These general orders set forth special rules or regulations and specified the daily routines that every soldier stationed at the post would be expected to follow. Orderly books preserved a written record of these orders. Because many of those serving at the garrison could neither read nor write, these orders were then read aloud to the soldiers while they were assembled together at parade on the day they were issued. Each company's orderly book also recorded administrative details specific to that company, including the type and duration of drills undertaken by the company, the assignment and completion of various fatigue duties, and the disposition of courts martial.[11]

The first orderly book was created by Col. James Mills, who commanded a detachment of Ohio Militia infantry. The document descended in the Mills family until at least the early twentieth century. In 1928, James Green transcribed the manuscript, added a brief introduction, and placed a typewritten copy of the orderly book in both the Cincinnati Historical Society and Ohio History Connection libraries.[12]

Among the administrative duties recorded by Mills was the sale of personal property owned by soldiers who had died while in service. If a soldier passed away while on campaign, his possessions were collected, inventoried, and then returned to his family or sold at general auction with the proceeds sent to his survivors. In the inventories listed here, the first was recorded at St. Marys while Mills's regiment was en route to the Maumee, and the remainder at Fort Meigs. These inventories provide considerable insight into the material culture possessed by soldiers at the post beyond that issued by the military such as uniforms, arms, accouterments, and equipment.

The second orderly book was created by Capt. Daniel Cushing, the commanding officer of Cushing's Company of the Second Regiment, U.S. Artillery. That orderly book has been published twice before, in 1944 and again in 1975. The original document is held in the local history and genealogical collections of the Toledo–Lucas County Public Library.[13]

Sgt. Greenbury Keen served in the First Regiment, Second Brigade of the Pennsylvania Militia from October 2, 1812, until April 29, 1813. His company was at Fort Meigs from February 2 through April 17. His diary is held in the Library Archives Collection of the Ohio History Connection. The document "Picture of a Soldier's Life" is an excerpt from a letter written by an unnamed member of the Petersburg Volunteers (almost certainly Alfred M. Lorrain) published in *The Weekly Register* on May 8, 1813.[14]

A Regimental Book for the 1st Reg't, 3'rd Detachment of Ohio Militia Containing Orders Received and Issued by Colonel James Mills of Butler County and State of Ohio, February 6 to August 4, 1813

CAMP MEIGS, APRIL 23, A.D. 1813

The following hours are appointed on each fair day for drilling the troops:

From 10 o'clock A.M until 12 o'clock A.M. [*sic*, P.M.]; from 3 o'clock P.M. until 5 o'clock P.M each clear day. The troops will be taught, under their respective company officers under the superintendence of field officers, the position of a soldier without arms, to mark time, forming, dressing, facing, marching and wheeling in the manner prescribed in Duane's handbook, the adopted system for infantry.[15] The troops must be perfected in this lesson before they will be suffered to proceed to the second or third drill. The commanding officers of [each] corps will hold the officers commanding companies responsible for their company's turning out promptly at the hours prescribed for drilling.

GENERAL ORDERS, CAMP MEIGS, APRIL 24, 1813

It is expected by the general that the arms, accoutrements, and clothing of the men will be in the most complete order. The general has begun to complain of the inattention of the police [i.e., cleanliness] of the camp. The sinks [i.e., latrines] have not earth thrown into them as often as is necessary. And the remains of animals are to be found in every part of the camp. The regulations for the preservation of cleanliness ought to be better observed. It shall be the duty of the Officer of the Day to point out to the commanding officers of the corps any defect as to the police of the camp under their control. And if any such defect or nuisance is not immediately removed, the Officer of the Day will report the officer neglecting it to the general.

COURT MARTIAL, CAMP MEIGS JUNE 21ST, 1813

Specification 1st, Ungentleman- and unofficer-like conduct being exhibited by Ensign William Dill to Sgt. Maj. John McCloskey in saying to the Sgt. Maj. when he was in the discharge of his official duties, that there were so many big bugs and under-strappers in the garrison that the men don't know what they should do, or words tantamount; implying that the Sgt. Maj. was an under-strapper who ought not to be obeyed or respected. Col. James Mills sent him a notification in the words following:

Ensign Dill,

It appears that you have been guilty of un-gentleman and unofficer-like conduct in your treatment to Sgt. Maj. John McCloskey this morning. You will therefore consider yourself suspended from any command in the company until you be reported fit for duty and will do well henceforward to be prudently reserved in your language.

Camp Meigs, May 16th, 1813

By virtue of a petition presented this day by the field officers of the Ohio Militia to the commanding officer of this garrison praying for an exemption from fatigue on the first day of the week or Christian Sabbath, except in cases of real necessity, the following answer was presented to Col. Mills, to wit:

Gentlemen,

I have received yours of this date wishing that the officers and men belonging to your regiment might be exempted from fatigue on the first day of week except in cases of real necessity. To this request, I can only observe that we are engaged in work of real and absolute necessity, such as the good of the service and the health of the troops require. And I can assure you gentlemen, if I thought differently, I have no disposition, having but a temporary command, to rescind any order or regulation General Harrison may have made.

Yours very respectfully,

John Miller, Col. 19th Regt., Inft. and Commandant

ST. MARYS—MARCH 8TH, 1813

Died this day at 12 O'clock William Marshal, a private, of the pleurisy, who belonged to Capt. McHenry's company of the Regt. Whereupon Capt. Shaw, Lieut. Vance, by order examined and took an inventory of his effects which consisted of: One dollar and twelve-and-a-half cents cash; one pair of nippers; one whetstone; three awls; one razor; one pocket knife; one lb. of tobacco; one spoon; one linen bag; one pair of woolen socks; one shirt; two waistcoats; one linsey coat; one hunting shirt; one white Roram hat;[16] and one pair of overalls.

Died on the 3rd of May A.D. 1813 of a wound from an Indian ball in the head, Eson Hibbs.

Inventory of the property and cash belonging to sd. Hibbs: Cash, one Doll., 12 cents; one hat; 1 coarse muslin shirt; pr. mittens; 1 cotton vest; 1 swan's-down ditto; 1 pr. of old pantaloons; 1 pr. ditto; 1 pr. shoe leathers, closed; 3 pr. ditto & thread; 1 pr. ditto uppers closed, lined, and bound; 1 light kit of shoemaker's tools; and 1 tomahawk.

Died on the 21st day of May Samuel Colby without complaint, supposed to be in a fit of some kind about daybreak—private in Capt. Hamilton's Company, 1st Regt., 3rd Detach., Ohio Militia. Whereupon Capt. Patrick Shaw and Capt. Theophilus Simonton examined and took an inventory of his effects which consisted of 1 roundabout; 1 surtout coat;[17] 2 shirts; 1 pair linen pantaloons; 1 par of socks; 1 pair of woolen pantaloons; 1 handkerchief; 1 belt & knife; 1 pair of mittens; 1 pair of shoes; 1 hat; 1 pair new shoes.

Died on the 28th day of May John Biram of a short illness. He was a private in Capt. Hamilton's Company, 1 regt., 3 Detach., Ohio Militia at Camp Meigs 1813

Whereupon Capt. Patrick Shaw and Capt. Theophilus Simonton examined and took an inventory of his effects which consisted of the following articles, 1 hat; 1 shirt; 1 vest; 1 comb; 1 cotton coat; cash, 6 1/4 cents; 1 pair corded pantaloons, 1 pair shoe leathers; and 7 twists of tobacco.[18]

Greenbury Keen's Journal of a Tour of Duty in the Northwestern Army under the Command of Major-General William Henry Harrison

February 17, 1813—About 4 o'clock this morning there were two men apprehended [i.e., observed]. The sentinel hailed them, "Who comes there?" They replied "Friends from the River Raisin." They said they wanted to get to the fire to warm them[selves]. After they got to the fire, they began to ask a great many questions concerning our strength, number of cannons, discipline; and in the mean time, the officer of the day came by and apprehended them as [i.e., believed them to be] spies. They were taken to Gen. Harrison; then he questioned them concerning their business. They said they lived at the River Raisin and that they had heard he was scarce of flour, and said that they had to let him know he might get a quantity of wheat and flour at the River Raisin by sending a small detachment; [but] word having been brought in the evening before of them receiving a reinforcement at Malden of 600 regulars, he suspected them to be spies and ordered them to be put under guard and handcuffed.[19]

March 28, 1813—Great quantities of fish are caught of different sorts, pickerel from 3–10 pounds, muskellunge from 3 to 40-pound weight, sturgeon from one to one hundred weight, cat one hundred. These fish are taken with spears or gigs by a man walking on the shore with a spear, the handle to be 12 feet in length. He dashes this into the water by random without seeing the fish, and often spearing two at one stroke.

March 30, 1812—About the break of day, myself and one more went to the river to spear some fish. We crossed the river in a canoe and in the space of thirty minutes we had 67 fish which weighed from 1 to 7 pounds. We caught them all by walking up the shore and plunging our spears in by random. Caught sometimes three and frequently two at a stroke. Many sturgeon have been caught of 90-pound weight and some more.[20]

Orderly Book of Cushing's Company, 2nd U.S. Artillery April 1813—February 1814

GARRISON ORDERS, FORT MEIGS, APRIL 9TH, 1813

For the future, in cases of alarm the troops are to repair immediately to their respective alarm posts. They will not be permitted to pass without the pickets on such occasions except by order of the commanding officer, the gates will be shut by the guards and kept shut by them till directed to open them.

No fatigue party is to be sent from the garrison without a guard with it.

One subaltern, one noncommissioned officer, and twenty privates of the dragoons will be kept in such readiness as practicable to make a sudden pursuit of the enemy on proper occasions. One subaltern, one noncommissioned officer, and twenty privates will be selected from the other corps and kept in readiness for the like purpose.

No men are to straggle along the river more than three-hundred yards either above or below the pickets without the written permission of the officers of the corps to which they belong; and where men are discovered committing a breach of this order, the officers of the guard the nearest to them shall send a party and apprehend them and confine them under a charge of disobedience of orders.

To preserve the health of the camp, it has become necessary to establish a rigorous police. The commanding officers of battalions and companies will see that the men remove from the vicinity of their tents and parade ground every species of filth and cause it to be buried without the garrison; and for the future to keep the tents and parade ground as clean as possible. It will be the particular duty of the regimental and detachment quartermasters to superintend the above mentioned police, and the officer of the day will visit the several lines and report all omissions of police duty.

For the future, the gates of the garrison will be shut at retreat beating under the direction of the officer of the day, after which no man will be permitted to pass out except by [the order of] of the commanding officer on special occasions. Of course the men will supply themselves with wood and water before that period.

As the men are thus prohibited from passing out in the night, the commanding officer of each company under the direction of his field officer, if any he have, will cause a sink [i.e., a latrine] to be made in a suitable place near his company, covered by a common tent, to which the men will repair at night and the sick in all seasons. The depth of these sinks must not be less than ten feet, if it can be avoided, and a small quantity of fresh earth must be scattered over their contents daily.

HEAD QUARTERS CAMP MEIGS, APRIL 22ND, 1813

Genl. Orders

The guards will in future when relieved be conducted to the outside of the camp and under the direction of the Officer of the Day, will discharge the loads in the guns at a mark. The best shot will receive a quart of whiskey, the second best a pint upon the order of the Officer of the Day.

General Orders, Head Quarters Camp Meigs, April 21st, 1813

The following prices will in future govern the sale of the Articles herein contained as Settled by a Board of Officers agreeably to a General Order

Coffee	$"—62 1/2
Refined loaf Sugar	"—62 1/2
Imported Brown Sugar	"—50
Maple Country Sugar	"—37 1/2
Tea—good Quality	3—00
Tobacco	"—50
Chocolate common	"—50
Do first quality	"—62 1/2
Maple & dissolved sugar Molasses	1—50
Molasses imported pr gallon	3—00
Whiskey when sold by permission	1—25
Brandy, Spirits and Rum	4—50
Pepper, pr lb	1—00
Soap hard	"—50
" soft	"—25
Butter	"—37 1/2
Bacon	"—25

Molded Cotton wick Candles	"—40
Common dipped Candles	"—25
Vinegar, good pr gallon	3—00
(By Order)	John O'Fallon
Actg Dy Adjt Genl.[21]	

Picture of a Soldier's Life: From a Private in the Petersburg Volunteers to His Friend in That Place, Dated Zanesville, [Ohio] March 28, 1813

When I last wrote you from Upper Sandusky, I confidently expected something of considerable importance would have transpired in a very short time; but, unfortunately, the war in this quarter is protracted to a much longer period than I at that time contemplated. Indeed, the best-informed people in the army think that nothing decisive can be done before the next winter. It will never answer to invade a country with militia; some will not cross the lines, others will not submit to any kind of subordination; and in fact, they would all rather be at home than courting fame on the embattled field.

The Kentucky and Ohio Militia have been discharged some time. The Pennsylvania and Virginia militia are to be discharged on the 1st of April: and unless other troops arrive, the camp will, in a great measure, be unprotected. None will be left except our battalion consisting of the Petersburg Volunteers and two companies from Pittsburgh (fifty men in one and fifteen in the other), together with about three-hundred-and-fifty regulars. James G. Chalmers (who is appointed paymaster for all the twelve months' volunteers with the rank of ensign) and myself left the rapids on the 8th. We have to remain here until the arrival of the district paymaster.

The next day after the date of my letter from Sandusky, we left that place for the rapids, together with three hundred militia under the command of Major Orr. We had with us twenty pieces of heavy artillery and a quantity of military stores of every description. We at this time knew nothing of the unfortunate events at the River Raisin. On the second day of our march, a courier arrived from General Harrison ordering the artillery to advance with all possible speed.

This was rendered totally impossible by the snow which took place, it being a complete swamp nearly all the way.

On the evening of the same day, news arrived that General Harrison had retreated to Portage River, eighteen miles in the rear of the encampment at the rapids. As many men as could be spared determined to proceed immediately to reinforce him. It is unnecessary to state that we were among the first who wished to advance. At 2 o'clock the next morning, our tents were struck and in half an hour, we were on the road. I will candidly confess that on that day I regretted being a soldier. On that day we marched thirty miles under an incessant rain; and I am afraid you will doubt my veracity when I tell you that in eight miles of the best road, it took us over the knees and often to the middle.

The Black Swamp (four miles from Portage River and four miles in the extent) would have been considered impassable by all but men determined to surmount every difficult to accomplish the object of their march. In this swamp, you lose sight of *terra firma* altogether—the water was about six inches deep on the ice, which was very rotten, often breaking through to the depth of four or five feet.

The same night we encamped on very wet ground, but the driest that could be found, the rain still continuing. It was with difficulty we could raise fire; we had no tents, our clothes were wet, no axes, nothing to cook in, and very little to eat. A brigade of pack-horses being near us, we procured from them some flour, killed a hog, (there being plenty of *them* along the road); our bread was baked in the ashes and the pork we broiled on the coals—a sweeter meal I never partook of. When we went to sleep, it was on two logs laid close to each other to keep our bodies from the damp ground. Good God! What a pliant being is man in adversity. The loftiest spirit that ever inhabited the human breast would have been tamed amid the difficulties that surrounded us.

The next morning, we arrived at Portage River (the headquarters of the North Western Army). During our stay at this latter place, we were in constant expectation of an attack. Several nights we went to sleep with our muskets in our arms and all our accoutrements fixed for action.

On the arrival of General Leftwich and General Crooks' brigades from Sandusky, we marched for the Rapids; the Kentucky and Ohio troops had then only six days to serve. In a speech made to them by the general, he pledged himself to take them to Malden in twenty days, which would have been the case if the cannon and military stores could have been got on.

When we arrived at the rapids, the advanced guard discovered on the opposite side of the river one of three persons who, two days previous, were sent to Malden with a flag, killed and scalped by the Indians. The other two, we have since heard, are prisoners at Malden—so little does our enemy respect the laws of nations.

The encampment is opposite the Michigan Territory in a fine situation, protected by nature in three quarters by a steep and high bank. The whole is piquetted in. The stores are deposited in block-houses built round the piquetting to the number of eight. All is nearly in a complete state of defense.

Along this river is the handsomest country I ever saw. There have been several fine plantations in the vicinity of the camp, but all is a scene of desolation. After Hull's surrender, the whole country was laid waste by the Indians. Every half mile there has been a house—the only indication of a habitation that now remains is their ruins that cover the ground where they once stood!

A few days after our arrival, a detachment was sent out, of which our company made part, to attack a considerable party of Indians fifteen miles the river. We started as night set in and marched all the way on the ice. About 2 o'clock, we came near the place where we expected to surprise the enemy. We were put in order of battle and instructed to proceed in silence

"Still was the pipe and drum—"Save the heavy tread and armor's clang,
"The sullen march was dumb."

In a few minutes their forces were in sight; they were in a bend of the river nearly a mile off. When within gun-shot, I could hear the men cocking their pieces. Our company, to a man, was even at that moment cheerful and gay! Fear was distant from our ranks, and I do sincerely believe that had the enemy not flown previous to our arrival we would all have realized the expectations of our friends. Some of their spies, as we have since heard from prisoners from Malden, saw us on our march, in consequence of which they made a precipitate retreat. We followed them within five miles of the River Raisin and returned to camp without any rest, except for two hours. We were twenty-one hours absent during which time we marched more than sixty miles.

The particulars of the last unfortunate account of the River Raisin you are already acquainted with, like in the failure on the expedition to destroy the *Queen*

Charlotte. Our company marched as far as the mouth of Lake Erie to reinforce the first party, but met them on their return.

We have all built small houses in front of the tents, which make us very comfortable. The camp duty is very severe, there being no tents or houses for the guard when off their post, so that it is equally as pleasant for them to be at their post as off, they being forbidden to leave the rendezvous of the guard. Every other day a man mounts guard, and the day that intervenes he is at work within the camp.

Major Alexander, who commands the battalion, is as fine a fellow as I ever knew. The most perfect harmony exists between the Pittsburgh Company and ours, they being the only two companies of twelve-month volunteers in camp; and all that wear a uniform, a generous emulation exists among them, which is of infinite service to both.

Officers and men all mingle together. We visit each other's tents of an evening, sing, tell stories, play music, and drink grog when we can get it, which by-the-bye is not often the case, suttlers not being permitted to sell spirits in the camp.

Poor Edmund S. Gee is no more! I saw him breathe his last. We consigned him to his mother earth with all the decency our circumstances would permit. We had it not in our power to dress his corpse in all the pomp and pageantry of sorrow. The tears of his companions, more eloquent than all the parade that sable weeds could bestow, were his due, and those he had. All the battalion attended the funeral—likewise General Leftwich, who requested the chaplain to perform a funeral service, a thing not done on any similar occasion.

Chalmers and myself will return to the camp in a few days. It is dangerous to travel the roads in small parties as the Indians are all round the camp. We will be obliged to remain in the settlement until some troops are going on.

The day before we left camp, a lieutenant was shot and scalped within sight of the camp. Another man was shot at, but fortunately had a Bible in his side-pocket, which arrested the course of the ball and saved his life.

There is one hundred miles of the road between this and the rapids without a single inhabitant—all a wilderness.[22]

~ CHAPTER 6 ~

First Siege, April 27–May 5, 1813

Towards the close of April a detachment of the 41st, some militia, and 1500 Indians accompanied by a train of battering artillery and attended by two gun-boats, proceeded up that river and established themselves on the left bank, at the distance of a mile from the site selected for our batteries. . . . At length every preparation having been made, a shot from one of the gun-boats was the signal for their opening, and early on the morning of the 1st of May a heavy fire was commenced and continued for four days without intermission.

—John Richardson, Cadet, 41st Regiment of Foot

As winter receded into early spring, Crown authorities undertook a determined effort to dislodge Harrison and the Americans from the rapids. Fort Meigs posed a direct and serious threat to British ambitions within the region. The American occupation of the rapids denied British forces use of the Maumee River from the rapids to its headwaters at Fort Wayne. It likewise prevented British forces from taking offensive action deeply into Ohio. If British forces advanced into Ohio from the north, American troops stationed at Fort Meigs could move to the east, severing their opponent's line of supply, reinforcement, and retreat. Moreover, Fort Meigs allowed American forces to operate with impunity in the area south and west of Detroit. Those operations did not pose a direct military risk to British forces at Fort Malden, but they did impact Britain's relationship with her Native allies within the region, and the American presence had already caused several Native bands either to switch their loyalty to the Americans or to declare neutrality in the contest. Lastly, British authorities were not naive about Harrison's intentions. They understood clearly that once the American general had amassed the men and materials necessary to undertake an offensive, he would move to repatriate Detroit and invade Upper Canada.[1]

On April 24, soon after the season's moderating temperatures opened the ice on Lake Erie, Brig. Gen. Henry Procter, the commanding officer at Fort Malden, launched an attack against Fort Meigs. A sizable flotilla consisting of the brig *Lady Prevost*, six other vessels of similar size, two gunboats, *Eliza* and *Myers*, and numerous bateaux carried the British expedition down the Detroit River and across Lake Erie's Western Basin, toward the mouth of the Maumee River. With Procter were 439 infantry regulars, most from the Welsh 41st Regiment of Foot and the Canadian Royal Newfoundland Regiment, 462 Canadian militia, and thirty-one Royal Artillerymen to employ the heavy siege artillery and howitzers accompanying the expedition. Traveling concurrently with the army, though over land, were a small detachment of Indian and Marine Department officials and a few civilian volunteers from the Detroit and River Raisin areas.[2]

On the April 26, an advance party of soldiers and Natives inspected the land on the north shore of the Maumee River immediately opposite Fort Meigs to determine its suitability for the placement of artillery batteries. On April 27, Procter sailed to Swan Creek a few miles upstream from the river's mouth and rendezvoused with Tecumseh, Roundhead, Blackhawk, and approximately 1,400 warriors, bringing the combined force of the invading army to about 2,400. Later in the day, the army sailed to within two miles of Fort Meigs. Establishing his base camp at long-abandoned Fort Miamis, a British installation erected to oppose Anthony Wayne in 1794 and now in ruins, Procter deployed his Indian allies to form a perimeter to the south around Fort Meigs while his troops constructed four artillery batteries immediately across the river from the American garrison.

At the same time, Harrison was working furiously to prepare his camp for the impending assault. Construction on the American post had continued until just days before the British arrival. Once completed, Fort Meigs was a large and commanding facility. Protected by an earth-and-log palisade, interior and exterior trenching, and earthen defensive works, and bristling with artillery mounted on five batteries and within seven blockhouses spaced irregularly along the fort's perimeter, the post housed a garrison of over 1,200 soldiers. Fort Meigs presented a formidable challenge to British aspirations, and Harrison himself boasted

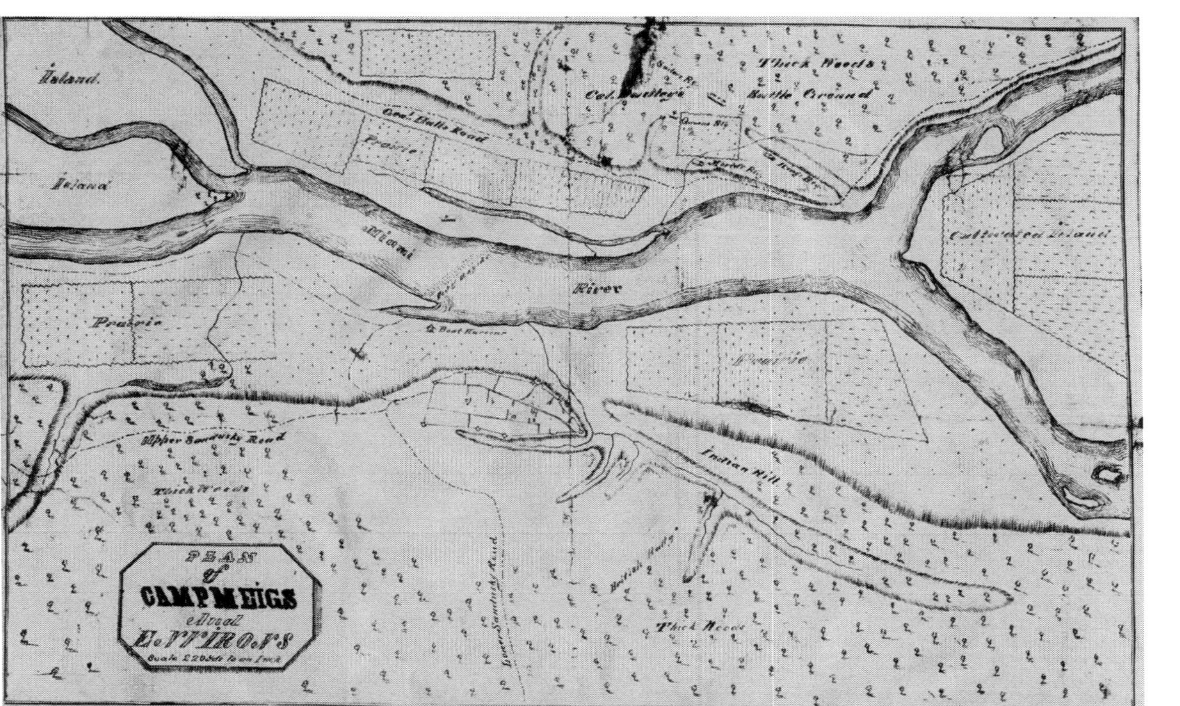

Drawn by Joseph H. Larwill in July 1813, this map shows the fort's stockade, blockhouses, the system of traverses, and earthen mounds thrown up inside of the fort, prior to the first siege. Courtesy of the Toledo–Lucas County Public Library.

to Secretary of War John Armstrong that he believed that the fort could "bid defiance to all the forces in Upper Canada."[3]

Nonetheless, Harrison and Capt. Wood both believed that in its present condition, the camp was vulnerable to the type of extended artillery bombardment it now seemed certain to undergo. Therefore, the Americans threw up two traverses, large earthen mounds twelve feet high and fifteen feet across at their base, parallel to one another running the length of the camp. These interior earthworks shielded the men from incoming artillery. In addition, the men excavated "bombproofs," small underground shelters placed at the base of the traverses that further protected them from exploding shells and ricocheting cannon shot.[4]

Lastly, Harrison and his officers reiterated the instructions to their men that would direct the American defense once the attack began. "Had the enemy attempted to scale the pickets (which we expected they would attempt)," recalled Samuel Walker serving with the Ohio Militia, "we would have g[iven] them a warm reception. The rifles first fired, then the muskets, then fall back and load our rifles; the volunteers to step forward and fire, we then to advance and fire again if they attempted to scale."[5]

From April 28 through April 30, both armies prepared their defenses. British gunners established four artillery batteries on the shore opposite Fort Meigs while the Americans did what they could to strengthen the post. Each side used their artillery to fire upon the other as these works were being completed, but the exchanges were tentative and probing in character, inflicting little damage. During the night of April 30, *Eliza* and *Myers* moved upstream to the foot of the rapids under the cover of darkness and fired upon the garrison, but with no effect.[6]

At 10:00 in the morning on May 1, a round fired from *Eliza* followed by a massed artillery volley from all of the British guns signaled the beginning of the siege in earnest. British gunners hurled 240 rounds into the American garrison throughout the course of the day while Native warriors harassed the defenders from the south, east, and west. Harrison answered with a constant, though measured, fire from his own guns. In this way, the battle continued for the next two days with neither side able to inflict significant casualties upon the other.

Before light on May 3, British gunners surreptitiously crossed the Maumee and quietly established a fifth artillery battery consisting of a mortar, a five-and-a-half-inch howitzer, and a single six-pound cannon some four hundred yards east of the fort. The new battery posed a significant threat to the fort's defenses.

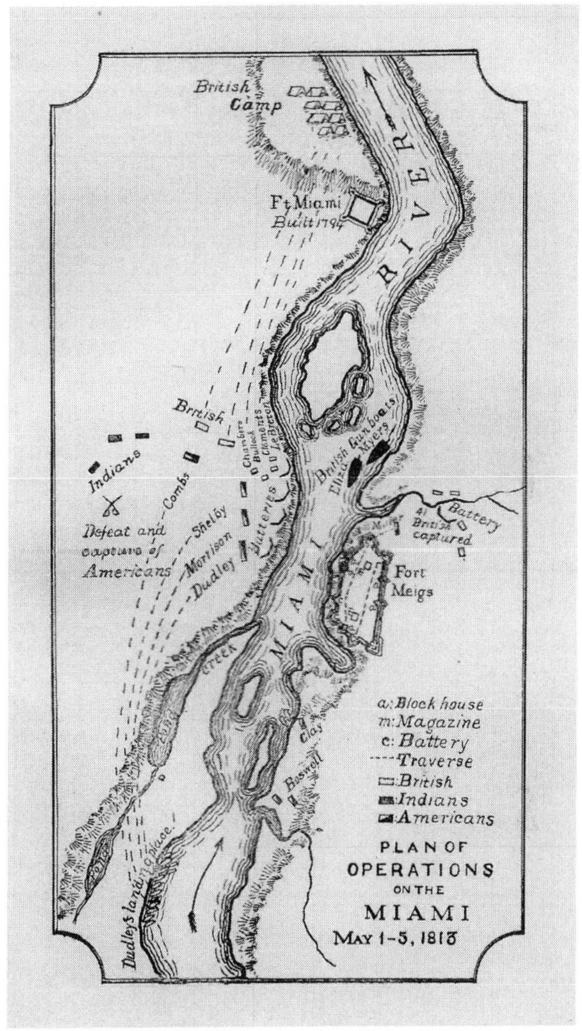

The first siege of Fort Meigs. This map shows the location of Fort Meigs, the British artillery batteries placed on both sides of the Maumee, and the location of the British camp near the remains of Fort Miamis. Three columns of Kentucky troops led by William Dudley successfully attacked and overran the British batteries immediately opposite the fort but were then lured into an ambush, where most of the Kentuckians were either captured or killed. Alexander Casselman, ed., *Richardson's War of 1812, with Notes and a Life of the Author* [Toronto: Historical Publishing, 1902].

The emplacement was positioned so that artillery rounds fired from the battery would sweep entirely through the length of the American post from the side, potentially inflicting many casualties and significant structural damage. Capt. Wood responded to the threat by erecting numerous "wing" traverses, short traverses projecting at right angles from the two main interior earthworks, to protect the men inside the garrison. But ultimately, it was the ineptitude of the

British gunners themselves who undermined the battery's effectiveness. "The person who was employed with the howitzer seemed a friend or possessed of very little skill in his profession," claimed Wood after the battle, "for notwithstanding he was but three or four hundred yards distant from the camp, yet not more than one out of four or five shells thrown ever came inside the lines. It was the opinion of many of our men that he certainly must be a friend and felt for our situation."[7]

Late in the evening of May 4, Harrison learned that 1,200 men making up a column of reinforcements from Kentucky led by Brig. Gen. Green Clay were in boats a few miles above Fort Meigs on the Maumee River, poised for their final descent to the embattled post the following morning. Harrison returned word that Clay was to divide his force and land eight hundred men on the north side of the Maumee opposite the American garrison, attack and destroy the four British gun batteries positioned there, return to their boats, and immediately cross the river to the protection of the fort. Clay's remaining four hundred men were to land on the south shore west of the post and fight their way into the American stronghold, dispersing the Indians harassing the fort in that location. As Clay's men completed their tasks, a strong detachment from the fort would move against and eradicate the new battery shelling the post from the east.[8]

Clay commenced the attack in early morning on May 5. At first, all went according to Harrison's plan. Clay personally led the detachment landing on the south shore, and he and his men confronted only slight opposition as they made their way into the American stockade. The attack against the east battery, led by Col. John Miller of the 19th Infantry, encountered heavy resistance and sustained numerous casualties, but was able to overrun the British position, render the guns inoperable, and return to the fort with forty-two prisoners.[9]

The assault against the main British batteries on the north shore, though, turned into a disaster for the Kentuckians. Led by Col. William Dudley, the detachment successfully surrounded and then occupied the British positions, disabled the enemy guns, and cut down the British flag without the loss of a single man. But instead of returning to his boats, Dudley allowed his men to chase what they believed to be retreating Indians into the surrounding woods. Native warriors, though, were not retreating; they were luring the Kentuckians into a carefully planned and skillfully executed ambush. In the running battle that ensued, Dudley and most of his senior officers were killed and nearly 650 of his men either lost their lives or were captured. Dudley's destruction was a stunning loss for the Americans.

Moreover, Dudley's men had disabled the British cannon by either removing the gun carriages' wheels or pounding their musket ramrods into the artillery's vent, a small hole at the rear of the cannon used to ignite the gun's powder charge and fire the piece. When British soldiers reoccupied the batteries shortly after the battle, they easily remounted the guns and removed the ramrods, quickly placing the guns back into service. The Kentuckians had paid dearly for Dudley's incompetence and gained nothing in return.

Although both sides were prepared to resume the battle following the Kentuckians' arrival, the actions on both sides of the river had seemingly exhausted each of the combatants. As the fighting ebbed, all grew quiet. The informal ceasefire continued to hold in the days that followed, and both Procter and Harrison sent envoys to one another to negotiate a mutual exchange of prisoners. Procter wished to resume the attack, but found that he could not. His Native allies, sated with captives and plunder taken from the ill-fated Kentuckians, began to drift away. In addition, the members of the Canadian Militia accompanying the expedition (along with their families) faced almost inevitable starvation the following winter if they were not permitted to return home immediately to plant their spring crops. They too began to evaporate. Procter's rations were running low, and dysentery and the ague had appeared among his troops. Lastly, on May 7, Procter received a dispatch advising him that the British post Fort York (present-day Toronto) had fallen, and he now believed that a large force of Americans could be deployed westward, either to attack Fort Malden directly or to cut off his retreat to Amherstburg. His forces ill and depleted, his provisions nearly exhausted, and wary of the possibility of an American counterattack from the east, Procter abandoned the siege.[10]

After his return to Fort Malden, Procter reported that his army had suffered thirteen killed, forty-one wounded, and thirty-seven captured during the engagement. Harrison claimed that the Americans had suffered eighty-one killed, seventeen within the fort during the bombardment and the remainder in the excursions against British forces on the south side of the river to his east and west. Harrison also listed 189 wounded during the battle. In addition, the Americans lost 650 men under Dudley. However, a Kentucky officer who served at Fort Meigs during the siege later insisted that Harrison's numbers were "too small by at least forty or fifty killed and an equal number in wounded."[11]

Despite these heavy losses, Harrison and his army still occupied the rapids. The Americans, therefore, still posed a significant threat to Detroit. Procter's objective when he moved against the rapids had not been to defeat Harrison and his army, but to destroy them. In this, he had failed. Procter's inability to reduce Fort Meigs meant that the Americans who occupied the post still remained poised to move against Detroit, and thus presented a potent obstacle to British security within the region. By any calculation, the campaign against Fort Meigs had been a stunning tactical victory for the British. But when Procter gave up the siege without dislodging the Americans, he ceded the strategic victory to Harrison.

The first four documents shown next are American. The first is the general order issued on April 29 in which Harrison exhorted his men to face the coming test with courage and valor. The next three documents, extended descriptions of the battle, were written by Eleazer D. Wood, Alfred M. Lorrain, and Alexander Bourne.[12]

Bourne was born in Wareham, Massachusetts, in 1786 and moved to Ohio in 1810, finding employment as a surveyor and cartographer in the Ohio Company's land office in Chillicothe. Drafted into the Ohio Militia in February 1813, he served as the adjutant in Lt. Col. Mills Stephenson's Regiment. At the conclusion of the conflict, Bourne resumed his career as surveyor with Ohio's General Land Office. In later years, he was named Adjutant General for the Ohio Militia and acted as one of the state's canal commissioners under Governor Duncan McArthur in the early 1830s. He died in 1849.

Bourne penned an extensive reminiscence of his life in the late 1840s, but the account remained with his family in manuscript form and unpublished for many years. In 1927, LeRoy Salsich, Bourne's great-grandson, transcribed the document and placed several typewritten copies in local libraries. In 1948, Neil Salsich, another descendent, edited and published that part of the memoir dealing with Bourne's War of 1812 service in *Northwest Ohio History.* The entire document was transcribed, edited, and published by Nicholas Benton in 2000 under the title *Memoir of Alexander Bourne 1786–1849 of Indian Neck Wareham, Massachusetts and Chillicothe, Ohio.*[13]

Bourne's recollection is lively, anecdotal, and filled with many entertaining vignettes. But it also betrays a hubris and naivety commonly encountered in militia accounts.

The next five documents were penned by British writers. The first is a daily journal kept by Maj. Peter Chambers during the Maumee expedition. Chambers served as the deputy assistant quartermaster general for the 41st, and sent a copy of his record to his friend Noah Freer, the military secretary for Sir George Prevost,

Governor General of British North America. The original document is housed in the Library and Archives Canada in Ottawa, Ontario. The version shown in this chapter is taken from a transcription published in volume 15 of the *Michigan Pioneer Historical Collections* in 1889.[14]

The second account was written by John Richardson. Richardson had volunteered to serve in the 41st immediately after the declaration of war in 1812 when he was only fifteen years old. Serving as a cadet, Richardson witnessed all of the important actions that his regiment was engaged in, including the fall of Detroit, French Town, and the sieges at Fort Meigs and Fort Stephenson. Following the war, Richardson published many accounts of his military experiences. Further, he also began to write novels based loosely upon his wartime adventures. As a result of these fictional writings, Canadian literary scholars today regard him as the chief creator of a distinctively Canadian literary tradition. The selection below is taken from Richardson's earliest account of his military service, "A Canadian Campaign: By a British Officer," published anonymously in 1826 in the British literary journal *The New Monthly Magazine.*[15]

The next document was created by Shadrach Byfield, a private in the 41st Regiment. Byfield's account is the only one created by an enlisted man serving in the 41st during the entire war. During the siege, Byfield served at the British battery established on the south shore of the Maumee, east of the fort. Severely wounded late in the war and forced to endure the amputation of an arm, Byfield likely created his account to supplement his income as a weaver following the conflict. This transcript is taken from Byfield's book, *A Narrative of a Light Company Soldier's Service in the 41st Regiment of Foot, During the Late American War*, published in 1840.[16]

The fourth and fifth selections are official correspondence. The fourth is the petition sent to Gen. Procter during the siege, from his militia officers, expressing their concern that if the siege continued, their continued absence from their homes would place them and their families in great peril in the months ahead. The fifth is Procter's official account of the campaign to his superior Sir George Prevost. Like Chambers's journal, both documents reside in the Library and Archives Canada and both transcriptions are taken from volume 15 of the *Michigan Pioneer Historical Collections.*[17]

The final document was created by the Sauk war captain Black Hawk (Ma-ka-tai-me-she-kia-kiak, or Black Sparrow Hawk). The Sauks under Black Hawk allied themselves with the British throughout the war, and Black Hawk was present during both sieges at Fort Meigs. Native accounts are extraordinarily rare, and extended reminiscences like the one presented here, rarer still. This narrative was created in 1833 when Black Hawk, following the Black Hawk War, was in captivity at Fort Armstrong in Rock Island, Illinois. While prisoner, Black Hawk narrated his autobiography to the garrison's Indian agent, Antoine LeClair, who translated it for J.B. Patterson, a local newspaper editor and journalist. Patterson published the autobiography in October of the same year, likely after editing his transcript of the oral interviews. In his narrative, Black Hawk has clearly conflated events occurring during both the first and second sieges of Fort Meigs, but nonetheless provides a unique perspective into Native motivation and action during the battle.[18]

Orderly Book of Cushing's Company, 2nd U.S. Artillery April 1813–February 1814

HEAD QUARTERS, CAMP MEIGS, APRIL 29TH, 1813

Genl. Orders

It is at length reduced to certainty that the enemy are about to carry into effect their threatened attack upon this post. The temerity of the attempt can only be accounted for by their ignorance of our strength or their reliance upon our want of resolution to defend ourselves. The general is confident that in both they will be disappointed. Can the citizens of a free country who have taken up arms to defend its rights think of submitting to a band composed of the mercenaries of reluctant Canadians goaded to the field by the bayonet and of wretched, naked savages? Can the breast of an American soldier when he casts his eyes to the opposite shore, the scene of his country's triumphs over the same foes, be influenced by any other feelings than the hopes of victory and glory? Is not this army composed of the same materials with that which fought and conquered under the immortal Wayne? Yes, fellow soldiers, your general sees your countenances beam with the same fire that he witnessed on that glorious occasion. And although it would be the height of presumption to compare himself to a hero, he boasts of being that hero's pupil. To your posts, then, fellow soldiers; and remember that the eyes of your country are upon you.[19]

Eleazer Derby Wood's Journal of the Northwestern Campaign, 1812–1813

On the 25th the combined British and Indian forces, consisting of 800 militia, 500 regulars and 1,500 Indians all under the command of Brig.-General Procter, arrived at the mouth and landed on the left shore of the Miami, and instantly threw a party of Indians across the river to observe and watch the conduct of our troops should any of them be sent to reconnoiter, as was the constant practice. The next day, the army was put in motion keeping its left to the river and arriving with the gunboats; and batteries in which were the artillery and ordnance stores, and advanced gradually up until it arrived on the 27th at old Fort Miami, situated as already described two-and-a-half miles below Camp Meigs and near the foot of the rapids. The bateaux were immediately unloaded and employed in conveying the balance of the Indians to our side of the river.

Today the camp was completely invested and on the following night, the enemy broke ground in four different places and were very industriously employed until morning when their works were discovered to be in a tolerable state of forwardness. No sooner were these nocturnal works discovered than orders were brought to bear to open instantly upon them; which orders were executed with alacrity and promptitude; and those works of one night's growth soon looked as if they had been but a moment's.

Understanding now perfectly the enemy's plan of attack and where each of his principal batteries were going to be erected, and the particular object of each, and knowing that we should be greatly annoyed in our present state by his artillery, it became necessary to entrench the army entirely anew, which of course must be done within the original lines of the camp. A plan for a kind of entrenched citadel had been some time before arranged and recommended by Captain Wood of the engineers to General Harrison as the only effectual security for the army in case the enemy should attack with artillery, and which in a measure had been mentioned by him. It had not only met his approbation, but he had on one or two occasions observed that he thought it had better be commenced and in a state of progression, that we might be the better prepared for the reception of the enemy in case he should come suddenly upon us.

Orders were given for Captain Wood to commence the new entrenchments. On the 28th in the morning, the whole army was set to work and continued in the trenches until "tattoo"; when, on account of darkness and rain, a suspension of their labors until reveille was recommended by the engineer to the general and readily approved of; the troops were accordingly dismissed with direction to the different commandants of parties to resume their stations in the trenches at break-of-day, which orders were strictly complied with.

Orders had been previously given in the forepart of the day for the troops to continue at work all night in the trenches; but they had progressed most rapidly through the day, and the night being a very bad one, it was thought that more labor might be accomplished the next day by letting the men rest than by keeping them all night at work. Never did men behave better on any similar occasion than did ours on this.

The Indians had now become extremely troublesome; there was not a stump, bush, or log within musket shot of the camp but what shielded its man, and some of them two or three. Unfortunately, we had not been able to clear the wood away to a sufficient distance on our left, of which circumstances those demons of the forest very readily availed themselves, and instead of remaining idle at the foot of the trees, they bounced into their tops with as much agility and dexterity as if they had been taught it from their infancy, and from those elevated stations, poured down into our camp prodigious showers of musketry; but the distance being so great, out of the numerous quantity of balls received in camp but very few took effect. Many of the men, however, were wounded and rendered incapable of performing duty for some time. This ethereal annoyance from the Indians certainly served as a source of great stimulus to the militia in camp, for notwithstanding their prompt obedience to orders and attention to duty, yet their movements were much accelerated by it, as will always be found in the case whenever musketry is brisk about their ears.

It is by no means astonishing that any kind of troops should act with energy and courage when situated as were those in Camp Meigs, one hundred miles distant from any settlement, in an impenetrable swamp, the camp entirely surrounded with Indians who filled it with musketry as thick as hail, no hope of relief, and the active preparations across the river for cannonading and bombarding the camp all announcing the *necessity* for the most spirited and vigorous resistance.

After the first day's labor in the trenches, one-third of the troops only were kept in them constantly, who were relieved every three hours by fresh ones. In this way we continued our operations, occasionally firing at the civilized savages across the river as well as upon the wild one in the woods, whenever the former exposed themselves *or the latter became too troublesome.*

The general was extremely active through the day, was everywhere to be seen in the trenches urging on the works, as well by precept as example. He slept but little, and was uncommonly vigilant and watchful through the night.

The first thing commenced to shield the troops against the annoyance of cannon, was a traverse of about twenty feet base laid parallel with the river upon the elevated ground, which was near the middle and running the whole length of camp. It was from ten to fifteen feet high and completed early on the morning of the 1st of May. An avenue, as it were, had been opened through the tents, and as many left standing on that side next [to] the enemy as possible to cover from his view our operations until the traverse should be completed, and which seemed from his conduct to have answered the purpose extremely well.

This particular piece of work was completed early on the morning of the 1st of May, just as it was discovered that the enemy had finished three of his principal batteries, had got his guns in, was then loading and bringing them to battery; when orders were directly given for all the tents in front to be instantly struck and carried into the rear of the traverse. This was done in almost a moment, and that beautiful prospect of beating up our quarters, which but an instant before presented itself to the view of the eager and skillful artillerists had now entirely fled, and in its place suddenly appeared an immense shield of earth obscuring from his sight every tent, every horse (of which there were 200), and every creature belonging to the camp. How disappointed must have been the indefatigable and skillful engineer on discovering the futility of all his works, and what a gloomy and hopeless prospect presented itself to the ardent and scientific artillerist!

Those canvas houses, which in a great measure had covered the growth of the traverse by keeping from the view of the enemy the operations about it, were now, with their inhabitants in them, entirely protected in their turn.

But as neither the general, engineer, or artillerist were convinced of the *folly* and *futility* of their works, everything being ready, the batteries must be opened; and five days of arduous cannonading and bombarding were necessary to produce *a thorough conviction.* At 11 o'clock at night, when all was again silent. As we sustained but little injury through the day, having but one or two men killed and five or six wounded (the latter principally by the Indians), and our supply of ammunition being quite inadequate to the necessities of a lengthy siege, we fired very little during the day, contenting ourselves in safety and listening to the enemy's music. Some shells and a few rounds of grape were occasionally fired at the Indians to drive them from their stations whenever they approached too near the lines, which, in consequence of their teasing, were kept in almost a constant blaze with musketry.

On the 2nd, at dawn of day, the cannonade again commenced with great vigor, and the batteries continued to play with considerable briskness through the day and with about the same effect as the preceding day. The position, however, of one of our magazines was discovered in the course of the day, and great hopes seemed to have been entertained by the enemy of effecting its destruction, the roof having been hit by a 24-pound shot. The whole of the batteries were instantly directed upon it, and the traverse not being of sufficient height to protect the roof, that part of it was pretty soon battered down, or rather blown off by a shell which fell and exploded directly upon its loft. No damage, however, was done to it.

As soon as the firing ceased in the evening, Captain Bradford (a most excellent officer), with a party of men, went to work, and before day had the magazine entirely repaired. Its loft had been covered with two tiers of large timbers with plenty of raw hides placed between them, so as to prevent the fire from falling down into the magazine in case of shells lighting upon it. These timbers were hewn on two sides and well spiked together.

It had been apprehended that the enemy, finding he could not affect his purpose by battering from the opposite side of the river, might take it into his head to establish batteries somewhere along our front or on one or other of the flanks, and in order that we might be prepared to receive him at all points, another traverse, parallel with the first and distant about one hundred yards, had been commenced, was soon finished, and the two connected by several short ones. This was done with a view to cut the space up so much that ricochet firing lengthwise the camp should be attended with no injury while the men were in their tents.

Our entrenchments now, in a manner, formed a complete citadel which could have been defended to great advantage, and would have been found extremely difficult to force had the enemy been able to have affected a passage at the first lines, which he never could done without sustaining an immense loss.

On the 3rd, at 10 o'clock A.M., our apprehensions respecting the enemy's crossing the river were completely realized, for it was now discovered by the fire of three of four pieces that he was already on our left with his cannon stuck in the edge of a small ravine. From a few of the first shots, some damage was sustained, but the best position had not yet taken, and by setting two or three 18-pounders to work upon those impudent fellows in the "bush," we were soon able to silence them for a time. An attack from the left having been anticipated, its consequences were, in a great measure, foreseen and guarded against. The person who was employed with the howitzer seemed a friend or possessed of very little skill in his profession, for notwithstanding he was but about three or four hundred yards distant from the camp, yet not more than one out of four or five shells thrown ever came inside the lines. It was the opinion of many of our men that he certainly must be a friend and felt for our situation. Be that as it may, he badly acquitted himself. In the course of the third day, we had two or three dragoons killed, several slightly touched, and a number of horses killed. In fact, it seemed to have been *particularly* an *unfortunate* day for the cavalry.

On the 4th, the enemy neither opened his batteries so early in the morning as he had been accustomed to do, nor did he fire them with his usual activity. The fire, though somewhat lively in the morning, grew less so through the day until toward evening, when it became quite dull; and everything about the batteries appeared as if the enemy were convinced that their labor was entirely lost and that a farther prosecution of the attack from that side of the river would only be attended with an immense waste of powder and ball, and ultimately prove of no avail.

From excess of fatigue and almost constant watching in the trenches through the night, our troops had become somewhat broken down. However, their spirits were yet good, and a little refreshment with a few hours rest were only necessary to render them as effective as ever. The garrison frequently showed itself above the works and occasionally gave three cheers, especially when the fire of the enemy was not brisk and when it could be done with safety. It always occasioned a most hideous *yell* from the Indians. These rascals appeared to be greatly delighted at the bursting of the shells in our camp, and whenever great or material damage was supposed to have been done by an explosion, they were sure to express the approbation by *yelping.*

At about 12 o'clock on the night of the 4th, Mr. Oliver, a young man who had been dispatched to meet General Clay who was supposed to be somewhere on the Miami, returned and brought information that the general was then within about eight miles of the camp with 1,200 militia, and that he would be able, in all probability, to reach Camp Meigs before day. Mr. Oliver left camp to meet General Clay on the 28th of April.

General Harrison immediately formed a plan for having the enemy's batteries across the river stormed and the guns spiked. Captain Dudley was furnished with spikes and directed to get out of camp as secretly as possible, to take a canoe and make the best of his way up the river until he should meet with General Clay, to whom he was to deliver the following instructions: That he must land the whole or such part of his troops on the opposite side of the river early in the morning as he might deem sufficient to storm and carry the enemy's batteries and spike their guns; the bearer of the order to act as a guide and to conduct the storming columns to the batteries. The magazines were likewise to be destroyed, and the troops instantly to return to their boats and recross the river to Camp Meigs. Captain Dudley reached General Clay in time to deliver his orders. Of the 1,200 men, 800 under the directions of Colonel Dudley (a man alike ignorant and rash, who had never heard a hostile gun) were ordered to land at dawn of day to perform this gallant service.

The troops were formed into three columns and moved down to the attack, but they did not reach the batteries until about 9 o'clock in the morning. On coming within 300 or 400 yards of the works, his men sent up a most tremendous yell (under an impression, I suppose, that a Kentucky yell was more to be dreaded than their arms), and pushed on without order or opposition and took possession of all the enemy's works almost without firing a single gun, and without the loss of a single man. The few artillerists who were about the batteries, on hearing this tremendous yell, took the alarm, snatched the colors from their standards, and flew with great precipitation to the main force below which was at old Fort Miami; nor were they easily overtaken. Colonel Dudley now found himself in complete possession of the objects of his enterprise, and he had nothing further to do but to spike the guns, blow up or destroy the magazines, and return with all possible celerity to his boats and cross the river before the enemy should have time allowed him to march the army up from Fort Miami and attack him in return.

But, great God! Neither knowing how to obey orders nor to profit by success, Colonel Dudley remained with his men upon the ground, gratifying a vain curiosity without spiking but a part of the guns and leaving the magazines entire until the enemy had ample time to collect his forces and return to repossess himself of his works and chastise in the severest manner the temerity, folly, ignorance, and stupidity of this most unfortunate commander. Yes, it seemed as if those miserable creatures were only waiting upon the theater of their success and glory for the enemy to be fully prepared to take ample revenge.

These batteries were situated near the bank of the river upon a small plain with a wood in the rear, and entirely edged with thick bushes except in the front; and the ground, on leaving the plain to go into the woods was considerably intersected with small ravines whose banks were entirely covered with under-mall brush.

After remaining in groups upon this plain in the most disorderly manner possible for about thirty minutes, the Indians returned and commenced a scattering fire from the edge of the bushes, which instantly drew the militia from the plain into the woods. In the meantime, a column of British regulars were marched along up the river until they came upon the ground just left by Colonel Dudley, when they halted, formed in order of battle, and advanced to the attack of his rear. Thus situated between two fires, his troops in the greatest disorder, skirmishing with the Indians in every direction, and possessing not the least knowledge of the local situation of the field of battle, what was to be expected, or what could be done by Colonel Dudley?

No human means within the control of this unfortunate officer could save him; his fate was fixed and the destruction of his corps inevitable. The contest was but short—a few minutes were sufficient to place this gallant corps of 800 Kentuckians at the mercy of a most *cruel, savage, and barbarous foe*, who only knew to conquer and slaughter. Of the 800 in the engagement, only about 100 were able to affect their retreat. Eighty or 90 of them got across the river to Camp Meigs and the balance escaped to Fort Wayne; 60 or 70 were killed and the rest taken prisoners.

Upwards of 600 were taken and marched under an escort of Indians to headquarters and confined in Old Fort Miami with a strong chain of sentinels round the works. The Indians were then permitted by General Procter to assemble upon the surrounding rampart and there, at their leisure, to amuse themselves by loading and firing at the crowd of prisoners until at length, they preferred slaughtering those wretched mortals in a manner more suitable to their savage feelings. They therefore laid by their rifles, walked into the slaughter-pen, seized such persons as they pleased, and leading them to the gateway, there tomahawked and scalped them without mercy or restraint.

Nine bodies were found lying in one pile near the gate of the fort after General Procter left the Miami. Many were found in other places tomahawked and scalped, and their bodies mangled in the most barbarous and inhuman manner. Colonel Dudley was found on the field of battle scalped, his breast cut open, and his heart taken out! He fell a victim to his own discretion and folly—and shared the fate of many of his brave countrymen who were less fortunate in escaping death upon the field of battle, as a more horrid one awaited them at Fort Miami. Long will Kentucky have cause to remember the 5th day of May as well as the 22nd of January, no less memorable for the massacre at Raisin.

Just as the unfortunate contest terminated on the other side of the river, another of much less importance took place upon our side, and within a few hundred yards of the camp. On attempting to land the balance of his men from the boats in which they had descended the Miami, General Clay met with considerable opposition from the Indians, who poured forth from the woods in great swarms and seemed determined that not a single man should reach the camp. The Kentuckians, wishing to see the works and their friends in camp, obstinately persisted in pushing on, and a sharp fire soon ensued. Such guns as could be brought to bear upon the enemy from the camp were played with great briskness. Lieut.-Colonel Ball with 200 dragoons and one battalion of infantry was sent to the assistance of General Clay, who by this time had been able to repulse the enemy and to get within a short distance of the camp. Being reinforced, he drove the enemy quite into the woods when orders were sent for the troops all to return to camp. In this affair he had fifteen or twenty killed and one man taken prisoner; the enemy's loss was somewhat greater. General Clay's men had got into camp, and that alone was all the advantage we could boast of. In fact, I thought it rather unprofitable business, for the lives of fifty savages will not, in my opinion, compensate for the loss of one single brave soldier.

Those guns which Colonel Dudley had failed to spike were played upon the camp and the rear of our troops during their skirmish with the Indians with great vehemence and considerable effect; this was truly perplexing and vexatious. That we should experience annoyance from these pieces, which but a few moments before were in the possession of our troops and might so easily have been spiked and rendered useless to the enemy, seemed almost insupportable. In fact, it was but too just to say that Dudley's conduct merited almost any fate that could possibly befall him.

General Clay and Colonel Ball having got into camp with their wounded, General Harrison determined to try one other experiment with the enemy; he therefore ordered Colonel J. Miller of the 19th regulars with 850 men to rally from two different places and to storm those batteries which were erected upon our left on the 3rd of May. This officer, always ready to distinguish himself, formed his men and moved along the small ravine until he came near the enemy without being discovered, but on rising the bank within fifty or one hundred yards of the batteries, he appeared in full view of twice or thrice his force. His men, however, were ordered to charge, which they did in the most gallant manner; and in a moment had possession of the batteries, and the guns were dismounted. The enemy were pursued some distance into the woods when orders were received for these brave fellows to return to camp, which they did, but suffered much from the Indians while returning to the lines. Two lieutenants and forty-one privates were the fruit of this affair. Our loss was about thirty killed and three times that number wounded. Many reasons tend to confirm a belief that the enemy's loss in this affair was much greater than ours.

Captains Croghan (now Colonel Croghan), Langham, and Bradford particularly distinguished themselves in this action (if such it may be called) as did several subalterns, among whom were Ensigns Shipp, Mitchell, and Stockton. The company of volunteers from Petersburg, Virginia particularly distinguished themselves by their intrepid and cool conduct while approaching the batteries under a heavy fire of musketry; Colonel Miller commanded his troops with conspicuous courage and gallantry, but being the only officer on horseback, it was out of his power to see what occurred on the flanks and in the center at the same time, or to get the requisite orders conveyed to those places, in consequence of which, the Indians came very near turning his right and getting into his rear, which had they gained, being at that time very numerous, it is more than probable that the consequences would have been terrible indeed. Lieutenant Gwynne, then commanding a company on the right, fought his men man-to-man for some time, and held the Indians in check until their maneuver was completely understood and Colonel Miller had time to counteract it.

It was now about 12 or 1 o'clock when all the firing had ceased, and each looked as if he had received all the injury that the other could possibly do him. The Indians were seen passing constantly to and from Colonel Dudley's boats, which were a short distance up the river, with immense loads of plunder. Flags were now passing between the two armies upon the subject of an exchange of prisoners, which ceremony the Indians soon availed themselves of by hoisting a white shirt or towel on a stick and then prowling along before us with heavy loads of plunder and in the most impudent manner.

In the course of the afternoon, General Procter had the audacity to summon us to surrender the camp; he was very properly answered and told that if ever he got possession of Camp Meigs, it would be under such circumstances as to give him greater claims upon the gratitude of his county than he possibly could have by its being surrendered into his hands—or words to that effect.

The day was extremely wet and cold, and having no comfortable places for our sick and wounded, both seemed to suffer much. But everything was done for them that possibly could be, and no means were spared to make them as comfortable as the nature of their situation would admit. The wounded had hitherto been lying in the trenches on rails barely sufficient to keep them up out of the water, which in many places, from the bleeding of the wounded, had the appearance of puddles of blood. These poor fellows were many times lying in that state without any other cover of shelter than that of the heavens.

It was now believed that General Procter, contenting himself with the partial success he had met with, would soon raise the siege and return to Malden; and without troubling us any more, on the morning of the 9th he accordingly left us.[20]

Alfred M. Lorrain, *The Helm, the Sword, and the Cross: A Life Narrative*

One afternoon as numbers were gathered together on the parade, two strangers, finely mounted, appeared on the western bank of the river and seemed to be taking a very calm and deliberate survey of our works. It was a strange thing to see travelers in that wild country, and we commonly held such to be enemies till they proved themselves to be friends. So one of our batteries was cleared forthwith and the gentlemen were saluted with a shot that tore up the earth about them and put them to a hasty flight. If that ball had struck its mark much bloodshed might have been prevented; for we learned subsequently that our illustrious visitors were Procter and Tecumseh.

The garrison was immediately employed in cutting deep traverses through the fort, taking down the tents, and preparing for a siege. The work accomplished in a few hours under the excitement of the occasion was prodigious. The grand traverse being completed, each mess was ordered to excavate under the embankment suitable lodgings as substitutes for our tents. Those rooms were shot-proof and bomb-proof, except in the event of a shell falling in the traverse and at the mouth of a cave. This gave occasion in the course of the siege for an English officer who had been taken prisoner and returned on parole to say to his general, "It is powder and shot thrown away to fire at that fort. I can compare the Americans to nothing but an army of ground-hogs. As soon as a sentinel cries 'Shot,' every man dodges under ground; and the ball has scarcely swept over the ground before they are on their feet again, inquiring into the damage." This observation of our prisoner was true as it regarded that portion of our men who were not on duty for the time being. But the shot did considerable damage to those who were necessarily at their posts.

The above works were scarcely completed before it was discovered that the enemy, under cover of night, had constructed batteries on a commanding hill west of the river. There their artillery-men were posted; but the principal part of their army occupied the old English fort below. Their Indian allies appeared to have a roving commission; for they beset us on every side. The cannonading commenced in good earnest on both sides. It was, however, more constant on the British side because they had a more extensive mark to batter. We had nothing to fire at but their batteries; but they were coolly and deliberately attended to; and it was believed that more than one of their guns were dismounted during the siege.

One of our militia-men took his station on the embankment and gratuitously forewarned us of every shot. In this he became so skillful that he could in almost every case predict the destination of the ball. As soon as the smoke issued from the muzzle of the gun he would cry out "shot," or "bomb," as the case might be. Sometimes he would exclaim "Block-house No. 1," or "Look out, main battery;" "Now for the meat house;" "Good-by, if you will pass." In spite of all the expostulations of his friends, he maintained his post. One day there came a shot that seemed to defy all his calculations. He stood silent, motionless, perplexed. In the same instant he was swept into eternity. Poor man! He should have considered that when there was no obliquity in the issue of the smoke, either to the right or left, above or below, the fatal messenger would travel in the direct line of his vision. He reminded me of the peasant in the siege of Jerusalem who cried out, "Woe to the city! Woe to the temple! Woe to myself!"

On the most active day of the investment there was as many as five hundred cannon-balls and bombs thrown at our fort. Meantime, the Indians, climbing up into the trees, fired incessantly upon us. Such was their distance that many of their balls barely reached us and fell harmless to the ground. Occasionally they inflicted dangerous and even fatal wounds. The number killed in the fort was small considering the profusion of powder and ball expended on us. About eighty were slain, many wounded, and several had to suffer the amputation of limbs.

The most dangerous duty which we performed within the precincts of the fort was in covering the magazine. Previous to this the powder had been deposited in wagons, and these stationed in the traverse. Here there was no security against bombs. It was therefore thought to be prudent to remove the powder into a small block-house and cover it with earth. The enemy, judging our design from our movements, now directed all their shot to this point. Many of their balls were red-hot. Wherever they struck, they raised a cloud of smoke and made a frightful hissing. An officer passing our quarters said, "Boys, who will volunteer to cover the magazine?" Fool-like, away several of us went. As soon as we reached the spot there came a ball and took off one man's head. The spades and dirt flew faster than any of us had before witnessed.

In the midst of our job, a bomb-shell fell on the roof and lodging on one of the braces, it spun round for a moment. Every soldier fell prostrate on his face and with breathless horror awaited the vast explosion which we expected would crown all our earthly sufferings. Only one of all the gang presumed to reason on the case. He silently argued that as the shell had not bursted as quick as usual, there might be something wrong in its arrangement. If it bursted where it was and the magazine exploded, there could be no escape: it was death anyhow; so he sprung to his feet, seized a boat-hook, and pulling the hissing missile to the ground and jerking the smoking match from its socket, discovered that the shell was filled with inflammable matter which if once ignited, would have wrapped the whole building in a sheet of flame. This circumstance added wings to our shovels and we were right glad when the officer said "That will do; go to your lines."

When retired to my cool subterranean lodge, I called a meeting of the whole cabinet of "Mansoul" in which after considerable discussion, the following preamble and resolution were unanimously adopted: "Whereas, Volunteering is a mere work of supererogation, and commonly founded on animal passions, and, moreover, brings no revenue of respect to our judgment; therefore, "Resolved, That this shall be the last volunteer service with us, come what will." To this I have strictly adhered, both in State and Church. Indeed, in our church, where there is such stupendous locomotive power, volunteering is truly ridiculous. Although I have generally gone where the determinate council have sent me, yet I still cherish an abiding and habitual diffidence about flourishing in a "forlorn hope."

The siege still went on with various success on both sides, the enemy becoming more formidable by experience and practice till the fifth of May. We will begin with that day by saying it was set apart by the authorities of the State of Ohio as a day of fasting, humiliation, and prayer. The infidel may say, "Pshaw! That was only accidental." But if that said infidel will take the pains to examine the papers and journals of the times, he will find that nearly all the victories which were gained in the last war by the American arms, were gained on fast-days.

On the fifth of May, a reinforcement under General Clay was descending the Maumee. The previous evening Harrison had sent a confidential officer to meet the force and give them the plan of operation. A division of the body was to land on the western shore and by a rapid and secret march, come down upon the enemy's batteries, spike their cannons, and then retreat down to the river under cover of our guns till they could be transported to the fort. The other division was to make their way down the river in their boats to the garrison.

As soon as this last division came in sight on the rapids they attracted the sole attention of the armies on both sides of the river. Meeting with some obstructions in the river, they were obliged to land. This they did under a heavy fire from the Indians on the eastern shore. A detachment, embracing our company, was marched out of the fort to cover the Kentuckians who were coming in. With little loss they entered the fort.

As soon as we had retired to the garrison, the Petersburg, the Pittsburg, and Greensburg volunteers, with some companies of regulars and Captain Sebree's brave militia, numbering in all four hundred men, were drawn up in a deep ravine outside of the picketing preparatory to a sortie. The object was to destroy a battery which had been constructed on our side of the river which had done us much harm, and which was supported by fifteen hundred Indians. The sally was also to be so timed as to divert the attention of the enemy from the approach of Dudley's command that was slyly stealing upon them.

The few moments immediately preceding the battle are, of all others, the most awful. Then, the soldier is capable of reflection, and the mental vessel, under the high pressure, moves fast. To counteract this, our first lieutenant, who had been nicknamed "Old Sluefoot," passed up and down our line encouraging the men. He was a wicked man, but had so many good traits withal, that he was very popular. "Boys," said he, "when they give the word, do your all to rush with a tremendous shout." And then he exclaimed with an awful oath that there was nothing under heaven like a shout.

At last the word was given—the charge made. As we cleared the ravine the whole forest was in a blaze. The continuous roar of the rifles was like the long roll of the drum—no intermission. The balls flew like hailstones, *pish, pish, pish*;

now and then *rap, rap*. In our passage to the woods we became exposed to the British battery on the other side of the river. They were not slow in playing their artillery on us; but we heard it not—we felt it not—we saw it not. With a blazing line before us and a crowd of anxious witnesses in the fort behind, we had no time for way-side chitchat and lateral sallies. Those who were in the fort said it was amazing to see how the balls plowed up the earth about our heels, and with what little effect.

But while the foe were engaged in this very act, Dudley's Kentuckians rushed down upon their rear took their batteries and spiked their guns. If they had then retreated to the river according to orders, happy would it have been for them. But unfortunately the Indian yell was raised in the forest. That was more than a Kentucky ear could bear. Our victors rushed to meet their mortal foe and a general slaughter ensued. After the siege while gathering up the dead, in several places were found the white and red man as they had fallen in single combat, locked in deadly strife.

This imprudence was not confined to raw troops. There was too much of it on our side of the river, for when our sortie was crowned with success, the eastern battery destroyed, and thirty artillery-men with two officers taken prisoners, our soldiers continued to drive the Indians till we were beguiled about three-quarters of a mile into the woods and the enemy began to outflank and get between us and our works. In this move Sebree's company became surrounded; but they fought desperately at close quarters, muzzle to muzzle and hatchet to hatchet till a regular company cut a passage through.

This militia company suffered more than all the rest of the detachment. We, however, considered that victory was on our side, for we retreated into a fort that was now comparatively safe. The enemy's guns were all silenced, and if they continued the siege, their only hope could be in storming, and this was most ardently desired on our side. We were afterward informed by deserters that this was their intention. The English general had engaged the Indians to assist him in this work at the breaking of the day. Some barrels of whisky, as part and parcel of the contract, were issued to the savages that evening and they spent the night in drinking and torturing the unhappy prisoners who had fallen into their hands. At the same time the company of Irishmen that we carried into Meigs were treated with American hospitality and regularly drew their rations, even to their whisky. They were profuse in their expressions of gratitude and their tongues moved as on a pivot.

Just before day-break Procter sent for the Indian chiefs and asked them if they were all ready for the storm. They answered "All ready! S'pose you take your braves and go before, and drive your nails into the big guns as Kantuc serve you; then we come -Indian much strong!" This, the English were not disposed to do. The next morning the dissatisfied Indians began to file off by companies and tribes; and the English general becoming alarmed, hastily raised the siege and retreated, leaving much of his baggage behind.

None of our company were left on the field. About twenty-five were wounded, some of them dangerously who recovered, and six died of their wounds. These, added to the sixteen whose deaths might be traced to their exposure in the Black Swamp, made our total loss twenty-two. . . . .

We have yet to speak of the slain, the wounded, and the dying, as these must be taken into the account in reckoning the cost. After the sortie, we visited the hospital. Reclining on a bed in one corner lay a gallant officer who was attached to the engineer department. He had rendered much service from the beginning of the war, and his courage was unquestionable. But now, in consequence of the irritation of his nerves by the roar of artillery, the bursting of bombs, the pain of his wounds, and his feverish condition, he had become as timid and as peevish as a child and was constantly apprehensive of being torn to pieces by a cannon-ball. "Lord, what is man! Poor, feeble man! Formed of the dust at first."

Stretched on a pallet lay Captain Jack Shore, "the darling of our crew." He had formerly commanded a merchantman, and although only a private in our company, and a sailor withal, he was better qualified for a military officer than any man in our corps. But he was a sailor; and that, in the landlubber's vocabulary, implies everything that is awkward and back-handed on horse or foot. He was related to General Harrison and had more than once taken tea with his distinguished cousin, "*sub rosa*," in the grand marquee. At the commencement of the cannonading, he had solicited a station in one of the principal batteries and handled the big guns to admiration. One of the guns was dismounted by a shot from the enemy, and an iron splinter pierced his leg. It was immediately extracted. The wound was considered unimportant, and was slightly bandaged. However, in a few hours it became distressingly painful and he retired to the hospital. He was now suffering in the last stage of lock-jaw. In his spasmodic agony, the smoke of his torment literally rose in a mist from his blanket. We gave him a hot bath, but to no purpose; he sank in death, lamented by all.

In another corner lay the handsome and delicate Cluff, mortally wounded. He was earnestly begging a messmate to read to him. In this he was gratified. We can not recollect the book that was used, but remember well noticing at the time that it was not a religious work. His comrade would read a few lines and then ask him how he liked it. With a vacant stare he would shake his head but immediately repeat, "Read, read." The thought struck me at the time that it was the Word of Life which he wished to hear from in that trying hour, but that he had not yet reached that point of contrition which would embolden him to express the humiliating request. And, alas! Alas! I had not moral courage to direct him to a source of comfort which had been so shamefully neglected by myself.

In a tent surrounded by his affectionate mess was nursed the brave, intelligent, and well-educated Booker. He spoke of death not only with composure, but sometimes with exultation. His hope was cheering; but it soon appeared from his conversation that it rested on the common opiate of dying soldiers: he was dying for his country. Although my stock of theological lore was very scant, yet it showed me that this would not do; but I durst not point him to a better foundation lest he might say, ironically but justly, "Physician, heal thyself." Precious young man! He was doubtless less faulty than myself. He felt that he was consummating the work which God had given him to do by sacrificing himself on the altar of his country while "I knew my duty, but I did it not."

We have not time to speak particularly of our fallen comrades. There they lie, each in his dusty bed deep in the cold banks of the Maumee, awaiting the grand reveille that will usher in the day-break of immortality "which shall their flesh restore." . . .

After the hasty retreat of the enemy, a detachment was sent out to scour the woods and gather up the dead. They brought in a great number and spread them out before one of the gates. They had been abused and mutilated in a most shocking manner. About midnight it fell to my lot to stand a lonely sentinel over this ghastly, silent congregation. The stars shone sufficiently bright to give effect to the scene. As I looked down upon them I became more astonished at myself than any other part of the creation. I felt truly like an apostate from human nature. A few months before, I could not feel comfortable in the idea of sleeping alone. The sight of a corpse could once afford me subject-matter of trembling for weeks to come. Even in the Black Swamp I had a tear to spare to the expiring pack-horse. But now, at this lonely hour while all the army were wrapped in sleep except a few widely-scattered sentinels, I could look down on this ghastly, disfigured group without even a tremor stealing over my nerves. I found that my heart had become wretchedly hardened by the scenes, sufferings, and conflicts of war. What particularly afflicted me was, I thought that all the social feelings and sympathies of my soul were clean gone forever; that I should no more feel with those who feel, or weep with those who weep.[21]

The Siege of Fort Meigs, Year 1813, an Eye-Witness Account by Colonel Alexander Bourne

In the latter part of April it was rumored that a British army had passed up the lake and would soon attack us. The Indians and Canadians were sent out two or three times as scouts to look out for the enemy, but they were either cowardly or unfaithful, and could see no enemy. On the 26th of April, the general ordered Captain Hamilton and his rifle company of the Ohio Militia to march down the river and find the enemy. He was brave, cool, and intrepid, fit for the most hazardous and confidential service, and soon returned reporting that the British were marching up on the other side of the river with a strong force; and we prepared to defend our post to the last extremity.

The British army of about 1500 men—regulars and Canadian militia and about the same number of Indians under Tecumpse—was commanded by Genl. Procter. They occupied the old British fort a mile-and-a-half below us and after reconnoitering our position, commenced three batteries for heavy cannon and one for mortars nearly opposite to our encampment and from 900 to 1200 yards from it. The batteries being completed and a small one commenced 300 yards in our rear, in the evening of the 30th of April the cannonade commenced. On this day some of the Canadians were missing and had probably deserted to their old master. So the genl. ordered [the] guard to be paraded and distributed at sunset and a new countersign, parole, and watchword given.

Just before night, the adjutant genl. informed that I was appointed adjutant of the day for the next twenty-four hours, and Major Alexander of the Volunteers field officer of the day, and requested me to inform him of it. I found him in the marquee of Col. Miller drinking brandy. He said he was unfit for duty and I ought to have told him sooner. I told him I had just been informed of it myself, and as it was nearly dark, nobody would perceive his inebriety, and that I would attend to his duties as far as it was admissible; and taking him by the arm, we went to his marquee and sat down, he lamenting his situation and I cheering him up. It had become very dark and we heard the report of a large cannon. I told him that was from the enemy and that we must go to headquarters immediately for special orders. He was afraid his situation would be discovered. I told him there was no alternative, if he did not go he would be sent for; and we then went. The general was standing in his marquee, surrounded by his staff. He asked me if I was on duty. I told him I was. He then said, "*Put out every light in the camp*," "that the enemy may lose his aim."

So I received the first order that was given after the firing commenced. I executed the order and returned to headquarters when the general and staff and the officers on duty set out on the grand rounds to see that all the guards were wide awake. It was extremely dark, wet, and muddy. We often fell down in the ditches, sometimes one or two upon the top of another, the British firing slowly with the least effect, for all their balls struck the bluff below us.

This was the first British cannon that General Harrison and most of the rest of us ever heard, and although we were completely invested by veteran troops, Indians, and wolves, we were not dismayed, and determined to defend the fort to the last extremity, for if we should surrender to a superior force, and an armament of twice our own, Genl. Procter could not prevent his 1500 Indians from taking our scalps.

The next morning the enemy opened all his batteries and poured in a constant stream of 24 pound balls and 10 inch bomb shells, his balls generally going through the front pickets and above our heads and lodging in the traverse bank; his shells falling and bursting, part of them inside of the fort and the others outside. We soon had a few men killed and wounded, and some mangled in a shocking manner, which was very revolting to my feelings at first, but I soon became accustomed to it. The cannonade and bombardment continued with but little intermission till the 5th of May, throwing us about 2000 large balls and shells and a quantity of large grape shot and hand grenades fired from cannon, and also some carcasses and other combustibles.[22]

Our most exposed blockhouse had the upper part knocked off and nearly demolished. We fired but little, reserving our small amount of ammunition for closer work, but sometimes dismounted some of their guns and probably killed and wounded some of their men. My blockhouse, No. 6 on the rear line, was situated so low that I would not fire on the enemy's battery in the rear, but it was calculated to rake the ditch with fatal effect if the enemy should storm the place on that line, and consequently I was well supplied with canister shot and port fire, and could load and fire four times a minute as long as the men could sponge and ram down, being in good health and almost insensible to danger.

I went to the adjutant general and told him to command me freely, and that I would do all I could for him in any way. He put me on duty as adjutant of the day every third day, and trusted me with some duties for *him* which were probably above my rank, and he evidently felt indebted to me. One evening during the hottest firing, being on duty, I was marching a small guard in single file over ground that was much exposed to the enemy's fire rather than go a long distance round under shelter of the banks. Genl. Harrison, who was not far off under shelter, became very angry and commanded me in a aloud voice to "order the men to run," and cursed me personally in the most horrid manner for exposing *his* men in that way, for he was naturally very passionate and sometimes very profane. I had before ordered the march in double quick time and would not let the men run in confusion, and so paid no attention to his order and coolly formed the guard under shelter of the main traverse and gave the officer his instruction.

As the general had openly insulted me before the principal officers of the army, my first impulse was to throw my sword down at his feet and let him arrest me forth with, but the next moment I thought of a better way, and saying nothing to him, I sheathed my sword and marched deliberately over the same ground, expecting every minute that an officer would be sent to arrest me, but none came that night. The adjutant general had been pleading for me.

The next morning the enemy did not open his fire till about 10 o'clock, and soon after breakfast I saw the general in his uniform attended by an orderly sergeant bearing his telescope coming towards my blockhouse and thought my time had come, but would he arrest me himself instead of sending an officer? Coming near, he said very pleasantly, "*good morning adjutant.*" I answered, "*Good morning General, I hope you are very well.*" He said he was apprehensive the British were building a battery behind a large quantity of dry ox hides on our west flank, and handing me his telescope, mildly asked me to reconnoiter the position and report my opinion in two hours. After the reconnaissance, I reported as my opinion that there was no battery there, nor any signs of intention to build one. This pleasant maneuver healed the breach entirely, and nothing more was ever said about it.

As the general was very sensitive on the subject of exposing his men, and lamented that any were killed or wounded, some persons thought he was a little defective in personal courage; but I know that is false. I saw him several times expose his person more than any commander-in-chief ought to, and believe he was naturally brave, and his bravery was very conspicuous in Wayne's battle with the Indians in 1794.

Captain Peters of Blockhouse No. 5 raised his gun up into the upper story so that he could bring it to bear on the battery in the rear, but the enemy's fire dismounted his gun and injured his blockhouse. As he had other duties, he left the blockhouse, probably intending not to remount the gun. I took his men, hauled up a pair of timber wheels, and was remounting the gun when the general came up to see what I was about. I instantly thought of the danger he was in if a ball of the enemy should come through the house, for a large number of spare muskets with fixed bayonets were standing against the wall next to the enemy, and if struck, would fly about like hail leaving no chance for escape where he stood, and was just turning round to beg him to leave the house when I saw he had turned about to go down.

Having mounted the gun, I fired three shots at the battery. I had never fired that gun before and did not expect to come very near until I saw how she threw her ball. The first shot fell short of the battery and ricocheted over it. The second struck the side of the embrasure and threw up a splinter. The third silenced the enemy's gun for about two hours; and this was the only opportunity I had to send them cold iron.

About the middle of the siege, Capt. Wood, the engineer, ordered me to take a fatigue party of the Ohio Militia and throw up a short entrenchment near the rear line and in front of my blockhouse. I commenced according to order. The ground was much exposed, being nearly in range of the magazine, at which the enemy were throwing red hot balls to blow it up; and these balls passed between the men and hissed and boiled in the bank. The men would leave their work and declare they could not stand it. I informed Capt. Wood that the men could not be kept at work. He then gave me an unlimited order on the commissary for whiskey and directed me to give it to them every half hour and make them drink it until they were insensible to fear but not too drunk to stand and work. He said, "*There is no other way; it must be done in extreme cases!*" And so I did it. The men then kept at their work, reeling and cursing the British and their hot balls until the work was finished. There were none killed or badly wounded.

Wood and O'Fallon were very friendly to me and the latter one day told me that Genl. Harrison would have me appointed a lieutenant in the U. States Topographical Engineers if I wished it. As I never intended to make Arms my profession, and only fought from a sense of duty and not for the love of fighting, I expressed no desire to enter into the regular army and the subject was dropped.

The siege exhibited several instances of great personal bravery and some of base cowardice. I had with me in the blockhouse two very brave men. Isaac Burkelon, a journeyman saddler of Philadelphia who went out as a substitute for a wealthy citizen of Chillicothe, and who was appointed on the march out sergeant major of the regiment, appeared to be wholly insensible to fear, and when any scouting party was ordered on dangerous service, he would volunteer and beg to go, although it was never his duty.

One morning in the hottest of the firing, he came out of the blockhouse to wash himself, and when I saw a large bombshell descending very near him, I ordered him to lie down instantly; but he would not muddy his clothes to save his life. And when the shell went into the ground within four feet of him, he would not lie down but only stooped a little, and the shell bursting the next moment, he was thrown down and nearly covered by the mud. He got up laughing and shaking himself, and appeared to enjoy the sport.

Another of my men from Ohio whose name was Bolenstein (a native of Germany), was a soldier of the Revolutionary War, about sixty years of age. Seeing a 10 inch bombshell fall just outside of the blockhouse and striking a sloping stump did not go into the ground, but bounded and then rolled swiftly on it, he jumped out through the embrasure and run after it. I told him it would burst in a moment and blow him to pieces. He kept on and said he would pull out the fuse. I knew he could not, for the British screw in their fuses. The sentinels on the walls, cocking and aiming their guns at him, hailed him to return or they would shoot him, for they had had orders to shoot every man outside without a written permission. He told them to fire away, he would have the shell anyhow. And fortunately for him, the fuse had not taken fire and he brought the shell in weighing nearly 100 pounds, for besides the powder, there were 96 musket balls in it.

F. Sutton, quartermaster of our regiment, was constitutionally a coward. He was so much afraid of being killed that he would not eat and said that he did not sleep during the siege. He generally sat crouched down behind a pile of three or four hundred barrels of flour, and while several men were looking and laughing at him, a 24 pound ball went through the flour just above his head, throwing the staves, heads, hoops, and flour over him. He jumped up and run down sideways into a wet ditch of two feet [of] water screaming "O, Lord! O, Lord;" and some of the men run to pull him out, supposing he would drown. I told them to let him lie there, he was out of the range of the fire and not worth pulling out.

When Capt. Butler's volunteer company of Pittsburgh [Blues] marched out with others to storm the battery in the rear on the 5th of May, they were fiercely attacked by the Indians on the right wing, and one George McFall, a saddler, seeing a large Indian shot down a few paces in front of the line and struggling in death, run to him right between the fires of both lines, scalped him, tied the scalp on his hat for a cockade, took his gun, tomahawk, knife and belts, and returned to the ranks. I saw him when he came in, and the scalp had been taken off and put on his hat so quick that the blood had run down nearly to the hatband.

Just before the siege I asked several of the officers if there was any plan or drawing of the fort, and they all thought there was none. I then determined to make one for myself, and when the drum beat for dinner, supposing that the officers would all be in their quarters, I took a sheet of paper and pencil and commencing at the southwest angle, paced the lines and estimated the angles all round from the right to the left, pacing also the sides of the batteries and blockhouses. As I was in undress uniform, the guards saluted and let me pass without any questions.

I then made a sketch from my rough notes and the next day, went round from left to right, correcting the first errors as well as I could, and finally put down all the interior works, positions of the several troops, officers' quarters, magazines, and etc. I knew that I might be liable to arrest for having a drawing of the fort in my possession without leave, for the commander-in-chief and principal engineers only are entitled to it, but one of the officers looked in while I was at work on it and discovered the secret. He saw that it was my own property, honestly obtained, and promised to say nothing about it, but the matter leaked out. I hid the drawing and the alarm subsided without any difficulty.

After the siege was over, I made a kind of wooden theodolite, divided it by a forked stick and other contrivances, [and] without scale, compasses, or any drawing instruments whatever, measured a base by pacing, and by a rough triangulation laid down the adjacent ground, the river, and positions of the British batteries; and suppose my drawing is the only one which now exists, for the public archives at Washington were all burnt by the British in 1814. And subsequently I made a drawing of the old British fort below Fort Meigs, which was a regular scientific work and one of their famous western posts.

It was known during the siege that a brigade of Kentucky Militia under the command of General Green Clay was on the march to reinforce us, and on a dark, stormy night about the 3rd of May, Captain Oliver was sent on horseback to run the gauntlet through the surrounding rapids about 20 miles from Fort Meigs; and returning safely through the Indians the next night, [he] gave the information. The next morning, May 5th, Genl. Harrison sent Captain Hamilton and part of his company to meet Genl. Clay and order him to detach 800 men to storm the British batteries on the north side of the river, spike their gun, cut down their wheels, and then immediately retreat towards our fort where they would be assisted across the river under the cover [of] our guns. Captain Hamilton carried the spikes and gallantly led on the storming party, and as the morning was foggy and the main British army being down at the old fort, and only the artillerists and a fatigue party at the batteries, they were completely surprised.

The 750 Kentuckians under Colonel Dudley stormed and carried the batteries in fine style; spiked the guns [and] cut down their flag staff and let it lay. But seeing some Indians in the edge of the woods (and every Kentuckian is crazy at the sight on an Indian), they rushed into the woods after them contrary to positive orders and the efforts of their officers, and pursued them into an ambush while the British army below hastened up, retook the batteries, raised up their flag again (for the Kentuckians thought it more honor[able] to fight Indians than to take a British standard); and attacking the Kentuckians in the rear, the contest was soon decided.

Col. Dudley and 220 of his men were killed; 180 retreated across the river. 350, including Capt. Hamilton were taken prisoners, marched down to the old fort, and after the Indians there had deliberately killed forty of the prisoners in the presence of the British officers, Captain Elliot stopped the massacre.[23]

On the same day two small batteries in our rear were stormed, the guns spiked, and two lieutenants and 40 privates of the veteran 41st British Regiment taken prisoners by Colonel Miller with a detachment of the regular infantry and volunteers. Our success was complete. We were reinforced by about 1000 men and rendered the enemy's cannon useless.

On the 6th of May Genl. Procter sent Major Chambers towards our fort with a flag of truce to propose an exchange of prisoners, and Genl. Harrison sent Major Hukill with a flag to meet him between the lines. Major Hukill's guard of honor, or escort, made a fine show. He was probably the handsomest man in the U. States, and with his rich dragoon uniform and Grecian helmet exceeded anything I ever saw. His officers and men also exhibited the finest equipment we could muster. They were in full uniform; the officers with splendid epaulets and ostrich feathers and the sergeants with silver-mounted swords, all borrowed for the occasion, astonished the British officers—outshone them five to one—for no British subaltern is allowed to wear bullion epaulets, but only embroidered shells on the shoulders.

On the 7th, the exchanges were completed and on the 8th, the British army raised the siege and marched off, having first attempted to unspike their cannon by heating them in burning log-heaps, but without success.[24]

Major Chambers to Secretary Freer, 13th May 1813

AMHERSTBURG, 13TH MAY 1813

Sir,

I have had not the opportunity of doing myself the honor of writing to you since 15th April last. I shall give you a concise account of our operations at the Miamis.

I have the honor to be, Sir, your most obedient humble servant,
Peter L. Chambers,
Major D.A.Q.M. General

SATURDAY, 24TH APRIL 1813

Sailed from hence at 10 o'clock A.M. Same night arrived at the Miamis, disembark'd the next day and encamped at Point en Chene. 26th, Went to the foot of the rapids to reconnoiter the enemy's position and decided for the position of the batteries. The enemy appeared to be in numbers; a large number of pigs, horses and cattle were driven in by the enemy on discovering us. Tecumthe and his brother the Prophet arrived, and eleven or twelve-hundred Indians.

27th, Embarked and arrived at Swan Creek four miles from Point en Chene, held a council with the Indians. Plan of operations agreed upon. 12 o'clock left Swan Creek and encamped at a small river about four miles from the old British fort. 28, Left this encampment and encamped at the old British Fort. The Indians cross'd to the enemy's side and kill'd a number of hogs and bullocks, took several horses from under the very guns of the fort. Extremely engaged all day in transporting our stores for the intended batteries. 29, A number of Shawnees, Winnebago's, Kickapoos killed several pigs and oxen under the enemy's guns. 8 o'clock P.M. all hands to the 24-pdrs, and after a hard struggle, succeeded in transporting them to the batteries (which were this day completed). In the course of the night, got up an 8 inch howitzer and all the platforms except two. Two 12-pdrs and two sixes, two 5 ½ mortars were all taken up.

30th, I accompanied Lt. Col. Warburton and made a reconnaissance on the enemy's side; approached so near to their fort that the riflemen fired several shot at us. I fired one shot at a number I perceived together with my rifle (one that General Brock presented me with).

Four Ottawa boys intercepted the Sandusky mail; it was guarded by three men who fled as soon as the boys fired. The eldest boy was only fourteen years of age.

7 O'clock, Pill went on board the *Myers* gunboat and in company with the *Eliza*, ascended the river about a half-a-mile; fired a shot from the 9-pounder every half hour. The enemy did not fire a shot at us.

1st May, 10 o'clock A.M. On a signal fired from the *Myers* the batteries opened, consisted of one battery of two 24-pounders and one six inch howitzer—one mortar [battery] of two 5 ½ inch, one battery of two 12-pounders, and a battery called the "Sailors" of one 12-pounder. We expect great effect from our guns. We were much disappointed the enemy had thrown up an impalement which in great measure sheltered them from our fire and there were a great number of traverses within their fort. The enemy fired occasionally at us without doing any injury.

2nd May, One battery still kept up a heavy fire, the enemy, as yesterday, sparing of his shot. The Huron Indians brought in a prisoner, one of a party charged with dispatches to General Harrison. The officer who had charge of it escaped.

3d May, I ascended the river as far as the Pottawattamie village fifteen miles from our camp. On my return the Shawnees and Roundhead were much dissatisfied with the ineffectual fire of our batteries. A battery of one 6-pounder, one 5 ½ howitzer, and one 5 ½ inch mortar was constructed within 300 yards of the enemy's fort. This day Captain Bullock, the grenadiers, and the light infantry was sent to protect our batteries. Still keeping up a heavy fire without effect.

4 May, One battery on both sides of the river keeping up all this day a heavy fire.

5 May, 8 o'clock A.M. Intelligence was brought in that the enemy were landing. Immediately ordered up to the battery and found them in possession of the enemy. After some time the enemy were driven out, and in about three hours from the time of their landing, they surrendered. It is with regret I state that a dreadful slaughter commenced on the arrival of the prisoners at our encampment. The Indians could not be repressed. One of our men was shot in the act of saving the prisoners. By the greatest exertions we succeeded in sending four or five-hundred prisoners on board the vessels.

I went over with a flag of truce, was blindfolded and taken into the fort. I saw General Harrison. He released our officers and men who had been made prisoners that day and treated them with marked politeness. An arrangement entered into for the exchange of prisoners. From this period until we left the ground, the militia and Indians leaving us hourly until our force was reduced to ten Indians including Tecumthe and very few of the militia.

We got off every article, not a single round shot left behind.

From the best information I can collect, the number of the enemy that landed was 1300, and from their own letters, only 141escaped; so the loss of the enemy on that day was about 700 killed and 500 prisoners.

P.L. Chambers

Major D.A.Q.M. Gl.[25]

A Canadian Campaign: By a British Officer

Far from being discouraged by the discomfiture of their armies under Generals Hull and Winchester, the Americans dispatched a third and more formidable one under one of their most experienced commanders, General Harrison, who, reaching Fort Meigs shortly subsequent to the affair at Frenchtown, directed his attention to the construction of works which rendered his position in some measure impregnate.

Determined if possible to thwart the views of the enemy and give a finishing stroke to his movements in that quarter. General Procter (lately promoted) ordered an expedition to be in readiness to move for the Miami. Accordingly, towards the close of April a detachment of the 41st, some militia and 1500

Indians accompanied by a train of battering artillery and attended by two gun-boats, proceeded up that river and established themselves on the left bank at the distance of a mile from the site selected for our batteries. The season was unusually wet, yet in defiance of every obstacle they were erected the same night in front of the American fortress and the guns transported along a road in which the axle-trees of the carriage were frequently buried in mud. Among other battering pieces were two 24-pounders—splendid guns which we had captured at Detroit—in the transportation of which 200 men with several oxen were employed from nine o'clock at night until daybreak in the morning. At length every preparation having been made, a shot from one of the gun-boats was the signal for their opening, and early on the morning of the 1st of May a heavy fire was commenced and continued for four days without intermission during which period every one of the enemy's batteries, within our range was silenced and dismantled.

The fire of the 24-pounder battery was principally directed against the powder magazine which the besieged were busily occupied in covering and protecting from our hot shot. It was impossible to have artillery better served; every ball that was fired sank into the roof of the magazine, scattering the earth to a considerable distance and burying many of the workmen in its bed, from whence we could distinctly perceive the survivors dragging forth the bodies of their slaughtered comrades. The officers whom duty or curiosity drew to the ground often pointed the guns; a favor on the part of the artillerymen which was generally repaid by a glass of rum or whiskey, both which liquors were extremely scarce with us and were prized accordingly.

Meanwhile, the flank companies of the 41st, with a few Indians, had been detached to the opposite shore within a few hundred yards of the enemy's works and had constructed a battery from which a galling cross-fire was maintained. Dismayed at the success of our operations, General Harrison, already apprised before our arrival of the approach of a reinforcement of 1500 men then descending the Miami under General Clay, contrived to dispatch a courier on the evening of the 4th with an order for that officer to land immediately and possess himself of our batteries on the left bank while he (General Harrison) sallied forth to carry those on the right. Accordingly, at eight o'clock on the morning of the 5th, General Clay pushed forward the whole of his force and meeting with no opposition at the batteries, which were entirely unsupported, proceeded to spike the guns in conformity with his instructions; but elated with his success, and disobeying the positive order of his chief, which was to retire the instant his object was effected, he continued to occupy the position.

In the mean time the flying artillerymen had given the alarm, and three companies of the 41st, several of militia, and a body of Indians, the latter under Tecumseh, were ordered to move on the instant and repossess themselves of the works. The rain, which had commenced early in the morning, continued to fall with violence, and the road, as has already been described, was knee-deep with mud, yet the men advanced to the assault with the utmost alacrity and determination.

The main body of our small detachment under Major Muir advanced against the American left and centre which had deployed into the woods, while Major Chambers, an officer whose gallantry in the field was ever remarkable, boldly attacked their right, then occupying the principal battery. On approaching the position he threw away his sword, and seizing the accoutrements and musket of a soldier of his own company who had been shot dead a moment before, called out in a voice and manner which was characteristic of the man, and which rather denoted indignation that the enemy should have had the presumption to carry the position than anything else, "Who'll follow me and retake that battery." I was immediately behind him at the time, and as enthusiastically replied (excited no doubt by the example before me) that I would. Lieutenant Bullock, who had been wounded over the left eye a day or two before on the opposite side of the river, yet who, when apprized of the capture of the batteries, had left his tent for the purpose of aiding in their recovery, together with Lieutenant Clements (of the 41st also) were a few paces in the rear, and these officers, followed by not more than a dozen men who happened to be near at the time, pressed eagerly forward in compliance with the invitation of our dashing leader.

It is a matter of perfect surprise to me, even at this hour, that our little force, which I have rather overrated, had not been annihilated to a man; for the Americans were in strength and of course perfectly under shelter, and the easy conquest we obtained (for they fled as we drew near to the battery) can only be attributed to the fact that their centre and left were being sorely pressed by the detachment under Major Muir and the Indians under Tecumseh. In an account of this action recently published by Captain Le Breton residing near Bytown, and then a Lieut. in the Newfoundland Regiment, that officer states himself to have been one of those who entered the battery with Major Chambers. Of course this is the fact, although my recollection does not embrace any other officers than those I have named, as being present on the occasion.

Driven from the batteries, the enemy in vain sought for safety in the woods. The murderous fire of the Indians which had already dispersed their main body, drove them back upon their pursuers until in the end there was no possibility of escape, and their army was wholly destroyed. A vast number were killed, and independently of the prisoners taken by the Indians, 450, with their second in command fell into our hands. A somewhat curious and characteristic anecdote may be related of a soldier (an Irishman) of the 41st, who being in a position in the woods isolated from his own party, contrived to disarm and make prisoners of three Americans who were opposed to him. On joining his company towards the close of the affair, preceded by his prizes and sweating beneath the weight of arms, he declared with great naiveté and indifference that he had with great difficulty surrounded, and made them his prisoners.

Of the whole of the division under General Clay, not more than 150 men affected their escape, and among the fugitives was that officer himself. The sortie made by order of General Harrison on the right bank of the river had a different result. The detachment supporting the battery already described, were driven from their position and two officers (Lieutenants Macintyre and Hailes) and thirty men were made prisoners. Meanwhile, it having been discovered that the guns on the left bank, owing to some error on the part of the enemy, had been spiked with the ramrods of their muskets instead of the usual instruments; they were speedily rendered serviceable and the fire from the batteries was renewed.

At this moment a white flag was observed waving on the ramparts of the fort, and the courage and perseverance of the troops appeared at length as if about to be crowned by the surrender of a fortress, the siege of which had cost them so much trouble and privation. Such, however, was far from being the intention of General Harrison. Availing himself of the cessation of hostilities which necessarily ensued, he caused the officers and men just captured to be sent across the river for the purpose of being exchanged; but this was only a feint for the accomplishment of a more important object. Drawing up his whole force, both of cavalry and infantry on the plain beneath the fortress, he caused such of the boats of General Clay's division as were laden with ammunition, of which the garrison stood much in need, to be dropped under the works and the stores to be immediately disembarked. All this took place during the period occupied in the exchange of prisoners. The remaining boats, containing the baggage and private stores of the division, fell into the hands of the Indians still engaged in the pursuit of the fugitives, and the plunder they acquired was immense. General Harrison having secured his stores and received the officers and men exchanged for his captives, withdrew into the garrison and the bombardment was recommenced. . . . .

Metoss, the head chief of the Sauks, was a tall handsome man about six feet in height and with features (as is peculiar indeed with the whole of this nation) essentially classic and Roman. When dressed, or rather undressed for battle, his body and limbs fantastically painted and his head ornamented with a handsome circlet of feathers, his tall and commanding figure presented the very beau ideal of an Indian warrior. He was a resolute man, and although by no means gifted with the eloquence or intellect of Tecumseh, was a sagacious and active leader—firm in his attachment to British interests and a most determined foe of the Americans for whom he had conceived a hatred almost as powerful as that which actuated the noble being who has just been named. The injuries inflicted upon his red brethren rankled at his heart and appeared to be ever present to his recollection. Still he could forgive an individual wrong, even when perpetrated by those whom he had so much reason to abhor—in proof of which, and to redeem the grossly maligned Indian character, the following touching circumstance may be related.[26]

During the early part of the siege, Metoss with his warriors frequently passed over from the left to the right bank of the river (where the 41st. flank companies were stationed in support of the small battery which had been constructed there) with a view of picking off such of the enemy as showed themselves above or without the ramparts of the fort. In these excursions the Sauks were generally successful, and the enemy seldom went to the river for water for themselves or horses without a shot from a lurking Indian. Metoss himself killed several in this way. One he contrived to make his prisoner, whom he kept in his wigwam, well secured. On the day following this capture, a favorite son of the chief—a fine lad of about thirteen—insisted on accompanying his father, notwithstanding all entreaty to the contrary. By this time the enemy had become so annoyed by the temerity of the Indians who, under cover of the night, used to creep so close under the fort that upon the appearance of any of them on the skirt of the surrounding forest, a shower of grape was instantly poured forth. Unhappily, on this occasion the American telescopes discovered Metoss and his son in ambuscade when a discharge of grape followed, and the poor boy was struck dead, dreadfully mangled in his bowels. Almost frantic with grief, the chief raised up the dead body, conveyed it to his canoe, and recrossing the river, hastened to his wigwam with the stern determination of sacrificing his prisoner to the names of the deceased.

Fortunately Mr. Robert Dickson,[27] who had brought the Sauks with him from the Mississippi and whose influence over the Indians has already been shown to have been great, heard of the circumstance in time to intercept Metoss on his way to his wigwam and to entreat that he would not destroy his prisoner, assuring him at the same time that if he did so, instead of surrendering him to himself as he proposed he should, His Great Father, the King, would hear of his refusal with unfeigned sorrow. Metoss, who had torn off the gay headdress with which he ever went into battle, at length yielded; and going to his wigwam whither his son's body had already been conveyed, he went up to the American, and severing with his knife the thongs by which he was fastened, took him by the hand and led him to Mr. Dickson, saying in a mournful voice "you tell me that my Great Father wishes it—take him;" and this noble hearted Indian, no longer able to suppress the feelings of his bereaved heart, wept like a child. The gaudy colors with which he was painted were soon replaced with black, and many months passed away before he was again seen to smile.

The body of the young Indian was buried the next day and, out of respect to the father, with all military honors. The funeral party, which was commanded by Lieut. Bullock, proceeded to the wigwam of Metoss where the body of the young Chief was laid out—his little rifle, with some powder and ball, and a supply of provisions, according to Indian usage, being placed at his side. About a dozen of the Sauk tribe, all painted black, were dancing what seemed to be a solemn war-dance around the body when suddenly Metoss rushed frantically into the midst of the group and exhibited every painful evidence of the most violent and ungovernable grief. With difficulty he was removed from the body of his child when the corpse was taken up and the party proceeded towards the grave which had been dug in the midst of our encampment on the left bank of the Miami. The black painted Indians slowly followed, and after the British party had fired the customary three rounds, they discharged their rifles several times as fast as they could load.

The fierce wild air of the warriors whose countenances evinced the strong desire they entertained of avenging the untimely death of the fallen youth, the originality of their costume markedly contrasting as it did with that of the officers and soldiers present at the ceremony, and the somber silence which prevailed, heightened in effect by the deep gloom of the forest in which they were assembled, composed a wild and romantic picture in which melancholy grandeur shone principally conspicuous.

When the expedition subsequently returned to Arnherstburg, Metoss, who had embarked in General Procter's boat, was frequently observed to be in tears. He later conceived a strong attachment for Lieut. Bullock, principally by reason of that officer having commanded the funeral party of his son. He made him a chief of his tribe and requested, as a great favor, that he would assent to an exchange of names. This was of course cheerfully complied with, for it was impossible not to esteem and like the untutored warrior who had so nobly and in so affecting a manner departed from the fierce Indian law which not only authorizes, but enjoins the sacrifice of life for life.

On the evening of the second day after this event, I accompanied Major Muir of the 41st, in a ramble throughout the encampment of the Indians, distant a few hundred yards from our own. The spectacle there offered to our view was at once of the most ludicrous and revolting nature. In various directions were lying the trunks and boxes taken in the boats of Gen. Clay's division, and the plunderers were busily occupied in displaying their riches, carefully examining each article and attempting to divine its use. Several were decked out in the uniforms of the officers; and although embarrassed to the last degree in their movements and dragging with difficulty the heavy military boots with which their legs were for the first time covered, strutted forth much to the admiration of their less fortunate comrades. Some were habited in plain clothes, others had their bodies clad in clean white shirts, contrasting in no ordinary manner with the swarthiness of their skins; all wore some article of decoration, and their tents were ornamented with saddles, bridles, rifles, daggers, swords, and pistols, many of which were handsomely mounted and of curious workmanship. Such was the ridiculous part of the picture; but mingled with these and in various directions, were to be seen the scalps of the slain drying in the sun, stained on the fleshy side with vermilion dyes and dangling in air as they hung suspended from the poles to which they were attached together with hoops of various sizes, on which were stretched portions of human skin taken from various parts of the body, principally the hand and foot, and yet covered with the nails of those parts; while, scattered along the ground were visible the members from which they had been separated and serving as nutriment to the wolf-dogs by which the Indians were accompanied.

Since the action of the 5th, the enemy continued to keep themselves shut up within their works, and the bombardment, although followed up with vigor, had affected no practicable breach. From the report made by the officers captured during the sortie from the fort, it appeared that, with a toil and perseverance peculiar to themselves, the

Americans had constructed subterranean passages to protect them from the annoyance of our shells which, sinking into beds of clay softened by the incessant rains that had fallen, instead of exploding were immediately extinguished. Impatient of longer privation and anxious to return to their families and occupations, the militia gradually withdrew themselves in small bodies while the Indians, enriched by plunder, and languishing under the tediousness of a mode of warfare so different from their own, with less ceremony and caution left us to prosecute the siege alone. Tecumseh at the head of his own tribe (the Shawanees) and a few others, in all not exceeding four hundred warriors, continued to remain.

The troops also were worn down by constant fatigue, for here as in every other expedition undertaken against the enemy, few even of the officers had tents to shield them from the weather. A few slips of bark torn from the surrounding trees and covering the skeleton of a hut, was their only habitation, and they were merely separated from the damp earth by a few scattered leaves over which was generally spread a great coat or blanket by the men, and a cloak by the officers. Hence frequently arose dysentery, ague, and the various other ills to which an army encamped in a wet and unhealthy position is invariably subject; and fortunate was he who possessed the skin of the bear or the buffalo whereon to repose his wearied limbs after many consecutive hours of toil and privation which those only who have acquired practical experience in the wild warfare peculiar to the country at that period can fully understand.

Such was the position of the contending armies towards the middle of May when General Procter (very naturally) despairing to effect the reduction of Fort Meigs, caused preparations to be made for raising the siege. Accordingly, the gun-boats ascended the river and anchored as near to the batteries as the lowness of the water would permit. Here the battering ordnance was embarked under a feeble fire from the enemy, and the whole having been secured, the expedition returned to Amherstburg, the Americans remaining tranquil spectators of our departure, nor offering further molestation.[28]

A Narrative of a Light Company Soldier's Service in the Forty-First Regiment of Foot, Shadrach Byfield

After this we were again sent to the Maumee Rapids with two gunboats and eleven or twelve pieces of ordnance, and landed about one mile and a half before we came to Fort Meigs (Fort Meigs is a strong fortification on the American side of the river) on the opposite shore. We then moved to nearly opposite the American fort and began to erect batteries. Our preparations were soon discovered by the enemy, and they endeavored to annoy us by opening their batteries upon us; but we persevered until we had completed the works with little or no loss, and we then returned the fire. We had a proof that our guns were doing execution, for one of our officers, with his glass, saw a man employed upon a building in the fort; he supposed he was covering their magazine with turf. This officer pointed out the man to one of our gunners who took an elevation and discharged the gun; the officer saw the man fall from the building.

Sergeant Smith and six of the light company (I being one of the number) were ordered to dig a place for to lay a mortar in front of the American fort. Sergeant Smith ordered me to go to the other battery and let the artillery officer know that the work was ready for the platform and as I came up from the work, I looked towards the fort and saw a smoke ascend and then fell to the ground, when a ball passed over me and struck into the earth. I then went and gave the orders that Sergeant Smith sent me with.

A few days after this, the grenadiers and light infantry were ordered back to the camp, and from thence crossed the river with a six-pounder and an howitzer, landed, and in the evening marched to within three or four hundred yards of the fort and occupied a ravine where the enemy's guns could not bear on us, and by the morning made platforms for the gun and howitzer and commenced a fire upon the fort. Here we remained some days, and at night sentries were posted in the woods, about thirty or forty yards from the fort.

While lying in the ravine one day, I went up to look round when a ball came near my head and struck a tree. I then looked round and saw an artilleryman shaving his comrade; the ball rebounded from the tree and struck the man that was shaved in his head. He died in the evening of the same day and left a wife and three children to mourn his melancholy fate.

One night as I was on sentry, I heard a person coming through the woods. He accosted me and gave me to understand that the Americans were coming down on the other side of the river. When I went off sentry I acquainted the captain with what the Indian had said, who treated it very lightly; but about ten o clock the next morning we heard a great noise and firing from the other side of the river. On looking towards our batteries we were surprised to see our colours down; 1300 of the enemy s troops had come down and got possession of the batteries, with all the ordnance, &c. We then received orders to re-cross the river, and I and one of my comrades had orders to take a box of ammunition and throw it into a creek to prevent its coming into the hands of the enemy. By the time we had done this the enemy had marched out of the fort, when my comrade said to me, "We can stop here; we have no need to go back to the fight," but I replied, "What, see your comrades fighting and not go back to help them? If you don't go back I will shoot you." I hastened back, but cannot tell how he acted.

When I joined them they were rallying for the charge. We charged them close under the fort, but were obliged to retreat because of their great guns, and were ordered to make the best of our way to the boats to cross the river. Several of the officers and men were taken prisoners.

After crossing the river we had orders to march towards the batteries as quickly as possible. When advanced about half a mile we met a party of our men with a considerable number of the Americans (prisoners) and were informed that on news being received at the camp that the enemy had taken possession of the batteries, the whole force were ordered under arms and marched for the batteries. Sergeant-Major Keynes with twelve men advanced in front and when they came in sight of the enemy, they commenced firing.

The Sergeant-Major was soon wounded in one of his arms, and lost several of his men, but that did not stop them; they were bold and courageous. The main force was not far behind and very soon the fight became general and continued about twenty minutes, when the Americans surrendered, but some of them escaped to the woods.

We passed our men and the prisoners and came to the batteries. The light infantry and a party of Indians received orders to go through the woods in search of those who had escaped.

I witnessed several affecting scenes in this pursuit. I saw one of our men and one of the enemy lying dead near together. I saw another of the enemy that the Indians had met with and scalped lying in a miserable plight and begging for water while covering over his head with boughs to screen it from the heat of the sun. A party of the Indians came up and found fault with us for showing any lenity to the dying man; and one of them instantly dispatched him with his tomahawk.

We took several prisoners in the woods and marched them to the camp. In this affair a considerable number on both sides were killed and wounded. The prisoners being secured and the detached men being come in, the Indians, who had lost many of their companions, began to manifest a disposition to be revenged on the prisoners, and actually fired amongst them and killed one of our men who opposed them in their cruel intentions. Our officers interfered and prevailed upon Captain Elliott and some of their chiefs to put a stop to their cruel proceedings. The prisoners were then put on board the boats for safety and put out into the stream. The flank companies were ordered back to the batteries where we encamped.

The same evening we heard that the American general had agreed to surrender Fort Meigs, and the next morning we were ordered back to the camp, and from thence we crossed the river with a flag of truce under the command of General Procter. General Harrison came from the fort with his attendants and met our general on the beach, who told him he was come to receive the fort, according to his proposal. The American general said he should not surrender. General Procter replied, "What, not fulfill your own agreement? That would be a violation of the honours of war." or words to that effect. He said he should not give up, for he knew his (General Procter's) strength was far less than his own; and further, that he knew his strength as well as he himself did. He was willing to exchange prisoners, and when that was affected, if they were not away in two hours he would open his batteries upon them. It was thought that the American general gained his information respecting our strength from four men who deserted from us the preceding night.

We exchanged prisoners and re-crossed the river. We then embarked the ordnance &c., went on board the boats with the remaining prisoners and sailed for Maiden. The enemy opened their guns upon us from the fort, but we were nearly clear of them, and sustained no loss.[29]

Statement of Militia Captains

CAMP MIAMIS, 6TH MAY 1813

Sir,

We the undersign'd officers of the first and second regiments of Essex and Kent Militia beg leave to state to you, as head of the militia, our opinion on the present circumstances of the militia-men and the district in general.

From the situation of our district last fall, but very short crops of grain were put in the ground, and these, as small as they were, will be render'd still less by the unfavorableness of the last winter: under these unfavorable appearances, the farmer had only the resource left of putting in crops of spring wheat, and should they be kept here any longer that of corn will be also be out of their power and the consequence must be a famine next winter. Indeed, the men are now detain'd with the greatest reluctance; some have already gone and we are apprehensive that it will not be in our power to detain them much longer.

We have the honor to be
Your obedient and humble servants,
Wm. Shaw, Captain, Kent Militia
Wm. Caldwell, Captain 1st Regt., Essex
Geo. Jacob, Captain, Kent Militia
Wm. Buchanan, Captain 1st Essex (Ditto)
John Dolson, Captain, Kent Riflemen
Wm. Elliott, Captain, Essex Militia
Wm. Sterling, Captain, Kent (Ditto)
Jas. Askin, Captain, 2nd Essex (Ditto)[30]

Brig. Gen. Procter to Sir George Prevost, May 14th, 1813

SANDWICH, MAY 14TH, 1813

Sir,

The usual communication being interrupted by the capital of the province being in the possession of the enemy, I have judged it expedient to make a direct report to Your Excellency of our operations and present state in this district.

In the expectation of being able to reach the enemy, who had taken post near the foot of the rapids of the Miami before the reinforcement and supplies could arrive for which only he waited to commence active operations against us, I determined to attack him without delay and with every means in my power: but from the necessary preparations and some untoward circumstances, it was not in my power to reach him within three weeks of the period I had proposed and at which he might have been captured or destroyed.

From the incessant and heavy rains we experienced and during which our batteries were constructed, it was not until the morning of the 1st Inst. the fifth day after our arrival at the mouth of the river, twelve miles from the enemy, that our batteries could be opened. Illness from excessive fatigue deprived me of the services early of the only artillery officer on an occasion when three would have found ample employment.

The enemy, who occupied several acres of commanding ground strongly defended by blockhouses and batteries well furnished with ordnance, had during our approach so completely entrenched and covered himself as to render unavailing every effort of our artillery, tho well served and in batteries most judiciously placed and constructed under the able direction of Captain Dixon of the Royal Engineers, of whose ability and unwearied zeal, shown particularly on this occasion, I cannot speak too highly.

Tho' our attack has not answered the purpose intended. I have the satisfaction to inform Your Excellency of the fortunate results of an attack of the enemy aided by a sally of most of their garrison, made on the morning of the 5th inst. by a reinforcement which descended the river a considerable distance in a very short time consisting of two corps of Kentucky Militia, Dudley's and Boswell's, amounting to 1300 men under the command of Brigr. General Green Clay. The attack was very sudden, and on both sides of the river. The enemy were for a few minutes in possession of our batteries, and took some prisoners. After a severe contest tho' not of long continuance, the enemy gave way, and excepting the body of those who sallied from the fort, must have been mostly killed or taken.

In this decisive affair, the officers & men of the 41st Regiment who charged and routed the enemy near the batteries well maintained the long established reputation of the corps. Where all deserve praise, it is difficult to distinguish. Captain Muir an old officer who has seen much service, had the good fortune to be in the immediate command of these branches. Besides my obligations to Captain Chambers for his unwearied exertions preparatory to, and on the expedition as D. A. Q. M. G., I have to notice his gallant conduct in the attack of the enemy near the batteries at the point of the bayonet, a service in which he was well supported by Lieutenants Bullock 41st Regiment and Le Breton of the R. N. F. Land Regt. The courage and activity displayed throughout the whole scene of action by the Indian chiefs & warriors contributed largely to our success.

I have not been able to ascertain the amount of prisoners in possession of the Indians. I have sent off agreeable to the agreement near 500 prisoners to the River Huron near Sandusky. I have proposed an exchange, which is referred to the American government. I could not ascertain the amount of the enemy's loss in killed from the extent of the scene of action, and mostly in the woods. I conceive his loss to have been between a thousand and twelve hundred men in killed and prisoners. These unfortunate people were not volunteers, and complete Kentucky's quota. If the enemy had been permitted to receive his reinforcements and supplies undisturbed, I should have had at this critical juncture to contend with him for Detroit, or perhaps on this shore. I had not the option of retaining my situation on the Miamis if it had appeared to me a judicious measure.

The mode in which the militia turned out raised hopes & expectations that were very far from being realized in the sequel. The day after the enclosed letter was received, half of the militia had left us, and the remainder declared their determination not to remain longer. I also received a deputation from the Indian chiefs counseling me to return as they could not prevent their people, as was their custom after any battle of consequence, returning to their villages with their wounded, their prisoners, and plunder, of which they had taken considerable quantity in the boats of the enemy. Before the ordnance could be withdrawn from the batteries, I was left with Tecumthe and less than twenty chiefs and warriors; a circumstance which strongly proves that under present circumstances at least, our Indian force is not a disposable one, or permanent, tho occasionally a most powerful aid.

I have, however, brought off all the ordnance, and indeed have not left anything behind. Part of the ordnance was embarked under the fire of the enemy. The service on which we have been employed has been, tho' short, a very severe one, and too much praise cannot be given to the officers & men for the cheerfulness with which, on every occasion they met the service. . . .

I have the honor to be, Sir,
With the highest respect,
Your most Obedient Servant
HENRY PROCTER
Brig. Genl. Comg.[31]

Life of Ma-Ka-Tai-Me-She-Kia-Kiak, or Black Hawk, Dictated by Himself

I soon concluded my arrangements and started with my party to Green Bay. On our arrival there, we found a large encampment and were well received by Dixon and the war chiefs that were with him. He gave us plenty of provisions, tobacco, and pipes, and said he would hold a council with us the next day.

In the encampment, I found a large number of Pottawatomies, Kickapoos, Ottawas, and Winnebagoes. I visited all their camps and found them in high spirits. They had all received new guns, ammunition, and a variety of clothing. In the evening, a messenger came to me to visit Col. Dixon. I went to his tent in which were two other war chiefs and an interpreter. He received me with a hearty shake of the hand and presented me to the other chiefs, who shook my hand cordially and seemed much pleased to see me.

After I was seated, Col. Dixon said, "Gen. Black Hawk, I sent for you to explain to you what we are going to do and the reasons that have brought us here. Our friend, La Gutrie, informs us in the letter you brought from him what has lately taken place. You will now have to hold us fast by the hand. Your English father has found out that the Americans want to take your country from you and has sent me and his braves to drive them back to their own country. He has, likewise, sent a large quantity of arms and ammunition; and we want all your warriors to join us."

He then placed a medal round my neck and gave me a paper (which I lost in the late war), and a silk flag, saying, "You are to command all the braves that will leave here the day after tomorrow to join our braves near Detroit."

I told him that I was very much disappointed as I wanted to descend the Mississippi and make war upon the settlements. He said he had been "ordered to lay the country waste around St. Louis—that he had been a trader on the Mississippi many years—had always been kindly treated, *and could not consent to send brave men to murder women and children!* That there were no soldiers there to fight; but where he was going to send us there were a number of soldiers; and if we defeated them, the Mississippi country should be ours!" I was pleased with this speech; it was spoken by a *brave!*

The next day arms and ammunition, tomahawks, knives, and clothing were given to my band. We had a great feast in the evening, and the morning following, I started with about *five hundred braves* to join the British army. The British war chief accompanied us.

We passed Chicago. The fort had been evacuated by the American soldiers who had marched for Fort Wayne. They were attacked a short distance from the fort and *defeated!* They had a considerable quantity of powder in the fort at Chicago which they had *promised to the Indians;* but the night before they marched they destroyed it. I think it was thrown into the well! If they had fulfilled their word to the Indians, I think they would have gone safe.

On our arrival I found that the Indians had several prisoners. I advised them to treat them well. We continued our march and joined the British army below Detroit and soon after had a fight! The Americans fought well and drove us with considerable loss! I was surprised at this, as I had been told that the *Americans could not fight!*

Our next movement was against a fortified place. I was stationed with my braves to prevent any person going to or coming from the fort. I found two men taking care of cattle and took them prisoners. I would not kill them, but delivered them to the British war chief. Soon after, several boats came down the river full of American soldiers. They landed on the opposite side, took the British batteries, and pursued the soldiers that had left them. They went too far, without knowing the forces of the British, and were *defeated!* I hurried across the river anxious for an opportunity to show the courage of my braves, but before we reached the ground, all was over! The British had taken many prisoners, *and the Indians were killing them!* I immediately put a stop to it, as I never thought it brave, but cowardly, to kill an unarmed and helpless enemy.

We remained here some time. I cannot detail what took place as I was stationed with my braves in the woods. It appeared, however, that the British could not take this fort.[32]

~ CHAPTER 7 ~

Dudley's Defeat

We drove them at all points a considerable distance from the river, in & through the swamps, continually running & fighting. Our troops saw no end of this thing. They became scattered & separated from their leaders, exhausted & worn down with fatigue. The enemy on horseback & foot were in front, rear, & on our flanks. Hopeless despair seized upon the spirits of the men. They became stupid & wholly unmanageable.

—Asa K. Lewis

Dudley s Defeat," the destruction of a column of nearly eight hundred Kentuckians commanded by Col. William Dudley destined for the relief of Fort Meigs on May 5, 1813, ranks as one of the most devastating disasters inflicted upon Kentucky during the entire War of 1812. Indeed, the loss is second only to that suffered by the commonwealth when Kentucky troops were overrun at the battle of the River Raisin in January 1813.[1]

The disaster, like all disasters, sprang from many causes. In early 1813, Harrison understood that as the six-month term of enlistment for many of his militia troops expired in late winter and early spring, the number of soldiers deployed to his army would necessarily decline, perhaps to the point where it could no longer operate effectively at the Maumee Rapids. In January, the American general asked Gov. Isaac Shelby of Kentucky to recruit and supply three thousand volunteers to his army, the number that Harrison felt necessary to continue the campaign against Detroit.[2]

Kentucky's response was disappointing. After much effort, only 1,200 men, many of whom were draftees or paid substitutes, mustered in Lexington in late March. Shelby placed the brigade under the command of Green Clay, a politically connected Revolutionary War veteran, land speculator, and plantation owner from Madison County. Clay divided his force into two regiments commanded by William Dudley and William Boswell, and began the march northward to join Harrison's army on March 31.[3]

Clay moved steadily, but the journey was disrupted numerous times by the actions of men unsuited by either temperament or training for the strict order and self-control demanded by military service. On the evening of May 4, Clay's force arrived at the head of the Maumee Rapids and prepared to begin its final descent to Fort Meigs at dawn the following day. Clay had nearly reached his objective, but his advance had been marred by pervasive insubordination, a flagrant disregard of military protocol, and a disturbing lack of discipline demonstrated by officers and enlisted men alike. Moreover, Clay had spent only one day in brigade- or regimental-level instruction training his men to maneuver and fight in formation. These circumstances boded ill for his force if and when it engaged a determined, resourceful enemy.[4]

At Fort Meigs, Harrison was also confronting serious challenges. From the siege's onset, Native warriors had successfully occupied the "Indian Hill," an elevated ridge above Fort Meigs immediately to the garrison's east, and harassed the defenders with small-arms fire. On May 3, a company of British gunners with three artillery pieces crossed to the south bank of the Maumee and established an artillery battery approximately two hundred yards behind the Indian Hill and about four hundred yards from the fort.[5]

At first, the new battery was ineffective, in part because of the interior traverses thrown up within the fort by the Americans, and in part because of the ineptitude demonstrated by the gunners manning the pieces. But the Americans realized that if the British advanced the gun to the crest of the Indian Hill and then placed the piece on an elevated platform, they could unleash a deadly fusillade from above the fort that would immediately compel the Americans' surrender. Throughout the first days of the siege, the British artillery positions on the north shore of the Maumee had been ineffective, inflicting some physical damage to the fort and its buildings, but few casualties. But this new battery to Harrison's east had made Fort Meigs untenable. For the moment, Procter remained unaware of his advantage. But once the British commander fully understood and then exploited this position, the fall of Fort Meigs was inevitable. Harrison needed to take bold, decisive action if he were to avoid defeat.[6]

The American commander sent word to Clay that he was to divide his force: Four hundred of his men were to land on the south side of the Maumee

A wealthy, politically connected plantation owner from Madison County, Green Clay led a column of Kentucky reinforcements to Fort Meigs in May 1813.

west of the fort and fight their way into the safety of the stockade, while the remaining eight hundred men would attack the British batteries on the north shore of the river, disable the guns, and immediately return to their boats and re-cross the river to Fort Meigs. While these actions took place, Harrison would send a strong force from the fort to destroy the new battery to his east, the exercise's true objective. The plan was overly complex and dependent upon a level of coordination, competency, and training utterly lacking in the troops assigned to accomplish it.[7]

The flawed plan was further degraded in its execution. Dudley and his officers failed to communicate Harrison's intentions fully to their men. Not a single junior officer or enlisted man landing on the north shore understood that they were to disable the enemy's guns, return to their boats, and then retreat to the fort. Lastly, when confronted with a vigorous counterattack by British forces, Dudley and his senior officers egregiously disobeyed explicit orders, and instead of retreating to their boats, allowed their men to be drawn into a deadly ambush where they were annihilated. Over 650 of the Kentuckians were captured or killed.

Following the battle, the survivors were herded to the ruins of Fort Miamis, a long-abandoned post built by the British in 1794 to oppose Anthony Wayne, where they were forced to run the gauntlet and some were executed by the Indians. Many of the Kentuckians later claimed that it was Tecumseh himself who put a stop to the indiscriminate killing. A few days later, the Kentucky prisoners were exchanged in return for British prisoners taken on May 5, ferried to the mouth of the Huron River on Lake Erie and, without weapons, rations, or in some cases adequate clothing, compelled to walk back to Kentucky.[8]

The first document presented here was written by Leslie Combs. In May 1813, Combs was a nineteen-year-old captain of a small company of "spies," or scouts, who had led Clay to the rapids and then supported Dudley's landing on the north shore. He wrote his report in May 1815 in response to a request from Clay seeking information about the engagement. Combs's letter was published in a small booklet under the title *Col. William Dudley's Defeat Opposite Fort Meigs May 5th, 1813* in 1865. The original letter is held in the Lyman C. Draper Collection of the Wisconsin State Historical Society.[9]

The second document is excerpted from a letter written by Asa Lewis, a private in Capt. John Clarke's Company of Infantry, to Green Clay a month following the battle. The letter is housed in the Ayer Manuscript Collection of the Newberry Library in Chicago, Illinois.[10]

The third reminiscence is by Thomas Christian, who served as a private in Capt. Archibald Morrison's Company of Infantry. Christian delivered these remarks at a reunion of War of 1812 veterans held in Paris, Kentucky, in 1870. His speech was later forwarded to A.T. Goodman, the secretary of the Western Reserve and Northern Ohio Historical Society, who published the oration in the society's quarterly bulletin in 1873. Christian's account, created fifty-seven years after the event, is highly romanticized, but still retains the ebb and flow of emotions experienced by the battle's Kentucky participants, from excited anticipation at the moment of landing and elation at the quick conquest of the enemy batteries, to abject fear, terror, and despair at battle's end.[11]

The final document is a report made by four Shawnees allied with the Americans who had fought alongside Dudley and his men. The four were captured by Natives fighting with the British and later released. Their description of the battle was delivered to Brig. Gen. John Wingate of the Ohio Militia on May 19. Thomas Duchoquet, Wingate's translator, interpreted the narrative as it was delivered. Wingate forwarded the message to Harrison on June 15.[12]

Col. William Dudley's Defeat Opposite Fort Meigs, May 5th, 1813

FAYETTE COUNTY, MAY 6, 1815

Dear Sir,

With feelings of painful recollection I proceed in compliance with your request to detail to you the particulars of a transaction as dishonorable to our late enemy as it was disastrous to us. When Col. Dudley attacked the batteries of the enemy opposite Fort Meigs, on the 5th of May, 1813, he advanced in three columns. The right, led by himself, carried them without the loss of a man. The middle was the reserve. The left, headed by Major Shelby, formed at right angles on the river to protect from below. This arrangement was scarcely made before the spies under my command (about thirty in number, including seven friendly Indians), who flanked at some hundred yards distance in the woods, were attacked by part of the Indian force of the enemy. Unacquainted with the views of Col. Dudley, they knew naught but that it was their duty to fight. For near fifteen minutes, with the loss of several killed and wounded, they maintained an unequal conflict.

In this time, Col. Dudley having affected his object, and fearing their fate, had advanced to their relief with the right column. The enemy retreated. Our troops,

Leslie Combs was only nineteen years old when he led Green Clay's troops to Fort Meigs on May 5, 1813. He was wounded and captured during Dudley's Defeat. Following the war, he became active in regional politics and served as a Whig for several terms in the Kentucky House of Representatives.

impelled more by incautious valor and a desire for military distinguishment than prudence, pursued. He then stood firm for a short time on his right and gave way on his left, which threw our line with its back towards the river so that every step we advanced carried us farther from under the protection of our fort. Whenever we halted, so did the Indians, and renewed their fire—we charged on them. They again retreated. In this way, with the loss of from thirty to fifty killed on our side and a number wounded, was the battle fought for upwards of three hours. How much the enemy suffered during this time 'twas impossible to ascertain from the circumstance of their bearing off their dead.

Soon after the commencement of the engagement we were forced to bring our whole force into action. The enemy was, during this time, receiving large reinforcements from the other side of the river which enabled him now nearly to surround us. Our troops were generally much exhausted owing to the swampiness of the ground over which they had fought and many of them with their guns wet, or without ammunition. In this situation, the enemy in much force, fresh to the battle pressed with a most destructive crossfire on our left. It gave way. Conscious of his advantage, with a desperate effort he advanced on the remainder. These, disheartened and confused, were ordered to retreat to the batteries. Unfortunately, this retreat soon turned to flight which all the efforts of the officers could neither prevent nor stop.

The best disciplined troops in the world are sometimes panic struck—then can it be surprising that militia, *under these circumstances*, and who had seen scarce thirty days service, should become so?

In small parties, by tens and by twenties, they arrived at the batteries, thereby falling an easy prey to the regular force of the enemy who, early in the action had retaken them from the right column. Thus, upwards of eight hundred men who had set out with the most flattering prospects of success, led on by imprudence were overwhelmed by numbers, cut up, and defeated. About one hundred and seventy only, having made good their retreat before the close of the battle, escaped across the river in our boats.

Immediately after the surrender, we were marched off towards Fort Maumee, one and a half miles below near the British encampment. We had gone but a short distance before we met the head of the left line of Indians who had been enclosing us. Having surrendered to Englishmen *entirely*, I expected we should be treated with that tenderness and humanity indicative of a noble mind and always due the *unfortunate.* What was then my astonishment when, so soon as we met the

Indians, *they began in face of the English guard of Gen. Procter, Col. Elliot, and other officers who were riding up the line*, to rob us of our clothing, money, watches, etc. Almost all lost in this way their hats and coats, some even their shirts, and some their pantaloons also. He who did not instantaneously give up his clothes frequently paid his life for it. No difference was made between well and wounded in this as well as what followed.

It would be almost impossible to relate all the acts of individual outrage that took place. I shall never forget the demoniac look of the villain who stripped me, nor shall I soon forget those who encouraged [him], since notwithstanding my request, they did not hinder him from doing it. I showed him my wound. T'was vain; before I could unfasten the bandage, regardless of my pain he *tore* my coat off from my shoulders.

I had gone but little farther before I saw ten or twelve men, lying dead, *stripped naked and scalped*. Near them were two lines of Indians formed from the entrance of a triangular ditch in front to the old gate of Fort Maumee, a distance, I think, of forty or fifty feet. The idea immediately struck me that all the prisoners ahead of me had been massacred. I determined, if such was the case, to go no further. Upon inquiring, a soldier told me they were in the fort and showed me the way, which was between those two lines of Indians. During this moment's delay, a man who was walking behind stepped before me; just as we entered the defile, an Indian put a pistol to his back and fired—he fell. I ran through without being touched.

My feelings were somewhat relieved at finding about two-thirds of the prisoners already within. How many were killed afterwards I am unable to say. We heard frequent guns at the place during the whole time the remaining prisoners were coming in. Some, although not killed, were wounded severely with war clubs, tomahawks, etc. The number who fell *after the surrender* was supposed by all to be nearly *equal to the killed in battle.*

We now hoped, however, that we were secure from further insult or injury—but no sooner had all the prisoners got in than the whole body of Indians, regardless of the opposition of our little guard, rushed into the fort. There seemed to be almost twice our number. Their blood-thirsty souls were not yet satiated with carnage. One Indian alone shot three, tomahawked a fourth, and stripped and scalped them in our presence. It seems to me, even to this day, whenever I think of this circumstance that I again see the struggles of the dying prisoner and hear him cry in vain for mercy. The whole then raised the war-whoop and commenced loading their guns. What were our feelings at this moment, he who has never realized can not imagine. A description is impossible. Without any means of defense or possibility of escape, death in all the horror of savage cruelty, seemed to stare us in the face.

Rendered desperate *by this idea* and the perfect disregard which the British evinced for that duty held sacred by all civilized nations (the protection of prisoners), much did we wish for our arms, and had we then had them, they would have been surrendered but with our lives. Or, had this been carried much further, the prisoners would, *at any risk*, have sold their lives as dearly as possible. *Tecumseh*, however, more humane than his ally and employer, generously interfered and prevented further massacre. Colonel Elliot then rode *slowly* in, spoke to the Indians, waved his sword, and all but a few retired *immediately*. After a short consultation with those who remained, they came and took from among us a number of young men of whom the British said they wanted to make sons, but we feared they took them as hostages for the lives of those Indians who were wounded.

Just at dusk, boats came up and carried us to the fleet, eight miles below. Notwithstanding the naked condition of the prisoners and the disagreeableness of the weather (which was rainy and excessively cold for the season) many of them were obliged to remain all night in the open boats in ankle-deep mud and water. The wounded were put into the holds of the different vessels where their only bed (and a good many had not even this) was the wet sand thrown in for ballast, without blankets or any other kind of covering. Provision was issued to them the next day about twelve. Their treatment afterwards was nearly as good, I am induced to believe, as the British could afford, being themselves scant of provisions. I feel myself particularly indebted to some of the officers for their politeness and attention.

Thus, sir, I have endeavored as briefly as possible to relate to you a transaction, the particular hardships of which are but little known. To describe the scenes which, altho' time may serve to ameliorate the poignancy of the feelings they gave rise to, can never while one spark of honor or fellow feeling is mine, be entirely effaced from my mind. I can not conclude this letter without testifying to the bravery and carelessness of danger displayed by the troops throughout the engagement. The only contest seemed to be while any hope of victory remained, who should first oust the enemy from his hiding places. And I am convinced when the retreat commenced, by far the greater part had no idea of surrender, but exhausted, confused, and overcome were forced to it on their arrival at the batteries.

I remain, with respect, etc.,
Your most ob't,
LESLIE COMBS, *Capt Spies.*[13]

Asa K. Lewis to Green Clay, June 9th, 1813

Dear Genl.,

. . . I then pushed on to the batteries, reached the first gun and attempted to break the carriage wheels of cast iron but could not, knocked out the lynch pins and etc. and threw them away. Saw no enemy here. The Col. came up at this moment from under the hill of the river followed by his men in disorder. The fire continues, and becoming more warm and heavy in the brush. Supposing the main body of the enemy then engaged with our men, I called to the Col. and told him I thought he had better move on and reinforce the troops engaged. He waved his sword over his head and ordered his men to follow and rushed into the woods. Here was the great error. I knew not the main body of the enemy lay a mile below us.

What number of the Indians we fought for near three hours, I could not tell. I saw but few of them dead upon the ground. They were seen to bear off their dead and wounded upon horses. We drove them at all points a considerable distance from the river, in and through the swamps, continually running and fighting. Our troops saw no end of this thing. They became scattered and separated from their leaders, exhausted and worn down with fatigue. The enemy on horseback and foot were in front, rear, and on our flanks. Hopeless despair seized upon the spirits of the men. They became stupid and wholly unmanageable.

I had, might and main, been seeking Col. D[udley] for some time. We occupied a range of country. I found the Col. at the head of a considerable body of men in motion in a direction about parallel with and down the river. I called to him and observed if he did not draw the men out of the brush, they could all be cut off. His reply was "Where is the river?" I pointed directly to it.

We attempted here to make a stand, form in some order, collect in the scattered troops and get off the ground. We succeeded in part. But now the spirit of battle was fallen. The enemy suddenly appeared, raised the yell and poured in a heavy fire. The men broke and ran! Every effort was used to halt and rally them. I exerted my voice and strength until both were nigh gone. All was vain and fruitless.

T'was a scene I shall pass over in silence. Shame and sorrow for Kentuckians overcame me quite, and I felt a wild unnatural wish at the moment, that some friendly ball might close the scene. Life was not desirable. Yet understand me aright. Our brave fellows, I must call them brave, acted as any other men similarly circumstanced would have done.

I am unable to say how far we were from the river when we ran. In this retreat the Col. fell. I reached the British batteries amongst the last. Our men had thrown down their arms as they arrived, and the front of the column of prisoners was out of sight, moving down the road to the British camp. We were indiscriminately stripped, some more bare than others. Commander Hall, commanding the British squadron in the Lake, saved me.

When I arrived near the old B[ritish] fort the Indians began to murder the men on all sides. Hall, to whom I owe great obligations, hurried me on to an old tent where I lay the balance of the day wrapped in an old rug. To heighten my misfortunes, Procter come to the tent and after enquiring who I was, upbraided me in the most unfailing manner with the conduct of our Govt. towards his; that we deserved the treatment we were receiving, etc. etc. I said little to him. He turned haughtily upon his heel and walked away.

That evening we were sent below and put on board their vessels. The private B[ritish] soldiers appeared solicitous to contribute all in their power to our comfort. No one gave us food or covering that night. I lay upon a coil of cable myself. The next day I was taken into the cabin of the vessel (*Nancy*) where afterwards I with several others, rec.'d very polite and hospitable entertainment from the Capt. (McIntosh).

Our men suffered much from the cold. None of us had a blanket, most without shirts. Capt. Irvine died on board the *Hunter* of his wound, being shot thro the lower part of the belly. Maj. Shelby had been missing and all believed him dead and very much lamented his loss. Afterwards he was brought down amongst us a prisoner to our great joy. He says when the men ran, he was exhausted and threw himself into a brush of hazel bush. After the surrender he was taken into the B[ritish] camp by a party of scouting soldiers. He had a cut upon his head 3 1/2 inches, which he says he expects was by his own sword when he once fell, but felt it not at the time. He is a brave man. I have no doubt [he] did his duty.

We were so scattered and the woods so thick, no man could see a tenth part of the events of the day. Many brave fellows fought and bled and have gained only disgrace! No officer or corps could distinguish themselves. A misfortune to which I hope none of our gallant country men will hereafter be subjected.

I might further detail some incidents, but my scrawl is already too lengthy.

Respectfully, Dear Genl., I Remain

Asa Lewis[14]

Campaign of 1813 on the Ohio Frontier: Sortie at Fort Meigs, May 1813

I again hear the tap of the drum that sounded in the little village of Athens, Fayette County, for volunteers in the winter of 1813, just upon the excitement of Winchester's defeat. I again hear the voice of my Captain, Archibald Morrison and see the faces of my fellow volunteers as they fall in line. Salutations are being received upon every side and the din of innumerable familiar voices are heard; alas! Only in the imagination, for those voices were long since hushed and those faces we will see no more this side of the grave. My father's "Good-bye, my boy,'" my mother's blessings and tears, all pass in review before me now.

Soon my loose warm jeans roundabout seems to be my most protecting friend as our rendezvous at Lexington has been far in the rear,[15] and we are upon a forced march across the swampy marshes of Ohio rendered almost impassible by incessant spring rains, to the relief of General Harrison at Fort Meigs.

One shower after another, and each one seemingly colder than its predecessor, is pelting us day and night. Upon brush-piles cut for the occasion we are compelled to sleep to keep above water. Our brave, kind-hearted and generous Colonel Dudley is busy encouraging his men and, aided by the other officers, doing all that can be done to lessen our sufferings; but continual wading in water is beginning to tell and the skin is peeling from our weary legs from the knee down; the well-clothed and well-protected camp followers, with their wagons of luxuries and drinkables, are extorting more and more as we leave civilization farther behind, and now a drink of their cider-oil is out of reach of two-thirds [of] the command and they have lost their popularity with both men and officers; consequently, another fatiguing day's march with the prospect of another night, twin-sister to the rest, plays havoc with the hucksters; the cider-oil wagons are upset, barrels are being rolled hither and thither. No orders to that effect have been issued, and without anyone seemingly to know who were doing these things or why they were being done, presto, the drinkables have disappeared and every soldier in camp suddenly forgets his fatigue and becomes Lieutenant General commanding innumerable hosts of invincible veterans.

Commands of officers in the heat of terrible battle are heard in every direction, innumerable game cocks are loudly crowing and all manner of songs and singing, concord and discord all around. This last jollification of our little command. Oh! How soon after was hushed forever on earth the joyful voices of almost every mess mate and friend I *there* had, and *then* so gay.

But a very few nights after, amid darkness and a pelting rain, we are cautiously and as rapid as practicable descending the Maumee to surprise Procter, whip the Indians, raise the siege, and relieve Fort Meigs; but ere we reach the fort, many of my companions' guns are full of water, as the pouring from their muzzles plainly indicates when they are brought from a perpendicular to a horizontal position prepatory to the bloody action soon to commence. Some faint signs of coming day and many indications of the immediate presence of our savage foe left no doubt in the mind of any one just then of a terrible conflict just commencing.

The morning of the memorable 5th of May was dawning. Officers and men were hurrying from boats and quick flashes and the keen reports of many guns pronounced the battle commenced. Many were being wounded around me. My captain, Archibald Morrison, had formed in good marching order and was under way when the brave Captain John Morrison was shot through the head, both eye-balls bursting clean from their sockets. Dying but undaunted, he orders his men forward to a post of honor where they could do their country good service and not waste their precious time with a dying man.

Officers and men then bounded forward, soon dispersing the besiegers and capturing the guns we were ordered to capture. And now flushed with victory and maddened by the sight of fallen, bleeding, and dying comrades, our brave Colonel Dudley and men could not resist the desire of following the retreating enemy and wreaking vengeance upon them for the loss of near relatives and friends. So without taking time to roll the captured guns into the river, after them we went; and had it not been for the dense forest and undergrowth, we would have made short work of them. But alas! That aid to the enemy was death to us. They formed an ambush, and securely hid from view had every advantage. Our futile attempts to dislodge them gave that portion of the enemy upon the opposite side of the river ample time to cross over in our rear completely hemming us in upon every side. Our case was then hopeless. Our ranks scattered, our brave Colonel slain, and most of the other officers mortally wounded seems sufficient to have unnerved the bravest hero, but even then many heroic deeds of personnel valor were enacted and I still occasionally heard the loud, shrill game cock crowing of one brave spirit who seemed determined to die game and cheer his comrades to the last. What became of him, who knows?

Louder and louder, nearer and nearer came the savage yells of the blood-thirsty foe from every quarter, and fainter grew the resistance offered by our thinned and dispirited ranks until bursting forth in our very midst, the deafening, demonic yells drowned all other sounds save the coarse, broad command "*ground* your *arms, surrender*," pronounced by British officers, banishing all hope of successful resistance. Captured, brave Dudley is defeated and we are prisoners in savage hands were the thoughts that then rushed into my mind, causing me to forget upon the instant to throw down my arms; but just then that same broad command, this time to me personally, "Damn your eyes, ground your arms or you will be slain," brought me hastily to my senses. Down went gun, off came knapsack &c, to hastily disappear beneath the mud and water, then ankle deep where I stood, and with my full weight I aided their exit from further service, pressing them as deeply into the mud as possible; then stepping towards where the prisoners were being collected, the first man I met with whom I was acquainted was old Mr. Bradburn, but he could give me no information as to the whereabouts of any of our messmates, as I was then the only acquaintance he had met since the surrender.

The sad fact was that but few of our particular mess were left to meet again upon earth, and soon, very soon, even his blood and brains were destined to bespatter me and others as the enraged savages tomahawked him in our midst. Now too late, we saw the error of surrendering to such a foe; and every soldier keenly felt the difference between dying in the heat of battle, contending for right, and the cold-blooded massacre that now plainly awaited him. For the few British who were with the Indians had no power to control them, being in almost as bad a situation as ourselves, the savages threatening to exterminate them if they offered any resistance to their inhuman desire to butcher the prisoners, and did kill one of them in my presence for begging the life of one prisoner, who had thrown himself under his protection.

Consequently the British aided by some of the Indians hurried us on as rapidly as they could down the river to an old deserted fort where they assured us that we could and should be protected. But the bloody tomahawk was busy along the whole route, leaving behind us a path of blood and scalped comrades. Matters growing worse and worse at every step, the savages becoming more and more enraged and bloodthirsty as we neared the fort, shortly before reaching which I was halted by some Indians and a sprightly stripling of some sixteen summers hastily proceeded to search my pockets; feeling much resentment, I suppose I must have exhibited some, for instantly two paint bedaubed warriors with uplifted tomahawks made a rush towards me and would, perhaps, have instantly buried them deep in my brain, but just then their attention was arrested by the glittering appearance of a brass inkstand the young savage had extracted from my pocket where in marching, it had rubbed to a glittering brightness equal to gold. The few silver dollars I had left soon shared the same fate of the inkstand, and amid the forward pressure I soon passed out of sight of my Indian boy and his captured goods which it seemed put him and his companions wild with delight. But getting rid of them could afford no joy or feeling of relief; for lifting my eyes, there stood a few hundred yards off the old deserted fort with thick lines of savages extending from either side of its entrance to the very spot where I stood, clubbing and tomahawking all they could of the terror-stricken prisoners as they made their wild, panic race for its entrance, where they foolishly hoped to find protection and safety.

Each one as he reached the head of the savage lines comprehended at a glance the nature of his situation. To hesitate was instant death, and without further orders each made his individual dash for life through the yelling savage lines with superhuman speed and agility. Many who were knocked down gained the entrance upon all-fours with astonishing speed. The prisoner in front of me received a deep gash in the shoulder as he ran, but succeeded in entering the fort. And now it was my time. The way was slippery with human blood and blocked in places by the slain. No time for thought or preparation. The loose, warm jean round-about which I before mentioned and which had done me so much good service through the long, cold, wet marches, was buttoned to the throat, and with a strength and speed that astonished me I made a bolt, but ere I had reached the prized entry, I felt a sudden jerk at the back of my head, saw a button strike the ground some feet in front, my arms were forcibly jerked back, and the precious gift of my dear old mother was lost forever without my having time to say good-bye, dear old friend roundabout.

A few more bounds landed me in the fort, or rather slaughter-pen; and here we seemed to be in, if possible, a worse situation than ever; for the savages rudely shoved the British sentinels aside and with unearthly yells, poured in upon us, killing and scalping as fast as their own crowded ranks would admit, while we, like terror-stricken sheep hemmed in by dogs or a parcel of hogs in a butcher's pen, were piled one upon another in one corner. Those at the bottom were being smothered, while those upon the top were being drenched with blood and brains.

Just then, suddenly as the lightning's flash, the yelling ceased, the uplifted war clubs descended harmlessly by the side of the now shamed warriors, and above the groans of the dying and the prayers of the living is heard the brave Tecumseh putting a stop to the massacre, shaming his warriors for behaving like squaws.

The few now left are saved from death, but the little band or remnant of the once proud regiment of 800 brave Kentuckians are still destined to undergo much suffering, for nakedness, cold, hunger and death still waited upon and thinned their ranks; and the exposure while being taken prisoners down the Maumee to the lake or place of exchange, proved too great for almost all of us, and many perished from it before reaching home, while the most of us were a long time in recovering. The cold was intense upon the water in open boats, and for three days and nights we had nothing to eat save a mess of horse-beef that we much relished and wished for more. At the mouth of Huron River we were turned loose without sufficient clothing to keep us warm, without money, and nothing to eat save one ration sent to us by General Harrison. He would have done more for us, but it was out of his power.

From that point we had to find our way home as best we could through an almost friendless country, traveling a very circuitous route to avoid falling in the hands of Indians, each little party of friends taking a different way, agreeing to assist one another, for there were many sick, and some of the sick had to accompany each party. Our little party homeward bound was composed of Robert Simpson, Daniel Carter, George Sherwin and Joseph Franklin. On account of my sickness we had to travel very slowly, in fact, all of us were unable to stand much fatigue. I was so weak much of the time that it was impossible for me to get up, but when lifted upon my feet could manage to walk for several hours by occasionally leaning against something to rest, living much of the time upon slippery elm bark and begging our way as we slowly advanced towards the Ohio River.

We were sometimes refused anything to eat, but as we neared the river we fared better and the sick got occasional chances to ride. Meeting a chance to ride a led [*lead?*] horse belonging to a gentleman who was coming several miles in the direction of the river put me so far in advance of my friends that they never overhauled me again before reaching home. After this I found other opportunities of getting short rides which soon brought me to the banks of the river opposite Maysville then called Limestone. Here a gentleman let me stay all night and finding an opportunity of crossing to the opposite bank early next morning, I met with a strange coincidence, for just as I landed upon the Kentucky shore, I saw my father standing near the water's edge, and looking intently up the stream at a boat descending. He had just arrived and some thing persuaded him that I was near, perhaps in the boat. So intent was his gaze that he did not see me until I spoke. We were astonished at the strange meeting, both having arrived upon the spot almost simultaneously.

I soon arrived home amid the welcoming of many friends, and in much improved health, but so lean that all declared that I had grown at least two inches taller. The girls treated me to cakes and strawberries, the young men introduced me to their sweethearts, and the old gave me much praise, so I got along swimmingly for a few months, when serious notions of returning upon the war path disturbed my dreams for a few weeks. Finding my services were not needed I joyfully gave up the idea, went resolutely to work and, with God's aid, have succeeded in making a good provision for my family and, I trust, peace with my maker.[16]

Shawnee Chiefs to Harrison, 19 May 1813

Brother

This is to inform you that the young men that went with Genl. Clay has returned to this place [Fort Logan, on the Auglaize River near present-day Wapakoneta]. Two miles above Fort Meigs we were stopped by Captain Hamilton from going any farther by water. The colonel of the troops told us we would shoot after a while, but did not tell us we should have a battle. We then went in front until we got opposite the fort and where the British had a very strong battery of cannon. We pushed back the Indians at first for some considerable time, but the further we went, the more we met to oppose us until a general engagement took place.

We then stood in the front and encouraged the men to be strong and fight, but to very little purpose; the men stood as if they could not help themselves and got shot down very fast. We shot for our part until our guns got so dirty that at last the balls would not go any more into our guns. We did all we could to keep the enemy off, but the British, getting more numerous, and a great body of Indians, collecting from all parts, soon surrounded us in such a manner that it became impossible to escape, and soon became their prisoners.

It was some time before we were found out to be their enemies; many British took us to be their friends in the crowd, but the Indians soon knew us to be of this place. The Wyandots took us and directly stripped us of every thing we had and tied us very close, and struck us several times and pulled our hair from all parts. Then the Indians fell on our friends the Americans and began to knock them in the head, and mostly those that appeared well dressed and of consequence. Then the remainder were taken in the old fort. The British pretended to protect them but they were overpowered by the Indians, and one British soldier got killed amongst them for taking their parts.

Then after that, they took us to a camp in sight of the fort where they tied us to a large pole deep in the ground. In going, we met Walk Upon the Water, a Wyandot war chief; he took a stick and struck us about the head as hard as he could. We made a great whooping every time to shew him we were not afraid of death. They kept us two days at this place very close tied up so that our hands and arms were black, more so to William Perry as he provoked them by mocking them as despising them, and told them several times to knock him in the head.

The next evening Tecumseh came to us and shook hands with us and told the Wyandots, Pottawatomies and others to let us alone. We asked to be untied, for that we could see death as well as to be tied, and that we were not afraid of it. They then untied us after assuring them that we would not run away. When there, a flag came from General Harrison to make some arrangements with the British concerning the wounded men and prisoners, requesting to have them exchanging and that the British should clothe them and feed them, which we understood was agreed to. 200 were killed and 500 taken prisoner. After staying two days at this place they took us to the River Raisin sleeping one night on the way. We stayed three days at the River Raisin and was informed there that the amount of the British army [was] 2000 Indians and 1000 British and a few French. The British told the Indians to rest for one moon to make preparations to attack Genl. Harrison again, and assured them that have him they must; and Tecumseh said if the British should take him, that he would get him from them and serve him at his own pleasure. There is to be 1000 Indians mounted well equipped with pistols, swords, knives, rifles, and tomahawks.

The way we got clear and escaped death was through two of Blue Jacket's sons named James and George. They took us under their protection and saved us from our enemies. One gave a gun and the other a pistol to use along the road. Blue Jacket said the white people got their own men back again and exchanged them to make their friends glad. He said it was the same nature of the Indians. He knew very well those men would be lamented made him take their parts in distress, and that nobody would blame him for doing so. He offered himself to bring them safe to their town; but would not stay, but return to places where there were enemies. These same two brothers [i.e., sons] of Blue Jacket's saved Mr. Whitimore Knaggs and his son last winter. He had many disputes with the British on that account. He told us to assure his brothers the Americans that for all he was on the other side, he would be the friend of White people; and if peace took place he would return to this place. This is all we have to say at present, only we wish sincerely that everything should be taken in time as we are your brothers. We wish you well; please to send a copy to Mr. John Johnston, agent.

Tecumseh told them it was eight years since he was working to fix this war, and that he had everything accomplished, and that all nations from the north were standing at his word. We repeat again to be strong this time, and not to go and give yourselves up like the others. A great army ought to be raised, for many Indians will come from different parts in great bodies. They said if a thousand Americans had went last winter, they would have taken Malden very easy. There was no Indians there.

We are your Brothers,
Chiefs Black Hoof
Wolf
Snake
Butler[17]

~ CHAPTER 8 ~

Life in Camp, Summer 1813

The position of the militia comprehending the space along the eastern and southern boundary of the fort (the Ohio & part of the Kentucky Militia) is but illy swept, and the ditch bordering on this position contains a mass of filth and stagnant water which I am persuaded must greatly endanger the health of the corps if not of the whole garrison.

There is likewise a quantity of stagnant water in a cellar or hole at the northern battery.

The environs of the fort are prodigiously filthy and offensive, particularly on the northwest and northern & eastern quarters.

—Lt. Col. E. P. Gaines

Fort Meigs had successfully withstood a severe test. On May 10, the day after the British withdrawal, the garrison dug itself out from its trenches and began the enormous task of tending to its wounded, burying the dead, and repairing and rebuilding the battered facility. The British bombardment had destroyed the roofs of every blockhouse and storehouse within the camp, and as a result, much of the supplies and provisions contained within them had been ruined. Enemy shot had pierced the fort's stockade all along the post's perimeter, and two of the fort's seven blockhouses had been severely damaged. One of these blockhouses, located at the fort's northeast angle and the feature of Fort Meigs most near the British batteries on the north shore, was so extensively damaged that the Americans razed it completely. The garrison also leveled traverses, filled trenches, rebuilt the remaining blockhouses, and repaired picketing, storehouses, and magazines.[1]

The first siege had revealed that the post could be extraordinarily vulnerable if enemy forces occupied the Indian Hill, an elevated knoll immediately east of the fort. Capt. Wood added two new gun batteries to the garrison. The Henderson Battery, placed on the fort's northeast angle on an elevated redoubt protected by a high breastwork, could bring all of its guns to bear against the Indian Hill, while the second position, the Tennessee Battery, protected the previously battery-less west approach. The garrison also erected five picket-guard stations fortified with raised breastworks and surrounded by abatis, each an entanglement of sharpened posts and tree limbs used much like modern-day barbed wire. These stations, located about 250 yards from the fort, provided a formidable barrier extending along the post's east, south, and west angles to enemy forces attempting to approach the Americans.

Finally, Harrison began to reprovision the fort, moving forward large quantities of flour, biscuits, whiskey, salt pork, bacon, candles, shot, and soap from Forts Loramie, Amanda, and Winchester, while contractors drove large herds of cattle and hogs into the camp where they were slaughtered and processed into rations.[2]

As temperatures moderated, so too did the camp's rigid discipline. The post's officers fought a losing battle against their own men as they resisted or simply ignored the camp's regulations. General Clay, who had been placed in charge of the post in the siege's immediate aftermath, was determined not to have his authority undermined, and the post's general orders became filled with increasingly explicit instructions that stipulated the proper appearance of troops, noted the correct time and duration for drill, and listed the conditions under which bathing, swimming, laundry, and fishing could take place.[3]

Courts martial became frequent, three or four per day in some companies, and for all manner of infractions, from minor insubordination to vandalism, theft, drunkenness, disobedience of orders, sleeping while on guard, dereliction of duty, conduct unbecoming an officer, desertion, and assault. The penalties ranged from having the guilty "acknowledge his fault and ask forgiveness," to having one's whiskey stopped, extended fatigue duty at hard labor, or confinement in the guardhouse while wearing a ball-and-chain.

A general court martial convicted Nathan Osborn, an infantry private, of desertion on June 22, and sentenced him to carry a six-pound cannon ball fastened to one of his ankles by a chain for thirty-nine days, have his whiskey ration stopped for the same time, be kept at hard labor for the same time, ride the "wooden horse" for sixteen evenings during evening parade, have half his pay stopped for three months, have half his head shaved at the expiration of his thirty-nine day sentence, and then be drummed from camp.

The wooden horse was simply a horizontal pole elevated enough that the feet of one sitting astride it would not touch the ground. Prisoners would straddle the pole stabilized by a cannon ball attached to each foot. The display was part corporal punishment, part public humiliation, part public object lesson for those who might privately be considering similar infractions, and partly for the purpose of displaying prisoners so that all in the garrison would know their status and recognize them on sight.

When Osborn was drummed from camp, his officers stripped him of all of his government-issued possessions, including firearm, blankets, regimental coat and hat, and other parts of his uniform, and then ordered that the company barber shave half his head (including one of his eyebrows) to mark him as a convict. At evening parade, a time when the entire garrison assembled together, he was placed between two drummers who, while playing a beating known as "Rogue's March," paraded him in front of every company in the fort, again to make certain that every soldier knew his identity and his status. After passing before the soldiers, the drummers escorted Osborn to the post's gate. Osborn continued through the gate and sentries closed it behind him. Osborn was unarmed and poorly clothed, had no provisions, carried no supplies, was marked as a criminal, would be shot on sight by either foe or friend, and now had to navigate a vast and inhospitable wilderness if he were to survive. Desertion was not necessarily a capital offense, and Osborn had not been given a death sentence, but at this moment, his prospects were dire.[4]

Although the fort's disciplinary lapses proved wearisome, only a few presented a serious threat to the post's continued security. However, one issue proved insidious: The camp suffered from a simple lack of cleanliness. Garbage was piled high on the ground, trash overflowed the ditches, and the carcasses of numerous animals remained unburied throughout the camp. Latrines were haphazardly placed and inadequately constructed, and the most basic rules regarding their upkeep and maintenance went unenforced.[5]

By June, an epidemic of dysentery, measles, mumps, and other ailments, the inevitable consequence of such an unhealthy environment, swept through camp. Harrison reported that the diseases were so prevalent that they had "seized almost every individual." Nathaniel Vernon, who served with the

Pittsburgh Blues, a company of volunteer infantry, claimed that after the first siege, the deaths in the garrison were so frequent that Harrison ordered a stop to the numerous funeral processions taking place within the camp, fearing the parades would trigger a deep and dangerous despondency among the sick and wounded who still survived. The "climate and hardships of the campaign were too much for them," Vernon recorded, "and they were cut down as by a pestilence." Eventually, illness claimed as many as ten men a day and reduced the number of effective, battle-ready troops to fewer than five hundred in a garrison of over two thousand.[6]

Col. William Anderson led 250 reinforcements from the 24th Regiment of Infantry to Fort Meigs in late June. By early summer, Anderson had become exasperated at the conditions he found himself confronting at the post. Supplies, discipline, sanitation, and the normal understandings that regulated how the camp was to be commanded were all deficient. Writing directly to Secretary of War John Armstrong on August 10, Anderson complained that the "250 picked men who marched with me here, without a second shirt to their back, have ever since been without soap to wash even that shirt." Since his arrival, his men had been forced to subsist on unsuitable rations of salted beef and then been mixed in with militia units and compelled to work under the command of militia officers. Of his original detachment of 250 men, seventy to eighty were on the daily sick report, he reported, all without the "hospital aid and comforts which ought to be furnished the soldier on such occasions." The cumulative effect on his command was distressing. "Those men who are here of the 24th are fast declining into the most relaxed habits" he admitted, "such as sitting down whilst standing sentry [and] sleeping on post."[7]

The first two documents that follow, detailing serious disciplinary transgressions within the camp, were taken from an orderly book kept by Capt. Peter Dudley of the Kentucky Militia. Dudley's company mustered in Kentucky on March 29, 1813, and served at Fort Meigs from May 5 through mid September 1813. Capt. Dudley was the nephew of Col. William Dudley, who had led his force to disaster while attacking the British batteries on the north shore of the Maumee on May 5. Dudley's orderly book is housed within the Kentucky Historical Society archives in Frankfort.[8]

The next two documents describe the unhealthy conditions found within the fort during the late spring and summer of 1813. The first was created by Lt. Col. Edmund Gaines of the 24th Infantry, who was ordered by General Clay to inspect the camp and then report his findings, along with any recommendations, to the camp's commanding officers. The report resides in the Green Clay Papers found within the Burton Historical Collection at the Detroit Public Library. The second was written by Samuel R. Brown. Brown was from Auburn, New York, where he was editor for the newspaper *Cayuga Patriot.* When the war began, he enlisted in Captain James McClelland's Company of Volunteer Light Dragoons, which eventually was incorporated into Major James Ball's squadron of the 2nd U.S. Regiment of Light Dragoons. During the war, Brown's company participated in the Battle of Mississinewa, both sieges at Fort Meigs, and the Battle of the Thames. At the conflict's conclusion, Brown published several books dealing with his wartime experiences, including *Views of the Campaigns of the Northwestern Army* (1814), *Views of Lake Erie* (1814), and *An Authentic History of the Second War for Independence* (1815).[9]

Although Brown intended his remarks to refer broadly to conditions throughout the Northwest Theater, many of his observations applied specifically to, and were drawn explicitly from, his experience at Fort Meigs.

The last two examples document the Independence Day celebration conducted at the fort on July 4, 1813. The Fourth of July was the great national holiday in early nineteenth-century America, and the signing of the Declaration of Independence in Philadelphia in 1776 was an event still within living memory of many Americans, including a number of those serving at Fort Meigs.

At the Maumee Rapids, the garrison observed the day with equal parts solemnity and enthusiasm. At dawn, soldiers awakened to a thirteen-gun artillery salute, one round each in honor of the thirteen colonies who had taken up arms against Great Britain during the Revolution. As the troops assembled on parade, General Clay issued orders canceling all fatigue duties and courts martial scheduled for the day. He then freed all those who had been convicted of serious offenses and who were then incarcerated, and commuted the sentences of those convicted of lesser misbehaviors, claiming that he was induced to "use this lenity alone from the consideration of this ever memorable day, and flatters himself that in the future, the soldiers under his command will better appreciate their liberty by a steady adherence to duty and prompt compliance to the orders of their officers." Lastly he ordered that all those reported fit for duty receive an extra gill (four ounces) of whiskey in their daily ration.

As the day progressed, the post's soldiers constructed a large bower near the fort's Grand Battery, the largest artillery position in the fort located in the garrison's northwest corner. In early afternoon, the camp's officers assembled beneath the bower for a "fine dinner" and to participate in a joyful, at times boisterous, observance of American independence. The ceremony began with a "national" salute, eighteen rounds in honor of the eighteen states then in the federal union, fired from two brass cannon on the Grand Battery.

Following the salute, the officers were joined by the band from the Independent Volunteers, consisting of fifes, drums, flutes, clarinets, violins, timbrels (a type of tambourine), and a bass drum. These musicians were then joined by the camp's martial music, every fifer and every drummer attached to every company then occupying Fort Meigs, perhaps as many as forty to fifty additional musicians. With Clay presiding and accompanied by the massed music, the officers raised eighteen toasts and sang eighteen songs. The tunes were familiar popular melodies and selections from traditional military airs of the day.

The toasts and tunes followed a familiar liturgy. Clay proposed the first toast, part proclamation and part warning to America's foes: "The day of our freedom, its blessing to all the world. It should admonish our ancient and inveterate enemy Great Britain that what was purchased by the blood of our fathers, their sons will ever be ready to maintain," followed by the singing of *Yankee Doodle.* Further toasts eulogized Washington, honored Jefferson, Madison, and Harrison, praised Congress, lamented the passing of fellow soldiers who had fallen previously in combat, and demanded that the nation's enemies "Go to the devil and shake yourself!" The observance concluded with a final toast to wives, sisters, and girlfriends far away and the singing of *My Heart from My Bosom Would Fly.* Following the ceremony, the individual companies within the garrison gathered within their camps to celebrate the day with equal enthusiasm. According to Adam Walker of the Ohio Militia, one company of volunteers butchered a steer for a barbecue and drank their toasts punctuated with "music and loud cheers."[10]

The documents below are the general orders for the 4th of July as recorded in the James Mills orderly book and an article detailing the day's activities that appeared in the newspaper *National Intelligencer* on July 29, 1813. The full documentation for the day is extraordinarily complete, especially in its recording of the use of military bands on the western frontier. These two documents, coupled with Cushing's diary, detail occasion, venue, instrumentation, and repertoire for the band during this significant celebration.[11]

Order Book of Capt. Peter Dudley's Company of Kentucky Militia

GENERAL ORDERS, CAMP MEIGS, AUGUST 30TH, 1813

... the general has seen with regret the inattention of sentinels at this fort, and orders "that in future they shall not set down their guns or hold converse with any person other than those authorized by existing regulations, and that they pay the accustomed honors to officers on passing them." Soldiers should not disgrace their profession by such a loose manner of doing their duty, and every officer is enjoined to take notice of such neglect in future. It is alone through the officers the soldiery looks for precept and example, and through them the commanding general expects a reformation.

GENERAL ORDERS, CAMP MEIGS, SEPTEMBER 9TH, 1813

At a general court martial ordered to convene the 3rd instant, for the trial of Resin Smith and such prisoners as would be brought before it, was tried Alvin West, a private in Capt. Metcalfe's Company Kentucky Militia on the following charges, 1st., for mutinous and riotous conduct in Camp Meigs on the night of the 3rd Sept. 1813 by preventing me (then corporal of the guard of artillery) from discharging my duty by seizing the gun of the guard who was then on his way to relieve a sentinel and using threatening language and striking me in the face. Charge 2nd; for violation of a general order by creating a disturbance and noise in Camp Meigs after tattoo on the night of the 3rd Sept., 1813.

(signed) Joseph Tensley, Corpl. in Capt. Cushing's Company.

To which charge the prisoner pleaded "not guilty." The court, after an examination of the testimony and mature deliberation, find the prisoner guilty of the charges exhibited against him and sentence "that the prisoner, Alvin West, a private in Capt. Metcalfe's Company, 10th Regiment Kentucky Militia, be sentenced to perform the police duties of the camp for the space of ten days."

The general commanding disapproved the above sentence in a general order of the 6th instant and ordered the court to reconsider. The court met pursuant to the general order and reconsidered the sentence, and on mature deliberation pronounced the following, "that Alvin West, a private in Capt. Thos. Metcalfe's Company of the 10th Regiment Kentucky Militia be sentenced to wear a ball and chain around his ankle and perform the police duties of the garrison for the term of ten days and be confined in the guard house every night while under punishment."

P. Dudley, B Maj. & president of the court[12]

Police of Fort Meigs, July 17, 1813

The ground occupied by the 17th, 19th, & 24th U.S. Infantry is tolerably clean. The adjacent ditches, however, in many places contain filth and trash that ought to be immediately cleared away. The same may be said as to the position of the Independent Battalion of Volunteers as well as that part of the Kentucky Militia occupying the N. western side of the great traverse.

The position of the militia comprehending the space along the eastern and southern boundary of the fort (the Ohio & part of the Kentucky Militia) is but illy swept and the ditch bordering on this position contains a mass of filth and stagnant water which I am persuaded must greatly endanger the health of the corps, if not of the whole garrison. There is likewise a quantity of stagnant water in a cellar or hole at the Northern battery.

The environs of the fort are prodigiously filthy and offensive, particularly on the northwest and northern & eastern quarters.

The state of the ditches and environs of the fort, I apprehend, cannot fail to destroy the health of the troops. I therefore take leave to suggest the necessity of a general fatigue (of the whole of the troops off duty) for a day or part of a day to clear off the dirty rubbish and sweep the ground for a short distance around the fort.

E. P. Gaines, Lt. Col. 24th Regt.
Officer of the day[13]

Views of the Campaigns of the Northwestern Army, Samuel R. Brown

ABUSES IN THE ARMY

If it be a fact that in the armies of the U. States, disease kills three to where the enemy does one, the evil claims the prompt and serious attention of government and ought to be remedied. It is a melancholy fact! I will premise, in the first place, that our northern frontier from the French Mills to Detroit, is, at certain points and especially at every military station, extremely unhealthy. The diseases incident to the climate are agues and fevers of different kinds. The British side of the lakes is as bad, or worse.

I will briefly state what I have seen, and with no other view than to aid in the correction of the evil, I last summer visited the northern frontier, volunteered in the service as a private, to ascertain by experience and ocular scrutiny the police of our camps and the condition of the sick.

The science of health was as no part of the general's study; other cares engrossed his thoughts. Hygeia and Mars were not in habits of intercourse. The stench of the camp was insupportable; men sickened and died in their tents. The little medical aid they received was administered in most cases by downright quacks. At Detroit, several houses were occupied for the benefit of the sick; they were dignified with the name of hospitals! The smell of the rooms was enough to make a well man sick in five minutes. It was as much as one's life was worth to enter them; yet the sick were sent there to recover their health! Poor fellows!

In an army, death soon loses its terrors. The loss of a soldier excites very little interest. The surgeons and doctors are not very solicitous to evince their professional skill, even if they chance to possess it.

The officers fared very little better. Even Col. Johnson suffered beyond measure in his passage from the Moravian town to Sandusky. One of Governor Shelby's volunteers was shot through the neck: ten days afterwards, his wound had not been dressed; his situation was distressing. We left him at Portage; whether he lived or died I know not. He was a promising young man and bore his pains with the greatest fortitude.

The disease most fatal in the army is the flux, or camp distemper; malignant and incurable in most cases when opposed by empirical ignorance, but which every old woman in the country would cure in three days with a decoction of milk, pine bark and spikenard root.

I went frequently to the burying grounds to count the fresh graves and mark the progress of death. My heart sickened at the sight. By inspecting those of Detroit, Fort Meigs, Portage, Sandusky, Erie, Buffalo and Eleven Mile Creek, and by ascertaining the loss sustained by different corps, I was enabled to form a pretty correct estimate of the number of deaths by sickness. The aggregate was alarming.

Capt. M'Clelland's company of 12 months volunteers from Fayette County Pennsylvania, a very patriotic corps and the one to which I was attached, left Pittsburg on the 5th of October, 1812 forty-five strong. They were, for the most part, men of talents and property. They were discharged at Detroit last October and had lost fifteen of their number—twelve by sickness and three killed in battle; and it was doubtful whether several others, then sick, would ever reach home.

Almost every other corps in the army that had been as long in service suffered in the same ratio. The Chillicothe Guards, the Pittsburgh Blues, Payne's, Markle's and Garrard's cavalry, Hopkins' United States dragoons, Puthuffs and Kisling's infantry, the Petersburg Volunteers, all of Ball's legion, and whose respective losses I had the means of correctly ascertaining, lost nearly every third man. The Petersburg Volunteers, as fine a company as ever trod the earth—men in the prime and vigor of life, the flower of Petersburg, left home 101 strong. At the time of their discharge, which was in October 1813, they had lost twenty-seven of their number, twenty-two of whom perished by disease; several more remained seriously indisposed. I question whether more than seventy of these brave fellows will ever see Petersburg again. Such was their patriotic ardor that they left business which was lucrative—their homes the seat of elegance and ease—their friends, parents, wives, and children—marched more than one thousand miles to encounter the inclemency of the seasons—the toils and dangers of war—the horrors of disease, *to serve their country*, which they most faithfully performed. I will not attempt to describe my feelings when I saw such men borne by their comrades to a rude and solitary grave.

From what I have heard and seen, I am induced to believe that the loss by disease sustained by the northern army is in the same proportion. . . .[14]

A Regimental Book for the 1st Regt't, 3'rd Detachment of Ohio Militia Containing Orders Received and Issued by Colonel James Mills of Butler County and State of Ohio, February 6 to August 4, 1813

CAMP MEIGS, JULY 4TH, 1813

General Orders: The general announces to the troops under his command the return of this day which gave Liberty and Independence to the United States of America, and orders that a National Salute be fired under the superintendence of Captains Gratiot and Cushing. All the troops reported fit for duty shall receive an extra gill of whiskey and those in confinement and those under sentence attached to this corps be forthwith released and ordered to join their respective corps. The general is induced to use this lenity alone from the consideration of this ever-memorable day, and flatters himself that in the future, the soldiers under his command will better appreciate their liberty by a steady adherence to duty and prompt compliance to the orders of their officers, by which alone they are worthy of the blessings of that Liberty and Independence—the only real legacy left us by our fathers. All courts martial now constituted in this camp is hereby dissolved. There will be no fatigue this day.[15]

Fourth of July in Camp, *National Intelligencer*, July 29th, 1813

CAMP MEIGS, JULY 4, 1813

The officers of the garrison were invited to celebrate the day with the commanding general. Their attendance was general from the different corps of regulars, independent volunteers, Kentucky and Ohio Militia. Upwards of one hundred officers, including staff were present.

The assemblage was preceded by a national salute from the guns of the garrison under the direction of Capts. Gratiot and Cushing.

General Clay (assisted by his aid-de-camp, Major J. H. Hawkins) presided. Col. Anderson of the 24th Regt. U.S. Infantry (assisted by Major Robt. Butler) acted as Vice-President.

The repast, though humble, was not the less cordial. Every eye proclaimed the Fourth of July as the day most dear to America—most animating to the patriot's bosom.

After partaking of soldier's fare, the following toasts were drank, accompanied by martial music and the band from the Independent Volunteers.

1. The Day of our Freedom—Its blessing to all the world. It should admonish our ancient and inveterate enemy, Great Britain that what was purchased by the blood of our fathers, their sons will ever be ready to maintain. *Tune—YANKEE DOODLE*
2. The War—May its issue prove that the only republic of the earth is competent to assert and maintain its rights. *HAIL COLUMBIA*
3. Our Enemies—the British—their red allies—domestic traitors—The day of retribution is at hand. *GO TO THE DEVIL AND SHAKE YOURSELF*
4. Our Rights at home and upon the ocean—What Nature's God hath guaranteed, let no earthly power wrest from us. *HAIL LIBERTY*
5. The Tories and apologists for the wrongs done us by the British government, where they ought to be, kissing their monarch's toe. *ROGUE'S MARCH*
6. The bleaching bones of our fellow-soldiers (whose cold-blooded butcheries were sanctioned by British officers) demand from our government retaliation. *ROSLIN CASTLE*
7. General Washington's Valedictory Address—May every real American feel and practice its precepts whilst the scoff and scorn of good men point to the wretches who use it as a cloak to hide their treason. *COLUMBIA, COLUMBIA, TO GLORY ARISE*
8. The memory of our father, time brightens his fame. It will flourish forever. *WASHINGTON'S MARCH*
9. The memory of Wayne—Holy be the sod on which we tread. It was here he conquered our savage foes. *STONY POINT*
10. Gen. Butler and the valiant heroes who braved and met the savage hatchet—while we mourn their loss, we will emulate their valor. *ERE AROUND THE HUGE OAK*

11. Jefferson—While he stood at the helm, all was well. May time prove he anchored the vessel of state into the harbor of safety. *JEFFERSON'S MARCH*
12. His successor, Madison—Firm in the path of virtue; undaunted amidst the ravages of party faction; vigorous in the prosecution of the war. The nation will support him. *MADISON'S MARCH*
13. The members of Congress who voted for the war—May they live to see its honorable issue; they will live ever-after in the affections of the people. *LET TRUTH AND SPOTLESS FAME BE THINE*
14. Genl. Dearborn—Silent be the tongue of defamation: slanderers, vipers, hide your heads. *TURKS MARCH*
15. Gen. Harrison—When the impartial historian records his preservation of Fort Meigs, the reader will find a monument which no time can decay. *HARRISON'S MARCH*
16. Gen. Winchester and his brave fellow-sufferers—Though unfortunate in battle, they still live in our affections. *THE SOLDIER'S RETURN*
17. Our brave brothers of the ocean—Ever flourish the laurels entwined round their brows by a grateful country. *AMERICA, COMMERCE, AND FREEDOM*
18. The Fair of our country—We have their hearts in the field of battle. When the battle is over, our hearts shall be yielded to them. *MY HEART FROM MY BOSOM WOULD FLY*[16]

~ CHAPTER 9 ~

Second Siege, July 20–28, 1813

About 2 o'clock a tremendous heavy firing of small arms commenced immediately on the Sandusky road about 3 or 400 yards in the woods, accompanied with the war-whoop of the Indians and all the confused noises of a severe and obstinate engagement. The firing was incessant and grew nearer, that of musketry appeared to predominate. The Indians' rallying yell never ceased; they seemed to be pressed, and beat in towards the fort as though they were giving ground until the heat of the battle appeared to be immediately in the edge of the woods, which is not farther than 200 yards distant from the garrison . . . Every mind was indignant yet distrustful whether it was our friends, who might possibly be coming to our relief and engaged with the enemy? Or was it a stratagem on their part to induce the garrison to make a sortie?

—An Officer of Respectability

Procter had been bitterly disappointed in the outcome of his first assault against Fort Meigs. Almost at once after his return to Malden, he and other Crown authorities began planning for a second expedition against the American outpost. But as spring turned to summer, British forces found themselves confronting numerous challenges that limited Procter's ability to take effective action against Harrison and his army.[1]

Casualties, illness, and demands for members of the 41st in other theaters of the conflict had greatly reduced the number of regulars at Procter's disposal. If he mounted an expedition against the rapids, it would take so many troops that those remaining at the British post would be incapable of defending themselves against either a counterattack from Fort Meigs or from an assault from American troops to Procter's east.[2]

Second, British forces at Fort Malden had begun to experience shortages of provisions, forage, and supplies. Procter's line of supply remained open, but had constricted considerably in late spring, particularly after American forces captured Fort George, opposite Niagara, in June 1813. By late spring, Procter was complaining to his superiors about his lack of pork, beef, clothing, shoes, Indian supplies, trenching tools, guns, gun powder, and ammunition. By summer, these deficiencies had become acute. British authorities responded only by telling him that the "stores you require must be taken from the enemy, whose resources on Lake Erie must become yours."[3]

Lastly, in June, Capt. Robert Barclay had arrived in Malden to take command of the British naval squadron already on Lake Erie and to augment the British naval force through the launching of *Detroit*, presently under construction at the Malden naval yard. When ready, he was to move against and destroy the American naval force commanded by Oliver Hazard Perry now being built at Erie, Pennsylvania. To arm *Detroit*, Barclay had taken possession of nearly all of the artillery used by Procter when he had attacked Fort Meigs in April. In early summer, therefore, the British commander simply had too few men with too few supplies and inadequate armament to mount a meaningful offensive against the American post.[4]

Like Procter, his Native American allies had also been frustrated at the outcome of the first investment of Fort Meigs. For the moment, they remained loyal and ready to bear arms on behalf of the British, but the lack of regulars made the army appear weak, the lack of trade goods diminished Procter's ability to negotiate with his allies, and the lack of provisions made it impossible to keep a large force of Native Americans in the area and at his disposal for any length of time.[5]

In late June, Procter's situation changed dramatically when Robert Dickson led more than a thousand additional warriors into the British alliance. At the outbreak of the war, British authorities had sent Dickson, a fur trader and interpreter with the British Indian Department, to recruit allies among the Indian nations in northern Illinois, Wisconsin, Minnesota, and the upper Mississippi Valley. Dickson had succeeded admirably. Through his efforts, more than fourteen hundred warriors were now streaming into Detroit to join the campaign against the Americans. The new recruits were a welcome addition to the offensive arsenal available to Procter, but the number of Natives inundating Detroit threatened to overwhelm his meager supply of provisions and stores. To employ this new force effectively, the British general needed to act quickly and decisively.[6]

Native American scouts had kept the British well informed about events at the rapids throughout the spring and summer. Procter understood that Fort Meigs was physically stronger, had more provisions, supplies, and ammunition, and housed a far larger garrison than it had during the first siege. He also understood that his small force of regulars and light artillery was incapable of battering the post into submission. Therefore, Procter and his Native allies, led by Tecumseh, Roundhead, and Black Hawk, agreed that they would move quickly against Fort Meigs, but instead of attacking the post directly, would use subterfuge to lure the Americans out of the fort, where they could then be destroyed by the expedition's large force of Indian auxiliaries. Procter launched the attack in mid July, advancing to the rapids with nearly 3,500 Native warriors but only about 350 British regulars and a small number of small-caliber cannon.[7]

The attacking army reached the rapids on the evening of July 20 and again established its base at Fort Miamis. At dawn on the 21st, a force led by Tecumseh attacked one of the newly erected picket-guard stations surrounding the fort, killing several of the American defenders and wounding others. Then they drove off a number of beef cattle, oxen, and horses and established a perimeter around the fort to its west, south, and east. American artillery and the picket-guard stations kept the enemy at bay and forced the attackers to remain beyond effective musket range. Within the camp, the Americans fully anticipated that they were to again undergo a sustained artillery siege followed by a massed assault against the stockade. The garrison spent the day frantically erecting new traverses across the length of the fort's interior and mounding over the post's powder magazines with dirt and sod. "What are not at work," observed Capt. Cushing, "are at the pickets giving battle."

Over the next few days, Procter did what he could to exaggerate the size of his army. Immediately after landing, British forces established their camp near where they had bivouacked during the first investment. Curiously, this time they erected their tents on an elevated knoll within full view of the American garrison. Procter likely had employed his soldiers to erect far more tents than he had soldiers, to suggest to the Americans that he had deployed far more troops than actually existed.

Native forces maintained a brisk and nearly constant fire into the post with small arms throughout the investment. Mounted warriors continually rode back and forth in full view of the fort on both sides of the river. Each morning began in the British camp with the firing of an artillery salute that was answered by a second that the Americans supposed to be from a fieldpiece manned by a British force held in reserve at the mouth of the Maumee River. A band of music loud enough to be heard clearly by the defenders serenaded the British camp at daybreak and sunset, and Procter exercised his troops by having them fire heavy musket volleys throughout the day. His soldiers occupied the site of the British artillery batteries used during the first siege and appeared to construct new ones. And on the 25th, he broke camp on the north side of the river, crossed the Maumee *en masse*, and, in an overtly provocative move, reestablished his camp out of sight of the Americans, but only about a mile from the fort on the river's south bank. The stratagems were effective. Clay believed that he faced in excess of two thousand regulars, while others within the fort estimated that the enemy force consisted of more than a thousand regulars and six thousand Native warriors. All predicted that the British force intended to take the post by storm.[8]

On July 25, the fifth day of the siege, the Americans were surprised to hear no morning gun and see no enemy soldiers or warriors. Instead, they were met only with a deep and foreboding silence that continued throughout the day. As evening approached, war drums began to beat within the British camp and continued until long after sunset. That evening, Capt. Joseph McCune rode into camp with news from Harrison. Harrison told Clay that he was at Camp Seneca (present-day Old Fort, Ohio), about thirty-five miles from Fort Meigs, with a large force of reinforcements. But he believed that Clay was strong enough to defend himself, and that he and his additional troops would not try to relieve the American fort. Instead, Harrison would hold his force in reserve in case the British moved against either Upper or Lower Sandusky.

At two o'clock in the afternoon the following day, the woods surrounding the fort erupted in a furious burst of gunfire. By every appearance, Harrison had changed his mind about sending reinforcements to the garrison, and now a column of American soldiers was engaged in a desperate bid to break through the Native American line and make their way to the stockade. Within the fort, the defenders could clearly hear two groups of combatants, and the fighting appeared to move closer and closer to the fort, only to recede and then draw closer again. But the noise was a mere ruse: a mock battle staged by the British and their allies to lure the Americans out and into the open. John Richardson, with the British, claimed that the battle was waged with such authenticity that "we were half in doubt ourselves whether the battle was a sham one or real."

Many of Clay's junior officers immediately demanded to go to the "column's" rescue despite the intelligence they had received the night before. But Clay, who trusted McCune's veracity, and who had witnessed firsthand during the earlier siege the consequences of Dudley's reckless disobedience, held firm, and instead of soldiers, sent several mortar rounds into the woods near the fighting.

The "battle" continued until mid-afternoon, when a severe downpour, "the heaviest thunder shower I have ever experienced" according to one of the Americans, ended the demonstration. The British took no action the following day, and on the 28th, they lifted the siege, boarded their transports, and sailed down the Maumee. From the rapids, Procter moved against Fort Stephenson at Lower Sandusky. There, a rash and reckless assault against the American post netted the British only heavy casualties before forcing the expedition's retreat to Canada.[9]

Fort Meigs had survived a well-executed and determined assault, but that victory had come at a price. In addition to the dozen or so men killed and wounded on the 21st, the contest had cost about four dead and a half-dozen wounded in the days that followed.

The second siege marked an important inflexion point in the Northwest campaigns. American efforts near Detroit had been marked by a long series of reverses. There had been no clear and unambiguous American victory in the Maumee Valley since Harrison had relieved a siege of Fort Wayne in September 1812. But the American victory at the second siege was unequivocal and marked the beginning of an uninterrupted string of successes starting at Fort Stephenson, continuing through Lake Erie, and concluding at the Detroit Theater's last major engagement, the Battle of the Thames, fought along the Thames River at Moraviantown in October 1813.

The first document presented here is a diary kept by an unnamed American officer during the siege and published in the *Weekly Register* on September 14, 1813. The second description is taken from John Richardson's first account of his wartime experiences, written under his own name, *War of 1812, First Series: Containing a Full and Detailed Narrative of the Right Division of the Canadian Army,* published in 1842.[10]

An Interesting Journal of the Second Siege of Fort Meigs, by an Officer of Respectability at That Place, *Weekly Register*, September 14, 1813

July 20. Tuesday night general orders were given for every officer and soldier to be vigilant, to lay on their arms and be ready to receive the enemy—which order proceeded from the discovery of a sail near the old British Fort.

21st. Wednesday morning at daylight the piquet guard posted at the east end of the fort were attacked and driven in by the Indians with the loss of five killed, one wounded, and three missing. The Indians immediately surrounded the fort and could be seen behind trees firing. Plunder seemed to be their principal object at this moment, and they turned their attention to the horses and cattle in the vicinity of the fort. Running up within gun shot of us, they succeeded in catching thirty or forty horses and fifteen yoke of oxen. The artillerists gave them several shot which made them very cautious in approaching the fort.

The British about this time were discovered landing their force at the old fort from two two-masted vessels and a numerous quantity of water craft. They pitched their tents on a flat convenient to the river and in full view of this place, but they quickly changed that plan, had them struck, and appeared to be fortifying the old garrison. In the evening, they fired an extremely heavy discharge of musketry by platoons.

22nd. Thursday. They beat reveille and fired a morning gun, which was answered by one at the mouth of the river, which gun was also answered by another supposed to be at Malden. The Indians were firing into the fort alternately throughout the day, but with very little effect. This day Lieut. Mountjoy penetrated to the fort with twelve or fifteen men, having been fired on by the Indians several times.

23rd. Friday morning. [Heard?] their reveille and gun which was again answered at the lake, together with delightful music on the bugle horn. A large number of horsemen were discovered; they came up the river and were passing and repassing continually. Indians firing as usual into the fort, a great number from the opposite shore.

In the evening they abandoned their encampment and landed all their forces on this side of the river immediately opposite the old garrison, where they established their headquarters. Tattoo and music at night.

24th. Saturday morning. Reveille, music, and gun, which was answered at the lake. Horsemen in motion again up and down the river. This day a sortie was made from the fort of about 200 regulars under command of Capt. Armstrong. They penetrated the edge of the woods and at that distance, marched around the fort; found four of our men who were killed on the morning of the 21st; brought them in. They were fired on by two Indians in ambush; no other discovery. The Indians kept up a very brisk fire into the fort this evening; no drum or music heard at night.

25th. Sunday morning. No gun, drum, or music; instead of which we had the yelpings of a war dance from the Indians. This day no discovery could be made of them but the smoke of their encampment; Indians fired a few shots, no tattoo or noise of any kind at night.

26th. Monday morning. All silence again; express returned from General Harrison, pressed closely by the Indians.

About 2 o'clock a tremendous heavy firing of small arms commenced immediately on the Sandusky road about three or four-hundred yards in the woods, accompanied with the war-whoop of the Indians and all the confused noises of a severe and obstinate engagement. The firing was incessant and grew nearer, that of musketry appeared to predominate. The Indians' rallying yell never ceased; they seemed to be pressed, and beat in towards the fort as though they were giving ground until the heat of the battle appeared to be immediately in the edge of the woods, which is not farther than 200 yards distant from the garrison. It was an alarming and momentous crisis; every mind was indignant yet distrustful whether was it our friends, who might possibly be coming to our relief and engaged with the enemy? Or was it a stratagem on their part to induce the garrison to make a sortie? It was a question which required the most decisive and prompt solution; and devolved upon the commander of the fort an immense degree of responsibility. He immediately declared it a sham fight; and as they commenced he let them conclude their own battle. We threw two bombs in among them—that rather silenced the heavy firing which continued fully an hour; however, they kept it up until night at intervals, as though they were killing prisoners. Just at the conclusion of the battle, a storm blew up with the most excessive rain I ever witnessed. A British officer was discovered on the point of a ridge during the engagement observing the movements of the garrison. The Indians gave their shot very briskly this afternoon.

27th, Tuesday. Silent both night and morning; none to be seen. A few shot from the Indians; large fires at night at the British encampments. During the siege only about six men were wounded in the fort, all slightly except one or two.

28th, Wednesday. No appearance of the enemy until about 12 o'clock when we discovered their fleet putting out of its harbor, which was a large bend on this side of the river that completely kept them from a view of this fort. Never until this moment could we form any opinion of their probable strength, having never shown their main body before. About one hundred and thirty or forty water crafts of different kinds, together with two double masted vessels, were seen; the small vessels were supposed to average twenty men each. What number were in the large vessels, we could form no idea of. The river was completely covered with their sail; they had a fine homeward breeze and were quickly out of sight.

The horsemen had kept their encampment about two miles above the fort. They were likewise in motion, directing their course down the river; supposed to be Tecumseh's squadron and, if so, about 800 strong, the same, no doubt, the deserters spoke of some time ago as being encamped on the River Raisin.

What number of Indians there were on foot is entirely conjecture, but it is reasonable to suppose that they were as numerous as at the former siege; and what the aggregate forces of the enemy were is a matter of much speculation here. Various are the conjectures; but it is the settled opinion of the better part of the garrison that they were at least 5000 strong.

The truth is, theirs has been one of the novel and extraordinary movements that could have been expected from an enemy. That they should advance openly in daylight, pitch a small number of tents in full view of us, strike them suddenly and change their encampment, make a display of their horsemen, have elegant music, give us a sham battle, invest the fort for eight days, and then retire without have any further communication with us either by way of truce or contest, is so mysterious and ambiguous a display of tactics as to render all a conjecture who the commander was. If he was a man of military talents, what could have been his object?

Had they intended a storm, surprise and secret movements should have been their ruling principle; but they seemed to have abandoned that policy by making their approach notorious. Had they anticipated a reduction of this place by artillery, they had advantageous ground and the most ample opportunity of erecting batteries, which they failed to do. Had their object been to cut off the communication and destroy reinforcements from other posts to this, they most shamefully neglected their duty, for all our expresses returned safe, and the circumstance of Mountjoy's arrival in open daylight was so remarkable as to be called a miracle by all. And should their whole movement have been grounded on the false hopes of success on the stratagem which they intended to practice on us, the result has shown how far they have been mistaken, and has attached to its projector the merited disgrace of so bad a resort, and has likewise reflected the highest honor on the commander of this garrison for his quick penetration of the deception.

What their real intentions were remain yet with themselves, for they have done nothing to disclose any of the views which might be thought important by us. For my own part, I will hazard my opinion as to this; that they had no particular motive, but have made all this parade to gratify the Indians who are continually pressing them to battle and who, I am told, are growing very hungry. This letter might easily have been comprised in the old saying of the King of France's troops, "The British marched their troops up to Fort Meigs, and then marched them down again."

Upon the whole, I consider their retreat as a disgraceful one, and the maintenance of this post on our part equal to a victory. This is the second defeat the combined army has suffered before the picketing of Fort Meigs, and long may it stand as a protection to the N.W. Army, and as an eyesore and subject of disgrace to the enemy, who in the former siege, with the heaviest rain of artillery they could produce, were not able to affect a solitary breach on this stubborn wall of oak."[11]

War of 1812, First Series: Containing a Full and Detailed Narrative of the Operations of the Right Division of the Canadian Army, John Richardson

Late in July at the earnest instance of Tecumseh, who had formed a plan for the reduction of Fort Meigs which he conceived would be crowned with the fullest success, a second expedition consisting of the main body of the 41st (Captain Derenzy having recently joined with those detachments of the regiment which had borne so conspicuous a part in the battle of Queenstown [Battle of Queenston Heights]), a few militia, and nearly a thousand Indians, accompanied by a few pieces of light artillery was undertaken against this fortress.

On our arrival in the Miami the whole of the regular force and guns were disembarked on the right bank of the river out of view of the fort, yet not far from the point where our light batteries had been carried during the late siege.

Tecumseh's plan was as follows. Immediately in rear of Fort Meigs and at right angles with the river, ran the road to Sandusky (distant about thirty miles), upon or near which the chief had been apprised by his scouts that General Harrison, who with a large portion of his force had left the fort soon after its relief from General Procter's presence, was at that moment encamped. Having landed some miles lower down the river, the whole of the Indian force was to march through the woods and gain unperceived by the troops in the fort the Sandusky road, where a sham engagement was to take place, leading the garrison to believe a corps hastening to their relief had been encountered and attacked by the Indians and inducing them to make a sortie for their rescue. The moment they had crossed the open ground intervening between their position and the skirt of the wood, we were to rise from our ambuscade and take them in the rear, making at the same time a rush for the fort, before the enemy could have time effectually to close his gates.

All the preliminary features in this plan (which certainly was one that gave every fair promise of success) had been completed, and we were awaiting with some interest and impatience the result when the heavy firing of two distinct parties suddenly commenced on the Sandusky road. We were all instantly, although noiselessly, upon the alert, but in vain did we look for any movement in the fort. Many of the garrison lined the ramparts in the rear and seemed to look out anxiously in the direction of the firing, but they gave not the slightest indication of a design to leave the fort even when the musketry had become so animated and heavy that we were half in doubt ourselves whether the battle was a sham one or a real. Either they had obtained information of our presence or they suspected the nature and object of the ruse, and we had the mortification to find ourselves utterly foiled in the grand design of the expedition.

Annoyed at the failure of his cherished scheme, Tecumseh urged upon General Procter the necessity of doing something before our return, and it being found out of all question to attempt the reduction of Fort Meigs with the light guns (6-pounders) which accompanied us, it was determined to change the theatre of operation to Sandusky. Thither the main body of the Indians proceeded by land while we re-embarked in our boats and descending again the Miami, gained Lake Erie, and thence the Sandusky River, on which the fort of that name is built.[12]

~ CHAPTER 10 ~

Reduction and Abandonment

We have nearly completed a fort at this place of the following descriptions, viz. About 110 yards square, a strong block house at each corner, pickets of fourteen feet in length and one in width, and let into the ground four feet. Against the pickets on the outside, earth is thrown up four or five feet high, and a ditch about six feet deep and five feet high, the side dug horizontally . . . It will be very strong.

—A volunteer in Capt. Dudley's company

The most significant factor shaping the prosecution of the war in the Detroit Theater was naval control of Lake Erie. Since the beginning of the conflict, Great Britain had held that advantage. Control of the lake allowed the unopposed movement of men and materials from the Niagara frontier all the way to Detroit, Michilimackinac, and beyond. British control also denied use of the lake to the Americans. American troops and supplies destined for northwest Ohio were necessarily obliged to undertake either a tedious and circuitous journey down the Ohio River to Cincinnati, up the Miami Valley, and west to Fort Wayne, Indiana, from which they could navigate the Maumee River to their destination, or an equally tiresome and difficult trek northward from Urbana through the Great Black Swamp. Control of Lake Erie, therefore, represented an enormous strategic and tactical advantage to whomever held it. By mid July, as Barclay prepared to launch *Detroit* from Amherstburg and Perry's squadron neared completion in Erie, Pennsylvania, American and Canadian authorities both understood that British control of Lake Erie would soon be challenged significantly when the two forces met in a decisive naval confrontation that would, in large measure, determine the remaining course of the war.[1]

Fort Meigs had been built originally as a forward supply base and staging area to allow Harrison to accumulate the men and supplies that would permit him to undertake an invasion of Upper Canada once military circumstances near Detroit enabled him to do so. The possibility that Perry could wrest control of Lake Erie was the opportunity that Harrison needed to bring his anticipated campaign to fruition. By late July, Harrison had already written to Gov. Isaac Shelby of Kentucky requesting that he recruit, assemble, and advance to the rapids with a large force of volunteers to participate in the planned offensive.[2]

Perry's squadron took sail in early August. Harrison believed that if Perry's force was successful in defeating Barclay, that victory would permit the Americans to begin to move the men and supplies at Fort Meigs forward to take part in the planned invasion. Harrison also understood that the removal of men and supplies from Fort Meigs would render the large facility at the rapids indefensible and drastically change its purpose. The American outpost would still function as a link in the attenuated supply chain funneling supplies and personnel to Detroit, albeit at a much smaller scale than previously. But those supplies would not be stored and amassed. Rather, they would be sent on quickly to their destination. The small detachment of soldiers remaining at the post after the main body of troops was redeployed would be too few to adequately mount a defense if the now empty and unnecessary large post was attacked. Therefore, Harrison acted quickly.

On August 15, Harrison wrote to Clay at Fort Meigs ordering him to consult with Capt. Charles Gratiot and devise a plan that would contract Fort Meigs to a size able to accommodate three hundred men, but capable of being defended by one hundred, and suggested that the most expedient way to proceed would be to carefully demolish the existing post's stockade and blockhouses and use those materials to enclose a smaller area in the fort's northeast corner. According to Harrison, Gratiot was to design and then supervise the construction of the new fortification. Four days later, Clay responded that he and Gratiot had examined the site and concluded that the new fort should be placed in the post's northwest corner, be about 150 feet square, and possess a blockhouse at each corner.[3]

On August 19, Harrison, Perry, and their staffs met for the first time. Together, they assembled a plan in which Perry would engage and destroy Barclay's force using soldiers from Harrison's army to act as sailors aboard Perry's ships. At the same time, Harrison would move rapidly to advance his men and supplies to the mouth of the Portage River (present-day Port Clinton, Ohio) where, following Perry's anticipated victory, Perry's ships would then escort Harrison's army to the Detroit River and Canada.[4]

On August 21, only two days after Harrison's meeting with Perry, construction of the smaller fort had begun. The new post, sited as Gratiot had suggested in the existing fort's northwest corner, was to be square, 150 yards to a side, and surrounded with stockading built of pickets fourteen feet long and set four feet in the ground. On the outside of the fort, Gratiot ordered that earth be mounded up to within five feet of the stockade's top and a steep-sided ditch, six feet deep and five feet across, encircle the position. The new post was to contain permanent barracks and storehouses within the stockade to house and supply the reduced garrison. Blockhouses constructed at each of the fort's four corners would allow cannon from within to rake the ditch if necessary. By September 8, Lt. Joseph Larwill observed that the new fort was "nearly completed and considerable of the works of the camp reduced."[5]

In late August, Brig. Gen. Duncan McArthur of the Ohio Militia took command of Fort Meigs from General Clay. On September 10, McArthur and the garrison listened to the sound of a severe cannonading emanating from Lake Erie, understanding that they were hearing the sound of Perry's long-expected battle with Barclay. Anxious to learn the engagement's outcome, McArthur sent a small boat with a detachment of scouts to the mouth of the Maumee at first light on the 11th, but did not learn the result of the action until the night of September 12 when a courier from Harrison brought news of Perry's victory.[6]

The American success threw the post into a state of furious activity. Agreeable to the plan orchestrated with Harrison, Perry sent three of his ships, *Somers*, *Tigress*, and *Porcupine*, to the site of Fort Miamis, just below the head of navigation on the Maumee. Using canoes, bateaux, and shallow-draft river craft, McArthur and his soldiers ferried the supplies and equipment stored at Fort Meigs over the rapids to the abandoned British post, where they were then loaded onto the waiting vessels. When Fort Meigs was emptied, the post's soldiers marched to Perry's ships. Those who could find space boarded the vessels for the journey to Lake Erie, while those who could not began the march to the same destination. Harrison left Fort Meigs in the care of a small company of Kentucky Militia, soon to be replaced by increasingly smaller detachments of the Ohio Militia.

Life at Fort Meigs became no easier following Harrison's departure, and in some respects worsened. Basic supplies, including provisions and medical

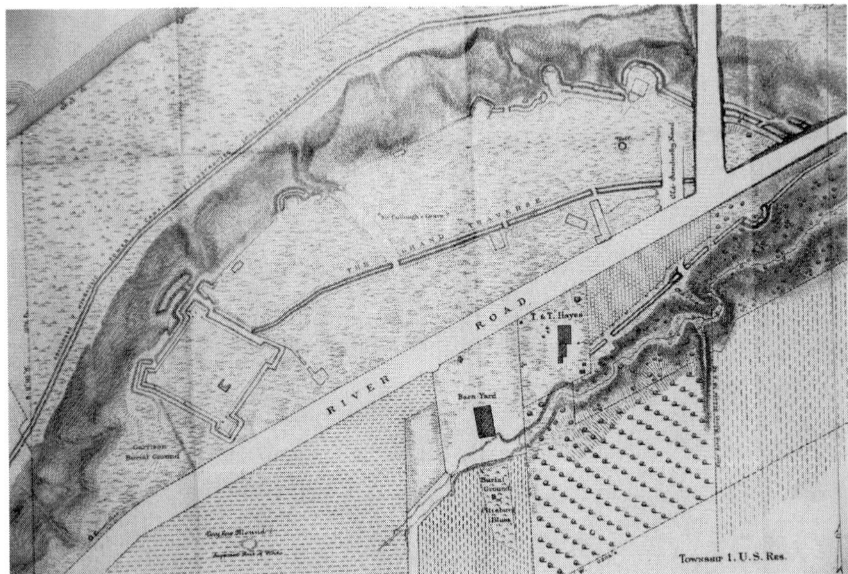

This map, showing the surviving earthworks at Fort Meigs in 1888, was created by Orlando Poe, the United States' chief topographical engineer. Although roads and structures had intruded onto the site, much of the post's perimeter earthworks and interior traverses remained intact. The outlines of the smaller fort, erected in August and September 1813, are clearly visible in the fort's northwest corner.

stores, became scarce, and declining morale contributed to a steady lessening of disciplinary standards. Illness continued to afflict the troops at the post, and in late January 1814, Gen. John Gano, the commander of the Ohio Militia, reported to Harrison that "at Fort Meigs, they have very few men fit for duty." Further, violence remained a constant possibility. On April 3, 1814, Capt. James Bonner reported that Indians had killed one of his men and had taken another prisoner within two hundred yards of the camp. In October 1814, a large party consisting of perhaps as many as fifty Native warriors raided the post, killed three men, and made off with fifteen head of cattle. Ohio Militia continued to occupy the fort until following the end of the war. In May 1815, the post was abandoned.[7]

The first document presented here is an extract of a letter written by a member of the Kentucky Militia describing the smaller post as it was being constructed in September 1813. The Worthington, Ohio, newspaper *Western Intelligencer* published the letter on December 29, 1813. The next document is a letter written by Harrison to McArthur following Perry's victory, urging the Ohio general to move his men and supplies to the mouth of the Portage River as quickly as possible. It is housed within the Duncan McArthur Papers held by the Library of Congress. The third writing is taken from a diary kept by Robert McAfee. McAfee served as a captain in Richard M. Johnson's Regiment of mounted volunteers. In September 1813, he was detailed to escort and then guard supplies from the fort as they were transported over the rapids and stored near Fort Miamis. Following the war, McAfee became active in Kentucky politics and eventually served in a variety of elected offices, including lieutenant governor during 1824–1828. In 1816 he penned a classic memoir of his wartime experiences, *History of the Late War in the Western Country*. His diary is in the collections of the Filson Historical Society.[8]

The next two examples are correspondence between officers at the fort and Maj. Gen. John S. Gano, who commanded the Ohio Militia in the waning days of the war. The letters, housed in the Western Reserve Historical Society and published by the Ohio Historical and Philosophical Society in 1923, hint at the growing frustration, both at the fort and at headquarters, over the deteriorating conditions at the rapids.[9]

Alexander Bourne wrote the last document in 1816, a little over a year after the military abandoned the post. Bourne had served at Fort Meigs during the war. In July 1816, while working as a surveyor for Ohio's General Land Office, Bourne returned to the rapids at the behest of the Ohio General Assembly to find a suitable site and then complete the preliminary platting for a town to be named in honor of Oliver Hazard Perry: Perrysburg. Bourne's description of Fort Meigs is the earliest surviving depiction of the site following the war.[10]

Extract of a Letter from a Volunteer in Captain Dudley's Company, to His Friend at This Place, Dated Camp Meigs, Sept. 1, the [Worthington] *Western Intelligencer*, Dec. 29, 1813

We have nearly completed a fort at this place of the following descriptions, viz. About 110 yards square, a strong block house at each corner, pickets of fourteen feet in length and one in width, and let into the ground four feet. Against the pickets on the outside earth is thrown up four or five feet high and a ditch about six feet deep and five feet high; the side dug horizontally. From the blockhouses each entrenchment can be raked completely by cannon. The fixments on the inside are yet to be made. It will be very strong. Today we commence the demolition of Fort Meigs—it will be completed in five or six days.[11]

Harrison to Duncan McArthur, September 15th, 1813

MOUTH OF PORTAGE RIVER, SEPT. 15TH, 1813

Dear Sir,

I am so desirous of getting to the opposite side of the lake as soon as possible that I am determined to take none of the artillery from Fort Meigs; the five eighteen-pounder carriages must, however, come, and one or two twelve-pound carriages; all the fixed ammunition for cannon and muskets except a small supply of the former for the garrison and about thirty rounds of musket cartridges for the garrison—as they will have a plenty of ball and powder this quantity will be sufficient. The flints also must be sent excepting a sufficiency for the garrison. None of the unfixed ammunition will be wanted, but all the salted provision and as much flour and biscuits as you can possibly bring with the means of transport you have.

Three of our vessels will set out today and will go as high up in the Miami as they can get; they will be there boarded by your boats as above directed. As soon as it is done you will come off with all the regular troops. I shall send you in the course of the day as many boats as we can spare. If the boats and vessels cannot take all the troops and their baggage, they must move down by land.

Hurry on then, my friend, as soon as possible. If you do not come on immediately, I must leave you. I calculate that it will take you but one day to embark your troops, stores, and baggage; if necessary, you must work all night.

Leave the command of the garrison with the senior officer of the Kentucky Militia that remains and send on to Lower Sandusky about thirty men (militia) under a captain to take charge of that post. Fort Meigs and Sandusky will both be relieved by Ohio Militia. Direct Col. Johnson if he has come on (or leave orders if he has not arrived) to wait at Fort Meigs for orders. I have a separate job for him to execute. Come on, for Gods sake, as soon as possible.

William Henry Harrison[12]

The McAfee Papers—Book and Journal of Robt. B. McAfee's Mounted Company, in Col. Richard M. Johnson's Regiment

Sept. 16th—Early we marched six miles to Fort Meigs and camped in the island above the fort which was covered with blue grass. In the evening, marching orders arrived for the fort, and all hands went to loading boats, and we were ordered to move camp in the flat below the old British garrison for the protection of the stores of the fort which were carried in their boats to be carried over to Canada in our larger vessels . . . Express arrived from General Harrison to move on everything.

Sept. 17th—We spent the day in guarding and securing the military stores and putting our arms in order.

Sept. 18th—Early, a heavy cannonading was heard in our camp on the lake, and three gunboats, one of which was in the lake fight, came up opposite our camp and took in the military stores of the army . . . The cannonading was from our schooners, one of which, the *Somers* of four guns, anchored near our encampment, each of the vessels had two masts. I was on board the *Porcupine* and near the *Tigress*, both of which had a 32 pounder on board. These were part of the ships that so gloriously conquered the *Queen Charlotte*, *Brig Hunter*, *Lady Prevost*, and three others on Lake Erie the 10th inst. They are strong and well built. Lt. Senate and several other officers who were engaged in the fight visited our encampment and breastworks. Great harmony and friendship prevailed . . .

The vessels were all loaded at sundown and stretched their sails again down the river, preceded by about 1,200 regulars and militia, some of whom went in boats and others on the land on the south margin of the river . . .

Sept. 19th—Up at half after 4 o'clock in the morning, and barges returned from the schooners and took the balance of the stores from our camp.[13]

Colonel John De Long to Major General John S. Gano, December 30th, 1813

FORT MEIGS, DECEMBER 30TH, 1813

Dear General,

. . . this is to inform you of our situation at this post. We are indeed very poorly supplied with flour of very inferior quality, and it appears without some other arrangement, we shall be entirely out. Although Maj. Fye has used every possible exertion to have flour brought from Winchester yet he don't seem to succeed. There is a quantity lying in the ice a small distance from [Fort] Winchester and no packhorses to be had. As I presume there is men whose duty it is to furnish these supplies, we hope their neglect won't go unnoticed by your honor, and [you will] cause such arrangements to be made as may be most conducive to the public. Although my hands is tied as to a command, but my wishes for the good of my country is still at my heart . . .

Sir, I remain with due respect your most humble servt.

John Delong, Col.

N. B. Sir, We are out of paper, so that we haven't paper to make provision returns and morning reports. I would wish you to mention to Maj. Lewis that if he don't fetch on paper to the commissariat, I don't know how we will make out for that article.[14]

General Orders, Head Quarters Ohio Militia, Lower Sandusky Feb. 2nd, 1814

MAJOR CHARLES FYE, COMMANDING FORT MEIGS

Sir,

I am surprised at information I receive from your post. The non-commissioned officers and privates, as well as others, report that your command is neither disciplined or subordinate, and from the letter received from Doctor Evans as to the sick, it must be evident you suffer every imposition to be practiced upon you and the other officers. For the good of the service and honor of the state, I expected better reports from the militia of our state. The troops on this line have performed an immense fatigue and many privations, yet have done their duty faithfully and are equal to regulars, and I was in expectation it would have been the case with all the troops. I am certain the men would do their duty if the officers would do theirs.

On the receipt of this, if you have not progressed with the addition to the fort, you may stop that work until an other officer arrives to take command and immediately attend to placing the old works on your present fort in the best possible state of defense; remove those buildings that are near the magazine to a remote distance; bank up the dirt around the magazine and see that there is no danger of fires communicating; see that the pickets are well lined and in good order; see the guards in proper order and that the men are exercised; exact from the quartermaster and others their duty, for I must believe the men are worthy the name of Ohio Citizens, soldiers zealous to maintain their honor and their country's cause, that they, with others, may have an honorable discharge when they have served out their tour.

I sent to Doctor Evans two lbs. tea, three & 3/4 lb. coffee, 24 lbs. sugar and 14 lbs. G. Salts for the sick. Your prompt attention and compliance with this order is expected.

John S. Gano, Major Genl.
Commanding Ohio Militia in Service U. S.[15]

Memoir of Alexander Bourne, 1816

. . . It was thirty-one miles from Lower Sandusky to Fort Meigs by the trail and marked trees then traveled, and I waited one day for company on this difficult and muddy road. We were fourteen hours in the mud and water from a late, heavy rain, and had to swim across Portage River. At the rapids of the Maumee, the appearance of the ground was much changed. Fort Meigs was nearly obliterated. The batteries, blockhouses, and pickets were removed, the ditches filled up, and corn had been raised on the field. The settlers who had been driven off by the Indians in the beginning of the war had returned and built several cabins, one for a tavern, one for a storehouse, and so on. One or two persons there had seen me in the army, and I was pleasantly situated.[16]

~ CHAPTER 11 ~

Cushing's Diary

Saturday, May 1st—*At 2 o'clock in the morning the British opened their artillery upon our garrison from their gunboats which lay one-and-one-half miles below us, but it was without effect. At 8 o'clock they hoisted the red flag at their lower battery and commenced firing with 24-, 12- and 6-pounders, and eight-inch mortars. They fired at us this day 240 shot and shells; did very little damage . . . We have not more than two killed and four wounded today.*

—Daniel Cushing

Capt. Daniel Cushing was the commanding officer of Cushing's Company, Second Regiment of U.S. Artillery at Fort Meigs during the War of 1812. While serving at Fort Meigs, he created numerous documents that detailed his service at the post, including his company's orderly book from April 1813 through February 1814 and a series of descriptive personal letters to family and friends. In addition, Cushing also maintained a personal diary, kept from October 1812 through July 1813. The diary describes the fort's construction and details the events occurring at the time of both battles as well as the mundane activities of daily garrison life. Cushing's diary is the most extensive and most detailed of the surviving records describing the events occurring at Fort Meigs during the War of 1812.[1]

In 1944 Harlow Lindley, the executive secretary of the Ohio State Archaeological and Historical Society (the administrative forerunner of the Ohio Historical Society, now the Ohio History Connection), published the diary and orderly book in volume XI of the society's *Ohio Historical Collections* under the title *Captain Cushing in the War of 1812*. Lindley was particularly well qualified to present these two documents. An authority on the Old Northwest's frontier and early pioneer history, Lindley had been born near Sylvania in Parke County, Indiana, in 1875. He attended Earlham College, and became a member of the history faculty there in 1899. While at Earlham, Lindley published widely on a number of topics relating to the Old Northwest. From 1903 through 1923, he also led the Department of History and Archaeology at the Indiana State Library. In 1923, he became the director of the Indiana Historical Commission. Leaving Earlham in 1928, he accepted the position of curator at the Ohio Archaeological and Historical Society in Columbus in 1929. He became the society's executive secretary in 1934, the position he held at his retirement in 1946. He died in 1959.[2]

In 1975, the Ohio Historical Society republished the diary and orderly book under the title *Fort Meigs and the War of 1812*. The book represented one of many initiatives undertaken in conjunction with the reconstruction of Fort Meigs and the opening of a new museum facility at Fort Meigs State Memorial the same year. In the 1944 publication, Lindley included a brief introduction that gave a short history of Fort Meigs and detailed Cushing's life. He faithfully transcribed both documents, but provided little annotation for either manuscript. The 1975 edition retained Lindley's introduction, transcriptions, and modest annotation, and added a brief preface by Joseph Thatcher, the Ohio Historical Society research curator who oversaw the new museum's development. The book also included photographs of archaeologically retrieved artifacts from the site, maps, drawings, and other objects that made up some of the exhibit material displayed within the new facility.[3]

The early history of both documents is unknown. In September 1891, Cassius Marcellus Clay, the famed nineteenth-century Kentucky politician, abolitionist, and son of Green Clay, speaking at Put-In-Bay on the seventy-eighth anniversary of Perry's victory, noted that "there is in the library of the Maumee Historical and Monumental Association (a forerunner of the present-day Maumee Valley Historical Society) a written order book by Captain Daniel Cushings [*sic*]." The material in the association's library was later donated to the Toledo–Lucas County Public Library, where it formed the foundation of that institution's current local history and genealogical collections. In 1944, Lindley claimed that both the orderly book and diary had been "found" in the library "some years ago." The library still retains Cushing's orderly book. The location of the diary is unknown; it has not been in the library's collections for many years and is presumed lost or stolen.[4]

The orderly book transcribed by Lindley is clearly an original document created by Daniel Cushing during his service at Fort Meigs. The diary, however, was not the original manuscript. Lindley noted in 1944 that the original diary "had been lost" and that the version held by the library was a handwritten transcription created by an unnamed editor in 1908. Lindley also observed that the 1908 editor had modified the document's original text to conform to contemporary spelling and punctuation, and had inserted subject headings that provided a degree of narrative context for the manuscript throughout the transcription. Even a casual reading of Lindley's transcription today reveals several errors of omission or transcription perpetrated by the document's 1908 editor that were incorporated by Lindley into his 1944 publication. Lindley was aware of these errors, and what little annotation he supplies throughout the manuscript is directed toward pointing out and correcting these mistakes.

The 1908 transcription of Cushing's diary also contained a serious omission. The entries from Sunday, April 25, 1813, through Tuesday, April 27, 1813, are absent from the 1908 diary. Lindley noted in 1944 that "here a few days of the diary are missing," but did not speculate as to whether the missing entries were removed from the original manuscript prior to its transcription in 1908, or were simply an error on the part of the manuscript's editor when the document was copied in the early twentieth century.

Fortunately, in 1813, James Taylor Eubank, a deputy quartermaster from Kentucky serving at Fort Meigs, copied a large portion of Cushing's diary into his personal letterbook. The material copied by Eubank consisted of Cushing's entries from April 25, 1813, through May 9, 1813, and includes the entries for April 25 through April 27. Eubank's letterbook survives today, housed within the holdings of the Kentucky Historical Society. Thus, by using the material found in the Eubank letterbook, it becomes possible to reconstitute Cushing's diary in its entirety.[5]

Cushing's diary documents the events occurring at Fort Meigs during the most significant part of its history. The following version of Cushing's diary, based on a typewritten transcript of the original document still in possession of the Toledo–Lucas County Public Library, includes the missing entries supplied by the Eubank letterbook, excises the portions of the diary added in 1908 and corrects the obvious misidentifications included in the 1908 transcription.[6]

The War of 1812 Diary of Capt. Daniel L. Cushing, October 10, 1812–July 31, 1813

October 10, 1812—I, Daniel Cushing, Capt. Of Artillery, 2nd Regt. marched from Lebanon—camped that night nine miles from that place—marched the 11th to Dayton—camped there until the 13th—marched from there to lower Piqua—camped there until the 25th.

We then marched to Urbana—arrived there the 27th, camped there until the 29th—marched from that place to Franklinton, arrived there 31st, camped near the church, stayed there three days, moved up the river a short distance, camped there until the flood drove us off. On the 8th of November, moved near the town on high land and camped there. Nothing new from day to day until the 24th.

The 25th [November 25th, 1812] One man died; buried him with the honors of war. On that day Col. Campbell left here with a detachment of 750 men, 600 cavalry, 150 light infantry, for an expedition on the Wabash, to pass through Dayton. On the 26th the command devolved on me at this place; some artillery, some dragoons, some infantry. This day commenced with snow but concluded with rain.

27th—By the general orders, moved the sick from the hospital tent into the court house. The day is windy but clear. Frederick Swaney went to the hospital this day from my company sick. Three men put into the river for getting drunk and fighting in their tents, took a bathing and returned to duty.

28th—Lieut. Meek returned from visit to Cincinnati—fetched letters from Mrs. Cushing and Capt. Ross, also from Major Van Horne.

Monday, 30th—This day made arrangements with Mr. Sullivan for timber to build artificer yards, called out five men for chopping wood and arranged teams to haul timber for the yard tomorrow. Put two men in the river for getting drunk.

December 8th—From the first to this day we have been engaged in fixing the building for the artificers, and putting down mill dams, and sending a boat up the Scioto, and repairing a flat to cross the river with public stores. General Harrison left this camp for the upper Sandusky on the 9th with all his suite, and gave me full command of all the troops at this place. All things went well until the 25th,

Christmas Day, when the devil got into the soldiers. From the 8th to the 25th we were steadily employed in building artificer shops and chopping wood and making coke.

27th—This day we are making out payrolls; shall receive our pay the 28th.

29th—General Harrison arrived here from Upper Sandusky; 30th he went on to Chillicothe.

January 1, 1813—I left Franklinton with my company for Upper Sandusky by the way of Worthington and Delaware—marched with thirty-four non-commissioned officers and privates, myself, and three lieutenants. It commenced raining early in the morning—continued all day. We moved off the old camp ground at 12 o'clock, marched four miles; our two wagons, one ammunition, the other baggage; both got stuck in the mud and could not move any farther that night. Rained very hard, became very dark, no tent pitched, no fire, nothing to make fire with, hemmed in with a very steep hill on one side and very wet and muddy bottom on the other. I sent all the officers and men to two houses in the neighborhood except two wagoners, my Black boy Ferguson, and four soldiers that stayed with me. It continued raining until about two o'clock that night then began to snow very fast. We made us a floor with rails from a fence, also burned rails for firewood. In the morning the snow was about four inches deep and very cold; still snowing; got something to eat, called all hands, pried up the wagons, doubled the teams and with much difficulty got one-fourth of a mile that day.

2nd—Stayed all night at Mr. Bears; the men all stayed in the house and barn; Lieut. Larwill and myself slept in the marquee. Unloaded a part of our loading, started for Worthington and arrived there about dark.

3d—Obtained the academy for the men. Myself and the rest of the officers put up at Col. Kilburn's. Continued snowing until some time in the night of the 3rd. Cleared off, very pleasant this morning.

The 4th I made a contract with Mr. Griswold to furnish the soldiers with provisions while waiting here. Left at Franklinton Corporal Finley sick, Nicholas Teal, Frederick Swaney, David Hart lame. I left with the goods five miles from Worthington Sergeant Morgan and five men. Sent back to Franklinton for a wagon and team to help us on to Worthington, which was furnished by Mr. Craig, Wagon Master General. The sergeant with the wagon and the goods arrived here on the 4th late in the evening but all safe. The soldiers were indulged this day, having been very much fatigued the last three days. They took great liberties, visited the towns, got drunk, quarreled and fought. Two or three got whipped and complaint came to me at my quarters.

I immediately visited them, quashed the quarrel and left them for the night. The next morning, the 5th, issued an order that no soldier should leave the barracks without leave of the officer of the day and if any soldier became drunk on duty, he should be punished without reserve; and if any non-commissioned officer was found drunk, he should be reduced to the ranks. Myself and lieutenants moved this day from Col. Kilburn's to the academy. All things are well this evening, the snow about fifteen inches deep.

6th—The Virginia troops commanded by Capt. McCrea came into town this evening and put up at the taverns. David Hart came to camp this evening from Franklinton; he was left lame there when we marched.

7th—The weather very cold and windy. My men hauling wood. Lieut. Meek not well. We had the pleasure of Mr. Robe's company last evening, a man of very small stature; weight only seventy pounds and thirty years of age, and one of the teachers of the academy.

8th—The Virginia troops left this place. I went to Franklinton in order to get sleds to take our ammunition and baggage, but find that the sleds will not answer. Returned back to this place tonight; find all things well. General Harrison came with me and all his suite bound for Upper Sandusky.

11th—Marched for Upper Sandusky, marched one-and-a-half miles past Delaware; camped without pitching tents, drew rations and forage to last to Upper Sandusky.

12th—Marched to Norton and camped there.

14th—Arrived at Upper Sandusky about sunset. The men took shelter with the Pennsylvania troops for the night. On the 15th we took our stations in the center and camped.

17th—General Harrison left here for the rapids.

18th—Received notice that we must march on the 20th for the rapids.

19th—Making preparations, and received notice that six companies were to march with us besides the Petersburg Volunteers.

20th—Waiting all day for the ordnance to get ready. At 3 o'clock received information that we could not march that day, but would march next morning at 8 o'clock without fail.

Thursday, 21st—At 10 o'clock the whole detachment paraded near the magazine, my company taking the right. The word march was sounded from right to left and all stepped off. We marched that day nine miles and halted for the night on a small branch of a creek. Major Robert Orr commanded the detachment from the Pennsylvania lines. All very well situated on a little stream of very good water.

22nd—This morning fine weather, clear and pleasant. Left the Sandusky Plains last evening, crossed small prairie and left that in our rear. One thing I have omitted in our march yesterday—that is crossing the ground where Col. Crawford had the battle with the Indians and was defeated, lost a large part of his men, fled before the Indians, was pursued, overtaken, himself taken prisoner, brought back and massacred. The place of his execution we passed by this morning on a small rise of ground just before we entered a very large prairie leaving an old Indian town on our right hand. The place said to be the place of Crawford's execution had four posts set up about ten feet high, two sticks of timber crossing at angles from one post to the other on the tops. In the center where those stick crossed there was another post that extended from the ground up through them with places to confine the hands and feet. We took a view of this and marched on through the prairie where we saw several Indian horses and passed on through a large, flat piece of land rather low. Soon came to a creek, passed that on the ice, approached another prairie, traveled on through that and approached a fine country of good land with very fine timber for three or four miles, then began the barrens. Marched this day eight miles with a great deal of difficulty—sleds broke, hames broke, chains broke. Crossed the upper end of large prairie, myself in front, the major and quartermaster in the rear. Night coming on I called a halt, laid out the ground to camp on and fixed out tents. The Petersburg Volunteers were late coming up as they fetched up the rear.

Saturday, 23rd—This morning the major was desirous that I should give the right to Capt. McCrea's company. I refused; took the line of march, marched on about one mile and met a white man and one Indian who had a letter from General Harrison to the major informing him of the first battle that General Winchester had with the Indians and British and ordering him to send on two twelve-pounders and three sixes with all possible speed to the rapids. The letter was dated the 22nd. Major Orr opened the letter and read it. His orders were to have me proceed with my company with the cannon. We held a council and concluded it was useless to alter our line of march as we had no cartridges with us for the guns.

Marched on three or four miles; met another express with another letter of the same date commanding the major to march on with all possible speed to the rapids with all the troops that he had with him except one company to be left with the baggage and the artillery; the express stating at the same time that General Winchester had another battle, was defeated, was killed himself, lost almost all his men killed and taken, and that General Harrison expected to be attacked in his camp at the rapids every hour. This battle was fought at the River Raisin. We camped early this evening in consequence of that, in order to make preparations to march early in the morning. A council was called of the officers at dark, and all agreed to march at two o'clock.

This evening came on to our camping ground four hundred-and-fifty pack-horses laden with flour and salt for the rapids. This night came on a very heavy rain. At 2 o'clock all the men out, but not ready to march; the packhorses took the front; it was agreed that we should take with us one six-pounder that was mounted and 36 rounds of fixed ammunition. At 4 o'clock I was ordered to march where the road was filled with packhorses, so that the men could not pass them any other way but to take the woods. The rain had softened the snow and mud to the rate that the packhorses made the road a complete bed of mortar about one foot deep. I found it impossible for the men to march in that way.

The intent of this day's march was to reach the rapids to relieve General Harrison. To march in the rear of all those packhorses I found we should not get half way this day; therefore, I led off through the woods with my company and passed all the horses in about four miles. Capt. Dunn, with a part of his company, followed me at daylight. We were about six miles from camp and passed Capt. Vance before day five miles from camp with his train of hogs, about four thousand in number. At 8 o'clock in the morning, we fetched in Hull's old track over the road that he traveled to the rapids last summer. Marched on to a small creek by the name of Carrying Creek; called a halt to take some little refreshment. While we were there, a man arrived from General Harrison who informed us that he had retreated from the rapids seventeen miles on this side of the same creek that we were on, but nine miles below where we were. We refreshed and moved on through the worst piece of road I ever traveled—up to our knees in mud and water almost every step. I arrived at headquarters about 4 o'clock this afternoon.

Sunday, 24th—From this time until dark the troops keep coming into camp, but not more than one half arrived this day. The Virginia volunteers and the Pennsylvania Militia were ordered to encamp out of the lines about forty rods up the creek, nothing to shelter them but the heavens and some scattering trees. They have neither tents nor camping equipage of any sort, it being all left behind with the ordnance and the traveling becoming so very bad it could not possibly come on. My company was ordered on the right of the whole army, but in no better fix than the above troops, but they were invited into tents with the troops that lay there. Myself and lieutenants were very politely invited by Major Harden and Doctor Logan to take part of their fare as lodging and victualing. This night it began to snow.

25th—I called on General Harrison. He ordered me back to the baggage in order to fetch it on as soon as possible. I applied to the quartermaster for a horse to ride, obtained one, left camp about ten o'clock, the road worse than the day before as the water had risen in every little creek to a great height.

When I arrived at the crossing of Carrying Creek, I found about twenty packhorse men with all their horses could not cross, as they thought these horses had been on by the army and left them loading. I met on the road from camp to this place about one hundred men that had not yet got to camp; among the number was Capt. McCrea, two of his subalterns, and about fifty of his men. This was about four miles from camp. I asked those packhorse men that were stopped above whether they did not intend to cross. They said not. I told them if they would assist me I would fix a bridge from the shore to the ice in the bed of the river that we could all cross in safety. They would not help; therefore, I went at it myself, made a bridge and crossed over safe. After I had got over, they were ready enough to follow me.

We came on about three miles when night came on. We stopped and built up a fire. Just as we had got our fire in good order, Col. Wells and Mr. Orderm came up from the army on their way. They stopped with us all night. I was without blankets or provisions in consequence of expecting to reach camp that night, or to meet the six-pounder that was behind where there were blankets and provisions, but in consequence of being detained at the river, I could not fetch either.

26th—Col. Wells, Mr. Orderm and myself started about daylight and were informed of a very bad creek to cross in about two miles. When we arrived there, I found the packhorses there that had our tents. They crossed on Sunday evening, but hearing that they could not cross Carrying Creek without difficulty, they stayed there. I gave the captain of the packhorse company a severe scolding for staying there all that time when he knew that the men were without. He promised me to start immediately.

There was with him at that place about two hundred packhorses that could not cross the creek. As they thought they were traveling the same way that I was, they had been there two days. Col. Wells and myself thought the water looked very bad. It was forty rods to the bend of the creek, covered with water and felled timber, and appeared to be very deep. The colonel thought that we could ride up the creek a short distance and find some place to cross. We rode about four miles, were satisfied it would not do, returned back and found the packhorses where we had left them with the tents. They had concluded not to start until next morning.

The colonel said to me, "Captain, what shall we do?" I told him I would cross the river at all events. "Well, if you do, I will also." I mounted my horse, plunged into the water, found it very deep but got safe to the creek and found a large tree fallen across the main stream. I dismounted my horse, took off my pistols and holsters, took them in my hand, walked over on the log, had to wade from the creek about twenty rods in water two feet deep, but got to shore. Found there Sergeant Mead and three soldiers with my six-pound piece; got them to assist us to fell trees from that side to a creek, swam over my horse safe and Col. Wells' and Mr. Orderm's also. That broke the way—the packhorses followed, but drowned one horse through carelessness. This evening, the 26th, I stayed here all night with the cannon and ammunition.

January 27th—Ate breakfast and started for our old camp, the road very bad. About 12 o'clock I arrived at Captain Vance's camp, who had charge of four thousand hogs. Brought a letter to him from General Harrison ordering him to return to Upper Sandusky with the hogs to have them butchered there. I arrived at camp about 3 o'clock but found the camp moved about one mile in advance, and were just pitching their tents. Brought an order to Captain Wadsworth from General Harrison to send all the teams and horses to Mr. Cruther's blockhouse for forage, but knowing that the Auglaize River was not passable in consequence of the high waters, we concluded to change the course and send to Upper Sandusky.

28th—This morning was occupied in fixing the teams and sleds with the horses for the purpose of going after forage. After the teams and horses had started, I concluded to follow after in order to meet General Leftwich, as he was on his march with his brigade somewhere between my camp and the river. I met him in about seven miles, did the business with him that I wanted and turned back again. They camped with two regiments within four miles of my camp, but Col. Connell marched to our old camp, one mile from our present camp, halted about dark, struck up fires and was very jovial when Major Scott came up and asked for Col. Connell. The colonel answered, "I am here."

"Colonel, you have used us damned ill; you have marched us too late. You are no gentleman." "I am sir. You are not in earnest." "I am, sir; you are no soldier, no officer, and no gentleman." "You lie, sir, if you say so." "You are a damned liar," said the major, and makes at the colonel, saying, "I can do as I please with you anyway you please." "You cannot," says the colonel, and draws his sword.

The officers interfered and parted them. The major left the company and went to his quarters. I stayed a few minutes and rode over to camp. At this place is a small creek, the name is not known; I call it "Duck Creek" in consequence of my getting ducked in it the morning we marched from that camp.

29th—This morning is fine and clear. General Leftwich with his brigade passed our camp about 9 o'clock in the morning, men all in high spirits. Our men are employed this day in building a blockhouse. About 2 o'clock the judge advocate went along on his way to headquarters. I sent word by him to General Leftwich to take along with him the six-pounder that lay at the creek called "Trouble," about twelve miles from this place. About sunset the captain of the packhorses arrived here with a note to General Leftwich from General Harrison to leave with us at this place what men he thought necessary to facilitate the movements of the artillery from this place. The note met General Leftwich. He wrote to me on the same, wishing me to send immediately to his camp for what men I wanted. I sent immediately back, requesting him to send me fifty or sixty men with their officers and all the axes and shovels that they could possibly spare. Nicholas Teal arrived here from the hospital in Franklinton, one of my company left behind sick.

This place is in no wise a fit place for defense or deposit for two reasons—one in particular is for want of water. We have no water here but what stands in puddles or what the Yankees call "slows." The other is the situation of the ground—it is a very flat country for a considerable distance around. No commanding spot. Our blockhouse is on a very flat piece of ground. We are at this time about fifty miles in our enemy's country in a complete wilderness without proper means for defense.

We have with us a very valuable property—four eighteen-pounders, four twelve, three six, all on sleds, and a large quantity of ammunition and public stores. I don't state this circumstance as a censure on anyone. Our being in this situation is in consequence of the late soft weather which has broken up the roads so that we could not possibly travel with our effects. The weather appears to be at this time favorable; has frozen very hard for three days and nights and still freezing. If our teams return from Upper Sandusky we shall leave here on the first of February.

January 30th—Froze hard last night, fine weather this morning. Our men still at work on the blockhouse. Mounted one six-pounder on a platform of logs in case of an attack; can move it with hand-spikes from right to left. The men arrived from General Leftwich this afternoon, about sixty in number. This evening regulating our guard lines around the camp making preparations for defense. Late this evening Lieutenant Tisdell of the Petersburg Volunteers arrived here from headquarters and brings the pleasant news of the fate of our army that was with Gen. Winchester at the River Raisin. I say pleasant fate for this reason—the first report came from headquarters was that Gen. Winchester had fallen and seven hundred of our brave men out of one thousand were killed and taken—but to the reverse of that, one man that was taken broke from them and arrived at Lower Sandusky, and states for a fact that Gen. Winchester was not killed but taken, and six hundred men with him. Mr. McCullouch, an express from Gen

Harrison on his way to Franklinton, brings the same intelligence, and as a fact also states that Gen Harrison will move his army from Carrying Creek to the rapids this day or tomorrow.

31st—This morning snowing, not very cold, nor yet very warm. Sent a lieutenant and ensign with a party of men to open the road wider from this to Hull's old road. The ox teams started from here to fetch forage from Sandusky returned back this morning, being ordered back by Captain Wadsworth as he found they could not go to that place and back in time for the horse teams and would detain us in our movement three days at least. At sundown all our packhorses and horse teams arrived from Upper Sandusky with flour and forage. Gen. Leftwich and baggage went past here on packhorses this day and Gen. Harrison's on packhorses and sleds.

February 1st—This morning preparing our artillery and baggage for marching to headquarters at foot of the rapids. We marched precisely at 12 o'clock with eleven pieces of artillery, the heavy pieces on sleds, the six-pounder on wheels. We have thirty-three teams in this detachment, most all sleds. I took the line of march, passed on about six miles when one of the pintles of the six-pounder broke.[7] I stopped to place it in a situation to move on, which flung me some ways behind the carriage. The front guard and pioneers kept on four miles; I pursued after them, came up with them, called a halt, waited until some of the sleds came up and ventured down a very steep hill; one sled knocked to pieces in the attempt. I waited some time for the teams to appear; they did not. I got on to one of the wagon master's horses and rode back, met several of the teams, continued on four miles back to the place where I left them or near that. Found my baggage wagon, one caisson, and one sled stuck fast in the mud. This being after dark and a number of men and wagons present, I ordered a fire built as quick as possible that the men might dry themselves and cook something to eat. Lieut. Tisdell of the Petersburg Volunteers was at this place; we got some bread and meat to eat, lay down on the snow; no tents pitched this night. All slept well, the howling of wolves very great.

Tuesday, 2nd—Rose early and mustered all hands; the wagons froze into the mud very much; cut them loose with axes, pried them out of the mud, ate breakfast and moved on, but with great difficulty; wagons sticking in the mud; sleds getting fast in the stumps in Hull's road. Overtook the detachment at Trouble Creek, they not marching but one mile this day.

Wednesday, 3rd—This morning made an early start; crossed the creek Trouble on a very sidling bridge made by my men and some others while they lay there with the six-pounder gun. Marched on very well this day, crossed Carrying Creek late in the afternoon on the ice, but made a safe crossing. Marched two miles, camped a little before sunset on a very good spot for that purpose.

Thursday, 4th—This morning marched about 4 o'clock; marched three miles to a black swamp. Found the water about eight inches deep on the ice for one mile; the men loath to venture on, the pioneers did not like to wade. I told them to hand me an axe and I would be the first man in the water and chop the first tree. This moved some of them; four or five followed me. We cleared the road, the teams came on, several got almost over when the heavy artillery began to break through the ice both in front and in rear. Wagons and sleds of every description shared the same fate, the water, mud, and ice being from two to four feet deep. From the time I first entered the swamp until sundown, I did not leave the water, but was from knee-deep to waist-deep all day wading in mud, water, and ice, prying out sleds and wagons, but got to Portage camp about dark with all our sleds and all our wagons but three. No time to pitch tents, slept outdoors this night.

Friday, 5th—This morning marched from this place, crossed Portage Creek safe, marched eight miles and camped on the same ground that Gen. Harrison encamped on the night he left the camp at Portage.

Saturday, 6th—This morning made an early start, arrived at the head of the rapids about 12 o'clock. Found it very difficult ascending the hills to get on the ice, but accomplished it in about one hour with all our effects. Found the ice sound so that we arrived at the foot of the rapids and at headquarters about 4 o'clock, all our ordnance and ammunition in good order. My company is quartered near the park on a very dry spot of ground.[8]

Sunday, 7th—This day nothing new; troops are employed in building blockhouses and the fortifications and stockading the camp. Lieut. Meek, my second lieutenant, has the superintending of one small redoubt for the purpose of planting one six-pounder.

Monday, 8th—This day employed in mounting one eighteen-pounder and three twelve-pounders. This evening we fired the eighteen-pounder for the evening gun with a ball at an old house across the river on an elevated spot—857 yards; fired a point-blank shot. Owing to the bad state the cannon was in and not having a full charge of powder for that distance, the ball fell short, striking the side of the hill, bounded, pitched into the house and stopped. Lieut. Larwill crossed the river and found the ball in the house. This day Col. Sutton was arrested by Gen. Tupper on a complaint made by Major Galloway.

Tuesday, 9th—Our spies that visited up and down this river to find out the situation of the Indians and British brought intelligence that they and some French people had discovered a party of Indians on each side of the river; the number they could not ascertain but thought there were about 200. The French came into camp with the spies and reported accordingly. Gen. Harrison this evening started off another company of spies with the same Frenchmen in order to ascertain if the statement was true.

Wednesday, 10th—This morning the spies returned and stated they saw the Indians above mentioned and they were in a war dance. The general ordered the commanding officer of each brigade to have a certain proportion of their men to be in readiness, to the number of 600 in all, to march at retreat beating this evening and 500 more to march in a short time after as a reserve if they should be wanted. They descended the river to the place, arrived there about 4 o'clock in the morning, but to their great disappointment the Indians had left their camps and driven off a number of cattle. The general called a halt, examined their camps and the neighborhood, discovered the route they took, followed after them about seven or eight miles but found they could not come up with them. I am mistaken in the day that the spies and the French came in with the news of the Indians being at the Miami Bay. It was on Monday, and on Tuesday evening our troops marched down to rout them, and on Wednesday about 4 o'clock they returned. They marched the distance of fifty miles in about twenty-one hours.

Thursday, 11th—Gen. Crook came into camp this day with about 500 men of the Pennsylvania line from Upper Sandusky. Lieut. Larwill very sick last night, but better this morning.

Friday, 12th—This day laying out the encampment in a smaller compass. Col. Sutton arrested by Gen. Tupper on a complaint laid in by Major Galloway.

Saturday, 13th—This day Lieut. Meek is appointed adjutant *pro tem* of the artillery. The militia of this state are decamping by companies of two, three, four, and six, as their times expire.

Sunday, 14th—This day Gen. Harrison sent off two companies of spies—Capt. Woods and Hinkston with a number of Indians—to reconnoiter this river as low down as the bay and to fetch in prisoners if possible. They have with them about sixty-five men and thirty Indians.

Monday, 15th—This day the Kentucky Militia cleared out for home as their times were out—Major Gano's battalion and Major Hardin's. A new order this day to build a battery on the front of the hill sixty or eighty feet long to plant our eighteen-pounders.

Tuesday, 16th—We mounted three eighteen-pound cannon this day—placed one twelve-pound cannon in the lower blockhouse. Gen. Harrison gave notice this evening that he expected to be attacked every night, ordered the artillery to have everything in preparation for the battle. I saw that all the twelves and sixes were supplied with ammunition. Four men were taken, two last night, two this evening; supposed to be British spies. They were about our camp taken by the sentinels.

Wednesday, 17th—This day very cold. Major Ball arrived here this evening with his squadron of cavalry from Lebanon.

Thursday, 18th—This morning Major Ball with his squadron moved from this place, ordered to Lower Sandusky. Made a short stay of one night. Col. Campbell arrived here this day with his regiment, Capt. Butler's and Alexander's volunteers. We have at this time four eighteen-pounders, four iron twelve-pounders, one brass twelve and four sixes mounted fit for battle.

Friday, 19th—Teams arriving constantly with ammunition and clothing.

Saturday, 20th—This day two howitzers arrived here mounted and plenty of bomb shells.

Sunday, 21st—Some snow fell last night. The troops are very busy building blockhouses, storehouses, and stockading. Two hundred-and-fifty men sent down the river to escort some teams from Lower Sandusky.

Monday, 22nd—This day very cold, all things going on very well; some more men sent to reinforce the escort, expecting to see some Indians.

Tuesday, 23rd—This morning Col. Poge's Regiment of Kentucky Militia left camp for home, their times having expired, and Col. Jenning's also. The spies and escort came in this day, did not see any Indians or British, the teams had returned back to Lower Sandusky.

Thursday, 25th—Cold. Preparing materials to fire the British ship, *Queen Charlotte.*

Friday, 26th—This day marched from this camp Capt. Langham with 140 men under his command for the purpose of crossing the lake on the ice by the way of Lower Sandusky to Malden, or within a very short distance of that place, to take possession of the *Queen Charlotte* and burn her down. Lieut. Meek with thirty men is with the detachment. His business will be to board the vessel and set her on fire.

Saturday, 27th—This day the teams are employed in hauling some boats up the river on the ice which lay not far below.

Sunday, 28th—I am sitting in a court martial. It commenced on the 26th. We had a sermon preached this evening by Mr. Badger,[9] he had a great deal to say about the River Jordan, a story that will not do for soldiers.

Monday, March 1st—Pointing the blockhouses and completing the stockading as fast as possible.

Tuesday, 2nd—This day came in two brigades of packhorses laden with flour and iron. We have at this time 600,000 weight of pork salted, and will have as much more by the time they are done salting, and as much beef.

Wednesday, 3rd—This day I began to get out the stuff for laying the floor to the Grand Battery; am still in court martial. The weather rainy and warm; the mud about 8 inches deep all over camp. Lieut. Meek obtained leave to go home today, as pleased as a child with a rattle.

Thursday, 4th—This day Gen. Harrison started for Cincinnati by the way of Lower Sandusky; took with him all of his retinue. Major Alexander with his battalion, a company of spies, and some Indians marched down to the mouth of the bay to cover the retreat of Capt. Langham if wanted. Gen. Harrison returned this evening to camp; could not pass that way in consequence of the lake being broken up.

Friday, 5th—This morning the general started again with all his suite by way of the blockhouse at Portage and to Upper Sandusky. The troops all arrived this day, both Capt. Langham's and Major Alexander's. They came back without success—the ice was too weak for their expedition.

Saturday, 6th—This day Lieut. Meek started for home. Corporal Warman died this morning about 11 o'clock. I have stated the return of the troops one day too soon. They arrived on Saturday, and Gen. Harrison left here on the same day at the same time.

Sunday, 7th—This day very cold. All hands to work at the battery. The Second Virginia Regiment moved within the lines.

Monday, 8th—Mounted one eighteen-pounder yesterday.

Tuesday, 9th—This day three of our men were fired upon by the Indians on the opposite side of the river while they were after grass for beds. One of them received a ball in his pocket, but lodged in his psalm book. They made their escape in haste. On the 6th, I had twenty-seven men transferred to my company from Capt. Bradford's company.

Wednesday, 10th—Lieut. Walker of the Pennsylvania line was missing last night. He was known by some of the company to have gone after ducks down the river yesterday. They went in search of him this morning; proceeded down the river about three miles, found him shot, tomahawked, and scalped. Also, he was poked under the ice. He was brought into camp about 9 o'clock this morning and buried this afternoon.

Friday, 12th—A very hard storm of rain, hail, and snow last night, and continues to snow almost all day. Clears off towards evening, cold. Hard times for wood, the water rising very fast in the river, the ice coming down the rapids in great abundance.

Saturday, 13th—This day clear, the snow all disappeared. At work at the batteries with all hands.

Sunday, 14th—Weather good. Water very high in this river; four feet higher than it ever has been since this country was settled. A number of hogs, horses, and cattle have been overwhelmed with the water and ice where the farmers' houses used to stand.

Monday, 15th—Lieut. Larwill left for home. I salt my beef this day.

Tuesday, 16th—One of my soldiers died last night by the name of Faircloth. I had him buried this day with the usual ceremonies. Lieut. Larwill returned this day; got defeated by the water that covers the whole face of the earth after leaving this camp one mile.

Wednesday, 17th—This being St. Patrick's Day some of our young waggish soldiers made a St. Patrick and placed it up against our quartermaster's chimney with the motto "The devil has come from Britain to see old Capt. Wheaton," meaning our old quartermaster. Rained and hailed last night and mud very deep all over the camp—not a dry foot in camp unless they stay close in their tents. Lieut. Meek left here yesterday with a party of men to proceed on to the Auglaize River, about 100 miles, after forage, which will be brought down in boats to this place. The Auglaize empties into this river.

Thursday, 18th—This day is cloudy and somewhat rainy with heavy wind. Capt. Wood, one of our engineers, arrived here with five other persons from Lower Sandusky. These are the first people that have arrived at this place from east, west, north, or south for seven days, and it has taken them four days to come thirty miles. The whole country is inundated with water and broken ice. Our camp is overwhelmed with mud and water; my eyes never saw such a place for mankind to live in—not a marquee or tent in the whole encampment but what has more or less mud and water in it, and what makes it much worse is for the want of wood. The timber is all cut off for a long distance from camp and there are no teams to haul any for the men; not a bushel of forage in this place; what teams we have cannot work for they have nothing to eat. Our men are very sickly; no wonder, lying in mud and water and without fire; not less than two or three men die every day and I expect the deaths to increase unless the weather changes very soon. The men this day have begun to catch fish. I bought one this evening for seventy-five cents; it weighed five pounds.

Friday, 19th—This day a party of men, about forty, went over the river expecting to see some Indians, but returned without. They saw several signs such as moccasin tracks and found some bunches of hair tied up that they had left. One man of the party that went over did not return this day; he was missing when they came to the boat, waited some time for him and crossed over. This day I have finished the Grand Battery, placed four eighteen-pounders in it ready for battle.

Saturday, 20th—A party of men went over the river this day in pursuit of the man that was lost yesterday; returned this evening without finding him. No doubt but that he has fallen a victim to savage and British fury. At this time this is the most romantic looking place that ever my eyes saw. To look from the battery on to the river and meadows is the greatest charm of any place that ever was in any country that ever I traveled in. The water is gliding through the meadows swiftly and covered with all kinds of water fowl, and the ice which was left by the high water on the meadows is without bounds from three to fifteen feet deep, and that over more than half of the bottoms.

Sunday, 21st—This day pleasant, not very warm, but clear. A party of men, sixteen in number, went over the river this afternoon in order to lie in ambush for Indians in the night. They went down as low as the old fort and stayed until after night and concluded to march back. On their way back the officer commanding the party being in front, ordered the men to fire in the bushes, saying, "There are Indians, there are Indians," and pointing to the place. The men obeyed, this being about 9 o'clock in the evening. The flash of the guns was seen and the reports heard in our camp, which caused alarm. Immediately the drums beat "To Arms," and every man who could lift his musket was on parade in ten minutes, although a greater part were in bunk, but it soon proved to be a false alarm and all returned to bed.

Monday, 22nd—This day warmer and windy. Col. Sutton was at this time attending to his trail; has put up with me since he arrived from Urbana with Capt. Black. Lieut. Meeks arrived here from Fort Winchester with several boats. Lieut. Larwill returned this day, it being the second time he has left here and returned. This day the mail arrived for the first time in two weeks. A small party of our men went up the river with a boat in order to save a man that had got flung out of one of the boats that Lieut. Meeks came down with. He got onto a rock, but the current was so rapid that they could not take him off and a boat was sent after him with six men. They got up the river three or four miles, discovered a party of Indians, about fifty in number, then returned and reported what they had seen.

Tuesday, 23rd—This morning a party of 250 under the command of Major Tod crossed the river in pursuit of those fugitives; also, another party in the boat pursued up the river after the man on the rock about four miles. Under cover of the advance guard commanded by Capt. Croghan, they got off the man, brought him safe to camp this evening; the front guard fell back toward the main body and they all encamped about four miles up the river on Gen. Winchester's old camping ground.

Wednesday, 24th—This morning the detachment all returned and saw no Indians, but came upon their tracks, but they had a long ways the start, and swamp very bad, so that the commanding officer thought it best not to pursue any farther.

Thursday, 25th—This morning Lieut. Larwill left for home the third time. We have a fine parcel of fish caught last night for the first time this spring. An express arrived here this evening from Franklinton, fetching news of 600 militia being on their way to this place and they will be here in five days.

Friday, 26th—Robert Parsons died last night, one of my soldiers. Col. Sutton left here this morning for home after being honorably acquitted by the court martial of the charges made against him by Major James Galloway.

Saturday, 27th—This day a general court martial convened, Major Stoddard president, for the trial of several soldiers. Nine members and the Judge Advocate constitute the court—Capt. Langham, Capt. Croghan, Capt. Elliott, Capt. Cushing, Lieut. Gwynne, Lieut. Frederick, and Ensign Ship are the members. There were three sentinels found sleeping on their post last night by the field officer of the day, Col. Evans. Two of them were from the Pennsylvania line and one of the Virginia line. Fine sentries to watch a camp against British and Indians, but it is as much as we could expect of militia. This evening a party arrived from down the river that had been from this camp under the command of Capt. Bradford after some boats that were left there by the Canadian French when they retreated from the mouth of the river. This party came up as far as the old British garrison then landed, built fires, refreshed themselves, and came on to camp.

Sunday, 28th—Snowing this morning after a very rainy night. One company of Virginia Militia leaves camp this morning for home. We are sitting on a court martial this day, tried Nathaniel Ewing for mutinous conduct to his captain.

Monday, 29th—Letters arrived from General Harrison to Gens. Leftwich and Crooks wishing their brigades to stay a few days longer. These calls and invitation will not do. The government has not been punctual enough in paying their troops for them to stay long. Major Tod sent his young man after his horse a short distance down the river this evening in company with some others; they all returned but his waiter, who is missing.

Tuesday, 30th—Major Tod sent an ensign and a party of men this morning after his waiter; they returned—reported they could not find him, neither could they see any signs of him or Indians.

Wednesday, 31st—This day a general court martial sentenced John T. Mosby, a private in Capt. Bradford's company for threatening to blow up the magazine and then to desert to the British, to be confined, tied to a post or log in a tent by himself one month, to have a handcuff on his right hand, to ride a wooden horse thirty minutes once a week for one month with a six pound ball fastened to each foot, to wear a ball and chain the whole time, to have one eyebrow and one side of his head shaved, and to be fed on bread and water only. After the time of confinement expires, he is to be drummed out of camp and taken over the line of the Indian boundary on the way to Kentucky. This evening two or three Frenchmen went down the river to fish, returned very soon, reported they saw some Indians crossing the river, but on seeing them, they returned back to the other side and the Frenchmen fled to camp.

Thursday, April 1st—This day fine weather. Mr. Smith arrived from Lower Sandusky, states that Lieut. Larwill left that place for Cleveland on the 27th or 28th ulto. Went on eight miles that day, having a young Frenchman with him as a pilot. They encamped for the night, made a fire, but soon after they had lain down the lieutenant heard something which he took to be Indians, spoke to the young man, told him he heard Indians and told him to listen, which he did. The Frenchman heard the noise, told the lieutenant that it was an owl and he would go and shoot it, which he did, but Oh! The report of the gun very much alarmed the warrior, he starts, he stops, he pants for breath, he hears the near approach of death, he does not stop to know the fate of his companion, nor to wait to know if it was the Frenchman's gun or Indian rifle that had won, but left his sword, his coat, his script; and through the swamp he nimbly skipped until he arrived at Sandusky's bank; the river wide, the current swift, and he himself without a skiff. He looked about and saw his fate, that there was no other escape but for him to try his active limbs and see if he the gulf could swim. He plunges in and struggles hard but could not reach the other shore; he turns about and with his eyes he sees the Frenchman, to his great surprise. The lieutenant supposed that an Indian shot the Frenchman, not him who shot the owl.

Friday, 2nd—This day all the Virginia troops but two small companies left camp, their times being out; also the Pennsylvania brigade except what volunteered to stay fifteen days—about 200. The command this day devolves upon Major Stoddard. The guards were moved within pickets last night for the first time.

Saturday, 3rd—This day four men arrived in camp from Detroit giving a very correct statement. They say that the British have in Malden and in Detroit about 600 regulars, 700 militia, and about 500 Indians. They further say that they contemplate an attack on this place as soon as the ice breaks in the lake, so that they can come with their vessels to fetch their artillery.

Sunday, 4th—We are often alarmed by the discharge of muskets. Night before last one of my men, a sentinel on the Grand Battery, discovered something part of the way down the hill; he hailed him three times, no reply; he then discharged his piece on him; the man cleared himself, took the course down the river. It is supposed it was an Indian as they came this morning about 9 o'clock, killed, tomahawked, and scalped one of our men with 250 yards of one of our blockhouses. The sentry saw the flash, heard the report, and saw the man fall. A party immediately under the command of Capt. Langham went in pursuit of them, followed them about eight miles but could not come up with them. It is thought they have killed one more or taken him prisoner as one is missing. Capt. Croghan with thirty was sent after Capt. Langham about 3 o'clock in order to cover his retreat if wanted. They all returned about dark this evening.

Capt. Langham reports that he heard two guns on his march; also reports they saw the Indians, but they got in the boats some distance below them and were crossing the river. He could plainly hear them shout as they crossed and heard several guns on the other side.

Tuesday, 6th—This morning fine and clear, all hands to work. I am with my company repairing the Little Battery, about 150 repairing the pickets, clearing off brush and small trees about the camp and preparing to build two small magazines to contain the powder. Capt. Wheaton, the quartermaster, left here this morning for home with about fifty or sixty militia whose time of service was out; also five or six men from Detroit that had lately come into camp. This day one of Capt. Bradford's corporals was accidentally shot by one of his men through the leg. The doctors were obliged to cut off his leg just above the knee.

Wednesday, 7th—This morning about 1 o'clock I went the guard rounds with the officer of the day, Major Tod. Found the soldiers very vigilant that were on duty. This day Major Hull arrived here from Cincinnati with ten of Major Ball's squadron of horse. He says Gen. Harrison will be here in three days with the remainder of Major Ball's squadron; also states that we shall have a reinforcement of infantry here in two days. The artificers are putting up watch towers around the within the gates.

Thursday, 8th—This day has proved to be a very unfortunate one to some of the men. Sergeant Kelly with six of my men went into the woods about half a mile from camp after timber. A party of Indians came upon them while they were unloading; they got between the teams before they showed themselves. As soon as the men discovered them, they started; three of them had their guns with them, the rest had set their guns up by a tree to help load. Felix Rudes, who drove one team, was shot dead, tomahawked and scalped in a most barbarous manner. Joseph Patterson and John Kelly were both taken prisoners, the rest made their escape unhurt. A party immediately pursued after the savages as soon as the news came to camp. This scene took place up the river from camp. Another party went down the river in order to intercept them when they came to their boats. Another party went down the river in boats. The first boat had twelve Frenchmen in it under the command of Mr. Peters; they got off first. The party that went by land got separated, a part of them returned to camp, finding themselves lost from the others and only five in number. The remainder pursued on about five miles and returned also. The Frenchmen that were in the first boat soon came upon the Indians about half a mile below where Lieut. Gwynn and his party returned back. The Indians, twelve in number, took two boats, five in each, ran out into the river in order to stop them. Five Indians stayed on land, which made fifteen Indians against twelve Frenchmen, and they in three parties. The Frenchmen allowed they killed five and wounded three that were in the boats. The Indians ran ashore, took in the Indians that were on the land and cleared out down the river. Seven of the Frenchmen were wounded, two very bad, five slightly, two must die.

Capt. Langham, with his party passed the Frenchmen soon after the battle, put on after them with all speed. There has been firing heard this evening down the river—it is expected that he has come up with them and given them battle. The party that first went after the Indians soon returned, came upon the tracks of the savages, found where they passed along the prisoners, found one of their guns, but found they could not overtake them and gave up the chase.

Friday, 9th—Major Ball arrived with his squadron, about 220 in number. They encamped on the bottom exactly in front of the Grand Battery. Gen. Harrison has not arrived here with the squadron as was expected. One thing I have neglected to state—Col. Stevens of Ross County, Ohio arrived here on the 8th with eighty or ninety men—some little help. Capt. Langham returned here this afternoon from down the river; he reports he went down as far as the lake and that the ice was all out of sight, nothing but the lake water to be seen. He also reports that he went ashore with a party at Swan Creek, which is about eight miles below this camp. He found in the creek fourteen Indian canoes, two of them were the two that the Frenchmen had the conflict with a little before. They were peppered full of holes with balls, and a large quantity of blood in both canoes. They also found four or five horses that they had left and shot them. It is supposed that they were the horses that belonged to the Indians that were killed and the rest had mounted and rode off. They destroyed all the boats but two, which they brought to camp.

Saturday, 10th—This morning about daylight, an alarm took place. Major Ball, who lay outside of the garrison with his squadron, had formed his men in two lines from the river to the hill under the walls of the fort; one on the right of the squadron, the other on the left. The line on the left was much the longest, as the distance was the greatest from the river to the fort. The lines had been formed some time when one of his lieutenants thought he saw an Indian. He was on the left of the left line, next to the fort on the side hill. He spoke to the sergeant that stood by his side, told him to shoot him; the sergeant spoke low and replied, "Perhaps it is one of our men out there." The lieutenant hailed three times; no one answered; the sergeant fired; they saw several things move which caused several of them to fire; the troops all were at their posts within the garrison very soon. The squadron were all moved within the pickets this day.

Sunday, 11th—This day windy and cold from the northeast. I finished the Little Battery this evening. The lines were formed all along the lines of pickets this evening; we found them all well manned. I have been today employed in having the ammunition distributed to all the cannon.

Monday, 12th—Gen. Harrison arrived here this day; Col. Miller with him with 100 regulars and 100 militia; had forage and salt on the boats. Capt. Nearing commanded the regulars. I fired a salute on General Harrison's arrival, fifteen guns—ten sixes and five eighteens.

Tuesday, 13th—This day is a day of general fatigue; both officers and soldiers employed in building breastworks, repairing the pickets, laying blockhouse floors, repairing the Grand Battery, digging a well, digging up stumps and cutting and fetching puncheons for the floors of the blockhouses.

Wednesday, 14th—This day Capt. Hamilton arrived here with fifty militia from Butler County. The men all employed as they were yesterday. We are expecting the British and Indians to attack us every night.

Thursday, 15th—Very cold and windy. One of the sentinels shot a horse last night supposing it to be an Indian.

Friday, 16th—This day preparing for an attack from the British and Indians. Our batteries, blockhouses and pickets are almost completed and traversed all around. Wm. Clarke, a private in Capt. Nearing's company, was brought out to be shot. All the troops on the ground were assembled. His sentence was read to him and he appeared unconcerned as to his fate. He was reprieved by the general. Major Tod supped with me this evening on turtle soup. I have been very much indisposed, but am better this evening. Capt. Wadsworth of the Pennsylvania Militia died last evening, was buried at 4 o'clock this afternoon. He was left sick when the brigade was disbanded.

Saturday, 17th—This day very pleasant. A party of Major Ball's squadron went down the river to Presque Isle to make discovery, but reported they saw nothing worth notice. Another party of Indians and whites went down on the other side. They were ordered to go to the River Raisin. Wm. Clarke had his head shaved and was drummed out of camp. This evening we are expecting an attack every day, but we fear they will not come.

Sunday, 18th—This day the Indians and white men that went down to the River Raisin on the 16th returned with three Frenchmen with them. These men say that the party of Indians that killed Rudes and took my two men prisoners passed by where they were with both of them; also state that the Frenchmen that went down the river after the party in boats that took their men killed six, two mortally wounded as they supposed, for one was shot through the breast, the other through both arms and breast. They say that Tecumseh with eighty Indians passed through there the 16th on his way to Malden; they also state that the British and Indians intend to attack us in ten or twelve days.

Monday, 19th—This day Col. Mills arrived here with 100 men, came down the river in boats from St. Marys, fetched 700 bushels of forage, forty barrels of whisky, 500 barrels of flour, all in good order. Most of these men were from Warren County—Capt. Simonton's rifle company and Capt. Shaw's militia.

Tuesday, 20th—This day a party of regulars and militia crossed the river for the purpose of clearing off the brush that the enemy should not have the advantage of them in fortifying, if they should have the presumption to come here to attack us. Gen. Harrison went over, took along with him Major Stoddard and others to view the ground. This evening Capt. Holt arrived here with about thirty-five regulars and 150 militia from Kentucky; a brigade of packhorses came with them fetched their baggage.

Wednesday, 21st—Capt. Holt with his company was attached to the artillery this day.

Friday, 23rd—This morning a very heavy rain; the river rose to a very high pitch. Capt. Holt moved his men on to my left this evening.

Saturday, 24th—This day I moved my company in front of the Grand Battery. The infantry began to drill.

Sunday, the 25th April, 1813[10]—Forty of Maj. Ball's Squad. went down the river to reconnoiter. They saw several tents pitched on the opposite side opposite Presque Isle & saw several Indians on this side. A brigade of pack-horses arrived with the 18-pound shot. Monday the 26, we placed one 18-pound cannon in Croghan's Battery and one in Wood's [Battery]. About twenty-three or twenty-four British came opposite to our camp or a little below & shew themselves & told some of our men that were at the river that they would dine with us next day unless we were very strong. They did not stay more than three minutes in sight before they took to the woods.

Tuesday, 27th—This day repairing the Little Battery and placing abitis in front of the Grand Battery. About one o'clock this day fourteen Indians and British came on to the same ground that they had viewed before, but were on foot; crept down a small gulley that hid them from our fort; a number of our men were fishing on this side. The first thing we saw of them from the garrison they were firing on our men who were fishing nearly opposite. We fired an 18-pounder at them and a second cannon was fired from the wood [i.e., Wood's] Battery.

I took good aim at them, the ball struck just over them. They fell down at the flash. They lay still until I had loaded again and Capt. Wood had loaded his eighteen- pounder in his loft. At length they started for the woods. Capt. Wood gave them a shot and I followed suit. They both struck very close to them; there were fourteen seen before we fired, and but twelve remained in the old fort where the remainder of their party were plain to be seen with a spy glass. This is the first time I have discharged a piece at an enemy in thirty years.

Wednesday, 28th—Last night we had the heaviest rain that I ever knew and very hard thunder. This morning we had the pleasure of seeing about 300 British down the river and a number of Indian and British came opposite to our fort and fired at our men that were on the river bottom. I gave them one shot with eighteen-pounder which made them leave their stations. Capt. Hamilton was sent down the river this morning. He reported that the British had landed on the other side about 1,500 or 2,000. We expect a hard fight this night. I have completed the abitis this evening in front of the Grand Battery. The whole army was at work this day, one third at a time, heaving up a traverse through the camp. A party of dragoons rode out a short distance from camp this evening; one of them received a ball in his arm from the rifle of an Indian—there was a party watching for our men.

Thursday, 29th—This day we are employed in finishing the traverse and making ready for battle for we have been surrounded by British and Indians for two days. We let loose our cannonade on them yesterday and have kept it up by spells all this day, and shall let loose upon them this evening with an eighteen-pounder that is already elevated.

Friday, 30th—We have been all day employed in traversing through the camp, playing upon their batteries with our eighteen-pounders, and throwing grape and canister shot at the Indians which are in our rear and on our flanks. We have had one man killed and 6 or 7 wounded by the Indians this day.

Saturday, May 1st—At 2 o'clock in the morning the British opened their artillery upon our garrison from their gunboats which lay one-and-one-half miles below us, but it was without effect. At 8 o'clock they hoisted the red flag at their lower battery and commenced firing with 24-, 12- and 6-pounders, and eight-inch mortars. They fired at us this day 240 shot and shells; did very little damage. They continued firing shells through the night, but not often, just enough to keep our camp from rest. We keep up a heavy fire on them all day from different parts of our camp. The Indians are very thick on our flank and in our rear. We have not more than two killed and four wounded today.

Sunday, 2nd—They kept up their bombardment all night, but not very often, enough to keep the men on the watch. This morning they commenced a heavy fire from all their batteries, both with cannonade and bombs, and our camp is completely surrounded with Indians and British keeping up a heavy fire of musketry and rifles. They threw at us this day about 350 shot, a large proportion of them red hot; we had about four killed, seven wounded this day. They keep up the business of sending over their shells this evening.

Monday, 3rd—This morning I gave them a morning gun at break of day which passed through their upper battery. They returned pretty much the same, and that all day. This day we discovered that they had a small battery on this side of the river about 300 yards on our right flank. The Indians had been for two days firing at our men from that direction which kept us from noticing what they were about. They opened on us from that battery one six-pounder and one five-and-a-half-inch howitzer, which made a complete cross-fire through our camp. This day we received about 516 shots from them and lost about the same number of men as we did yesterday, killed and wounded.

Tuesday, 4th—They still keep up their fire with shot hot and cold, and bombs; killed a few men, wounded some. This evening Mr. Oliver, who was sent out to meet Gen. Clay, came down the river in a boat; arrived here tonight about 12 o'clock. He brought the news that Gen. Clay and his brigade would be here by break of day. This put our camp in motion. Every man was up and preparing for battle.

Wednesday, 5th—This morning about 3 o'clock Gen. Harrison sent Capt. Hamilton, Capt. Shaw, and one other up the river to meet Gen. Clay with orders for him to land about 700 men two miles above camp on the other side of the river, proceed down to their batteries, spike their cannon and retreat immediately back to their boats, but to come down under the cover of my battery. They complied so far as to land the men, march them down to their battery, drive them from their guns, spike some of them, take down their colors, but did not retreat as ordered; pursued the Indians into the woods until about 200 of them fell into the enemies' hands and 100 supposed to be killed—the rest made their escape up their boats and arrived safe at camp, At the time, the balance of the brigade was floating to camp from where the men landed. The Indians and British kept up a heavy fire on them from the woods; then men left their boats fighting them. The cavalry with Major Alexander's Battalion sallied out and drove them into the woods and then retreated into the garrison. There were several killed and several wounded; the Indians followed them within 150 yards of the gate. This sally was made from the left wing of our camp. Another sally was made at the same time from the right wing by Col. Miller. He drove the British and Indians from their little battery, spiked their guns and howitzer, took about forty-two prisoners, of which two were officers. We had several killed and wounded. After the battle ceased, the British sent into our camp a flag of truce, the bearer of which was Major Chambers. Gen. Harrison permitted the two regular officers to return back to their camp; they gave us but two shots after the battle was over.

Thursday, 6th—This day no fighting. A complete cessation of arms on both sides. The flag passed both to and from each camp, and men employed in completing their bomb-proof; the weather very rainy and has been for three or four days, which puts out camp in a dismal situation.

Friday, 7th—The British are very peaceable; they have sent up a flag from the old fort, made arrangements to have prisoners exchanged, and have taken them to their camp this evening. The prisoners that they took from us are to be sent to Huron; we have sent down boats to transport them to that place; also, have sent down provisions and blankets for them.

Saturday, 8th—The rain still continues. We have not received any shots from the British this day; they appear to be making preparations to decamp; if they are not, they are laying some deep plan to annoy us. The Indians have not been on this side today as usual; in fact, there have been but very few seen this day on either side.

Sunday, 9th—Last night two men deserted from the British and swimming the river, came into our camp. They state on being examined that the enemy moved off the greater part of their cannon the night before last and the rest last night. They also state that the British and the Indians have all cleared out. They state further that news had arrived in their camp within 24 hours that Little York had fallen into the hands of the Americans. They state that the Indians had got mad and would not stay any longer in consequence of the British not letting them have a share in the plunder that was given up in this fort, for they supposed that we had surrendered as the white flag had been passing so very often. I have been out on the battleground this day; found several dead men, the most of them scalped and tomahawked. The British took down their colors about 10 o'clock this morning, went aboard of their boats and cleared themselves for Malden. We gave them a few stern shots as they left their camp and three cheers when they lowered their colors. Also, we fired a salute at 12 o'clock three times around the fort. The sight of dead men has become no more terrifying than the sight of dead flies on a summer day.

Monday, 10th—This is the first fair day we have experienced in eight days. A party of men crossed the river this afternoon in order to reconnoiter the battleground on that side and make discoveries of the dead that a party may go tomorrow and bury them. Theya reported that they saw but one dead man above ground, but saw several graves. The British left their camp in great haste by appearance, for they left behind one set of carriage wheels and a large quantity of shot and shells. I pitched my marquee for the first time this day since the siege, also the tents of my company.

Tuesday, 11th—This day a party of men went over the river in search of the men that were killed in the battle of the fifth; they found forty-five men dead and scalped. Amongst them was Col. Dudley of the Kentucky Militia and several officers of lower grade. The party dug holes and buried them. Capt. Holt with a party of the artillery crossed the river after the shot and shells that the British left; he found several, fetched them over and one large pair of gun wheels. Major Amos Stoddard of the artillery died this evening about 11 o'clock. His death was caused by a wound he received the first day of the siege, which was the first day of May. The wound was caused by a shell bursting over the Grand Battery.

Wednesday, 12th—This day Gen. Harrison left camp for the settlement. A short time after he had left the camp an express arrived here from Gen. Dearborn informing him that Little York had fallen into the hands of the Americans with 1,000 men. The letter also stated that the British magazine blew up and destroyed 200 of our men. Gen. Pike was amongst the sufferers. I had the remains of Major Stoddard buried today in front of the Grand Battery on the spot where he received the wound which caused his death. Another party crossed over the river this afternoon in search of dead men—they found two of the militia and three Indians. Major Tod, Capt. Langham, Ensign Butler Harrison, Lieut. Reeves, and several others started down the river in order to sail around to Huron and from thence to Cleveland.

Thursday, 13th—This morning Major Tod and the officers that started with him last night all returned; the lake was too rough for their boat. I have had all the shot and shells collected this day; find we have a large number more than we had when the siege commenced. The weather very fine, the men have fine fun fishing.

Friday, 14th—This day the militia left the ground in the rear of my company. I cleared off the ground they occupied and moved my company onto it. Three British regulars came into our camp this morning; they state that the British left them behind, but I expect that they have deserted but don't like to own it. The mail arrived this day; brings the pleasing news that Fort George was taken by the Americans as well as Little York.

Saturday, 15th—This day I moved my tent from the Grand Battery; had the bomb-proofs filled up in front of my camp. Andrew Nichelson died this morning about 4 o'clock. Major Hukill, Major Pintel, myself, and thirteen of my soldiers crossed the river this afternoon in order to reconnoiter the old British camp that they left in haste. We found several balls; also, a man came to us who was taken by the Indians on the day of the battle; he was taken to Brownstown and he and one other made their escape from that place, but the other got shot at the River Raisin by an Indian. He states that a large number of our men were killed by the Indians after they were taken; he says he saw twelve or fourteen shot down himself; he also states that the Indians have all returned to their towns.

Sunday, 16th—This day very pleasant. I have made garden; set out lettuce and planted radishes, etc. A party of men crossed the river, went down as far as the old British fort, saw three dead men that were killed the day of the battle; found several muskets, some cannon balls and one very large chain.

Monday, 17th—Fine weather this morning, my men in high spirits, fish plenty, no want of provisions, all that is wanting to have everything complete is a little whisky. I took sail in a small canoe this morning and caught sixty-two white bass that would weigh about one pound each, returned before dinner; caught them with a hook and line baited with a red rag. I moved two eighteen-pounders from the lower battery to the Grand Battery this day.

Tuesday, 18th—Nothing new this day. Our camp getting in fine order in respect to cleanliness. The men are becoming more healthy since the dry weather commenced. This evening has commenced with rain which will be very useful.

Wednesday, 19th—No rain last night as was expected. This day very pleasant, rather cold. I placed a sentinel at the Croghan Battery this day.

Thursday, 20th—My men are well employed fishing. Two lieutenants caught 375 with hooks.

Friday, 21st—This day I crossed the river with a party of my men, found forty-seven balls that we fired at them from our batteries and blockhouses during the siege; also, we found one Indian chief that was killed by a cannon ball that I fired from the Big Battery. A prisoner that we have here confirmed it to be true. At the time I fired at them, one of my men that was looking to see where the ball would strike said the ball had killed a man that was on a gray horse. This prisoner says that this is the man.

Saturday, 22nd—Fine weather; a number of men sick in camp, several died, not more than could be expected considering the severe fatigue and the badness of the weather they have experienced for the last thirty days.

Sunday, 23rd—This day I went over the river with twelve of my men in hunt of cannon balls; found some, found several dead men that were not buried. They were killed during the fight on the 5th. I went down as low as the old fort, discovered that there had been a large number of men buried there, several of ours and some of theirs. We returned back to camp about 2 o'clock; found several balls. Soon after I got back a very heavy tempest of thunder, wind, and rain commenced; continued the remaining part of the afternoon and until late in the evening.

Monday, 24th—The rain still continues very hard. Samuel Grossman, one of my soldiers, died last night.

Wednesday, 26th—This day Lieut. Hackley arrived here from Kentucky and several men with him.

Thursday, 27th—This day as usual, only our men cleaning fish that were caught yesterday with a seine. At two hauls, caught six barrels. Col. Miller, who commands at this time, thought it advisable to send a party of men, 120, up to Fort Defiance in order to fetch down a quantity of flour that is there. Having some suspicion that there might be some Indians about, he sent Capt. John and two other men in front. They left camp two hours before the party got ready, went up within one half mile of Roche de Bout;[11] discovered on this side six Indians and nine on the other side that they were on; retreated in haste, got back to the river as the party were crossing, came over and reported to Col. Miller. The party were all ordered back for the present.

Friday, 28th—This morning four men arrived from Detroit in a boat. They made their escape in the night. They state that twenty Indians had left Malden for the purpose of coming to lurk about this camp in order to catch a prisoner or two and intercept the mail as it comes through. This afternoon two mails arrived safe; Major Vorhees from Kentucky brought them in company with several others. The weather cold and unpleasant for the time of year.

Sunday, 30th—Rainy part of the day; measles and mumps very prevalent in camp at this time.

Monday, 31st—This day all the troops, both regulars, volunteers, and militia passed muster and inspection by Major Hukill.

Tuesday, June 1st—Nothing new this day except drawing seine; they caught a large quantity of fish.

Wednesday, 2nd—This day Conrad Deguire, one of my soldiers, died very suddenly. He had been sick for a long time, but had got better so that he was able to walk about the camp and to the river. At 12 o'clock his messmates called him to dinner, but he did not come nor answer. They went to the tent and found him dead. This afternoon Capt. Holt left camp with 100 men for Fort Winchester after flour and whisky.

Thursday, 3rd—This day Lieut. Gwynn and several others left camp for the settlements to recruit their health. Our mechanical work goes along very well, repairing gun carriages, axes, wagons, and small arms; the troops very industrious keeping the camp clean. Our wounded are in a fine way to recover shortly, all but one man. He must die very soon.

Friday, 4th—This day very fine weather—two men arrived here from Cleveland with a boat load of potatoes, 150 bushels; sold them all out in a few hours at $2.00 per bushel. They returned this evening. Dr. Marvin took passage to Cleveland for the purpose of recruiting his health. The above-mentioned wounded man died this evening. His name was Meek, one of Capt. Nearing's soldiers. Eight fine steers came into our lines this morning from the woods.

Saturday, 5th—Commenced raining about 4 o'clock this evening with heavy thunder, continues on until guard, still raining very hard. Capt. Phillips of the Ohio Militia arrested by Col. Miller for neglect of duty. I had for supper this evening a cup of tea and piece of bread only—high living.

Sunday, 6th—This day rainy by showers; killed three steers that the men might have some fresh meat.

Monday, 7th—This morning good news; an express arrived about 12 o'clock last night from Gen. Dearborn with intelligence that Fort George was taken by the Americans and that Gen. Prevost had the assurance to cross the lake to Sackets Harbor with 1,500 men and was completely defeated by Gen. Brown with a loss of 300 killed and taken prisoners.

Col. Miller, who commands at this place at this time in consequence of Gen. Clay's indisposition, ordered that there should be a salute fired at 12 o'clock this day of 18 guns. All the music in the garrison was paraded on the top of the Big

Battery where the salute was fired out of two brass twelve-pounders. We had drums, fifes, flutes, clarinets, violins, timbrels, and a bass drum. After the firing and the music, I had Gen. Clay, Col. Miller, and Major Sodwick to dine with Capt. Gratiot and myself. Dined on soup and roast beef, and for dessert, a plate of strawberries.

Tuesday, 8th—Rainy. Party arrived here this day from Lower Sandusky with seventy or eighty fat cattle, also a part of the men that went up the river with Capt. Holt arrived with some flour and some twelve-pound shot. Say they left at the head of the rapids thirteen boats laden with flour, the water so low that they could not come over the falls.

Wednesday, 9th—Cloudy this morning, threatening rain all day. In the afternoon, butchered fine beef. A party went this morning to help down with the boats and the flour; another party took up some pirogues to lighten heavy boats. Four o'clock commenced raining very fast. I took a stroll up the river this morning with Major Huckill after strawberries, found plenty. My garden looks very flourishing at this time. I have lettuce, large and small radishes, sage, mint, onions, peas, and beans.

Thursday, 10th—This day very warm, thunders some, rains a trifle. Col. Miller sent Lieut. Frederick and about forty men up the river to help down with some of the boats. They got up about three miles and met a party of Indians, about fifteen or sixteen in number, all on horse back. They fired at them and then retreated down on to the bottom and formed a line of battle. The Indians formed in a line also in the woods. The firing was heard at camp. A party of 100 was sent off immediately to their assistance. They crossed the river, the others being on that side, met them within one mile of camp, turned them back, and all proceeded up to where the boats were they were after. Fetched down the boats but discovered no Indians. Mr. Perry, one of the Petersburg Volunteers, died this morning.

Friday, 11th—This morning warm and cloudy. Major Huckill left here for the city of Washington by the way of Fort Defiance or Fort Winchester. He has with him Major Vorhees who is going on to Kentucky. Major Sodwick with 100 men going to Fort Winchester after flour and other stores. The three men that were sent up the river, Capt. Shaw and two others, returned about 11 o'clock. Their orders were to proceed to the head of the rapids without delay with orders to the commanding officer to come on with the boats as quick as possible. They report they have done according to orders, been up to the above place, delivered the orders, and state the boats will be here tomorrow. The also state that they came upon the trail of the Indians that were seen yesterday by Lieut. Frederick and party, but that they had made their way down the river. Mr. Dodds, one of the Pittsburg Blues, died this day

Saturday, 12th—This day Capt. Bradford dined with us. Capt. Wood joined mess with Capt. Gratiot and me on the 10th. Thirteen boats and several pirogues arrived here laden with flour, salt, whisky, soap, and candles. Several men with two horses and eight head of cattle were seen down at the old fort this afternoon. Sergeant Meldrum caught an Indian horse this day.

Sunday, 13th—A tremendous thunder gust last night with heavy rain and hail; this morning pleasant. Mr. Asa Stoddard, Major Spafford, and Major Farley arrived here with two boats from Cleveland laden with produce and dry goods. I got twenty-four pounds of butter, a bag of pickles, and a large cheese.

Monday, 14th—This day the gentleman that arrived here yesterday with produce sold to the amount of $1,500.

Tuesday, 15th—This day Gen. Clay took the command of the garrison, ordered a general court martial for the purpose of Q. M. Lea's trail, of the 19th Regiment. Isaac Simpson died this day, one of my soldiers.

Wednesday, 16th—This day two boats left here for Cleveland. Capt. McCray and Lieut. McGee with several of the Petersburg Volunteers went out in the boats for the purpose of recruiting their health, also six of my soldiers for the same purpose—furloughed for thirty days, Thomas Golden, James McCurdy, Robert Persons, Richard Gwynn, Francis Wartenbee, and William Shields. Gen. Clay ordered the traverse from the gate at the northeast end of the big battery that extended to the main traverse leveled, which was done.

Saturday, 19th—This day Capt. Hatfield arrived here from Fort Winchester with seven or eight boats laden with flour. I commenced reading the history of modern Europe, one volume. My men laid the Little Battery floor. A hard shower this evening.

Sunday, 20th—Last night one of Capt. Nearing's soldiers died while one guard. It is supposed he took something that poisoned him. He was opened by the surgeons; they could not discover any defects. Two men arrived here this day from Detroit. They fetch intelligence that the British are coming to pay us another visit; they will have 2,000 regulars and from 4,000 to 6,000 Indians. 2,000 of the Indians are to start from Brownstown tomorrow for this place and the British will be here as soon as the troops arrive from down the lake, which will be within a few days. This news has aroused us to arms within this garrison, and has induced us to put ourselves in the posture of defense as fast as possible. One party of men were sent over the river this afternoon and demolished all the batteries the British had hove up at the other siege. Another party was employed in clearing off the bushes for a long distance around the fort. I had my men employed in fetching up the gun carriages from the blacksmith shop and mounting the guns. An express has been sent to meet Gen. Harrison two or three ways; another is sent up to Fort Winchester to meet Col. Johnson to urge him on with all possible speed.

Monday, June 21, 1813—This day all the effective men within the garrison are on guard or on fatigue repairing the batteries, clearing off the woods around the camp, cutting, hauling, and placing abitis in front of all the batteries. Every man appears to be working for his own safety. Two Frenchmen and two others have been sent down the river as far as the bay to make discoveries; they will return tomorrow. I mounted all the cannon this afternoon and put them into their proper batteries and blockhouses. A soldier of Capt. Langham's company arrived here this evening from Fort Winchester; states that Col. Johnson is there with 800 mounted men.

Tuesday, 22nd—This day all the camp busily employed in strengthening the garrison wherever there appeared to be a weak place. One man arrived here from Franklinton; states that Gen. MacArthur is there with 500 regulars. He also states that there are 500 more at Upper Sandusky of the 24th Regiment. Eight men arrived here from Fort Winchester. A part of Col. Johnson's men arrived here from Fort Winchester, a part of Col. Johnson's regiment of cavalry. The regiment will be in tomorrow early in the morning. Two men arrived here from Kentucky this day; they bring no particular news. About 100 men have been for three days employed in clearing off the wood and bushes about the camp. A good deal of rain fell this evening. It is about nine o'clock in the evening and the Kentuckians are just approaching the ferry on the other side where they will encamp for this night.

Wednesday, 23rd—At 3 o'clock gun fire by the Kentucky cavalry on the opposite shore raised a horrid yell in imitation of the Indians. This is conduct very unbecoming an officer or soldier. They commenced crossing the river about 6 o'clock; about 12 they had all got over with their horses except what horses had strayed from their camp. When the gun fired, these horses all took flight. Several men were run over and very much hurt. One dead, the blow he received by a horse's foot broke his skull. My men completed the abatis in front of the Little Battery and repaired them in front of the Big Battery. Col. Johnson's regiment of mounted men encamped down on the bottom next to the river for the present. At 10 o'clock in the evening the boats that have the baggage of Col. Johnson's regiment are landing. They are laden with flour, whisky and pork; he left a part of them at the head of the rapids.

Thursday, 24th—This morning very cold and windy. A party of spies were sent down the river in order to make discoveries; came back and reported they saw three savages and several horses. It is expected we shall have another visit in a few days from them.

Friday, 25th—The weather still very cold, so much so that winter clothing is very comfortable. A party of spies returned this evening from the mouth of the river and state they saw nothing like Indians or British while they were gone.

Saturday, June 26th—This day warm and pleasant. The spies returned from down the river; report that they saw nothing like Indians or British. Lieut. Sanders and party arrived this afternoon from the head of the rapids with the boats and a part of the flour that Col. Johnson left when he came down. They left about 200 barrels rolled out on shore.

I have spent several hours in walking by myself around the garrison, both outside of the pickets and inside of the batteries. I find by examination that this place must have been a seat of war for ages past. In almost every place where we have thrown up the earth, we find human bones in great plenty. Yesterday the fatigue party that were digging a trench in the front of blockhouses No. 3 and 4 came on a pile of bones where they took out twenty-five skulls all in one pit. A tree had grown over the pit that was several feet over, say four. In walking around this garrison on the earth that has been thrown up, it was like walking on the sea shore upon the old mussel shells, only in this case, human bones.

Sunday, June 27th—This day very warm. The spies returned from down the river; they report they saw no signs of the Indians or British, but heard the report of eleven cannon out on the lake. Mr. Smith arrived here with two cows and two calves; brought sugar, coffee, tea, and cranberries. This evening we have radishes for the first time this season.

Monday, 28th—This morning Henry Fieldman, one of my soldiers, died of lock jaw. Capt. Langham with three others arrived here last night about 11 o'clock. They left Gen. Harrison with the 24th Regiment about fifteen miles in the rear. About 2 o'clock this afternoon, the general arrived with his two aides and an escort of ten of Lieut. Ball's squadron. I gave him the salute of fifteen guns. This evening about 6 o'clock Col. Anderson of the 24th Regiment arrived with his regiment of regulars, about 500 strong; brought their baggage on packhorses. Crandall, a man that arrived here from Detroit several weeks since, was put under guard this day by an order from Gen. Harrison on suspicion of being a spy.

Tuesday, 29th—This morning Col. Johnson with 200 of his mounted men crossed the river on an expedition to the River Raisin for the purpose of reconnoitering that part of the county. This afternoon 130 of Col. Johnson's mounted riflemen arrived here, a party that had not joined the regiment before. Q.M. Thompson of Col. Mill's regiment came in with them; they came by the way of Fort Defiance.

Wednesday, 30th—Today rainy by showers. Two hundred of Col. Johnson's men crossed the river this morning for the purpose of meeting him and the party that crossed yesterday and went to the River Raisin. They all returned this evening; brought in two French prisoners.

Thursday, July 1st—This morning Gen. Harrison left camp for Cleveland. Capt. Wood with him and 100 mounted men as an escort. An express arrived soon after the general left this place from Lower Sandusky with information that the Indians had been in that neighborhood; had killed one man and one woman and scalped them, and had taken seven prisoners. Col. Johnson with the balance of his mounted men are ordered to proceed immediately to Lower Sandusky. They will leave here tomorrow morning. A man, one of the Kentuckians that was taken by the Indians on the 5th of May over the river, came into camp this evening; made his escape from them ten days ago somewhere at the head of the River Raisin. He said that the Indians sent him with a young Indian to a small creek to wash some corn. He was smoking a tomahawk pipe as they went along and just as they got to the bank of the creek, the Indian before, he struck the tomahawk into the Indian's head and cleared himself, and has not eaten anything but weeds and bushes for ten days.

Friday, 2nd—This day the whole camp in motion. In the first place, Col. Johnson left his camp which was on the outside of the pickets on the bottom. His men commenced firing as they left the camp and continued firing until they got entirely out of hearing—*a great mark of bravery.* Another party left camp—Major Robinson, Major Wilson, and several of our Indians and some other people went up on this side of the river to Fort Defiance. Capt. Craig of Col. Johnson's regiment with his company was left behind. He and his lieutenant took it upon themselves to send a party up the river without orders, as they say, after packhorses. They sent twelve or fourteen and took along with them four men that were discharged from the service; their orders were to go along with Major Robinson and party, but were persuaded by those unruly militia to go with them. They went up on this side of the river five or six miles then crossed over; the Indians came upon them, killed and took the whole of them prisoners except two who have got into camp.

Capt. Langham was sent up the river with 100 men in order to collect some flour that was left at the head of the rapids in different places; took with him small boats to fetch it down. Several of his men that he had with him, but militia, without orders concluded to leave him and go on ahead. They fell in with four or five Indians who gave them a shot but did not kill any of them. All those that made their escape met Capt. Langham. They reported to him that there was a large body of savages, not less than 100. He returned back to camp on this side. Capt. Holt was sent up on this side with 200 men in order to assist Capt. Langham if wanted, but met him and all returned together. Lieut. Col. Gaines of the 24th Regiment was ordered to cross the river with 200 men and proceed up the river to where those men were killed; he has not returned this evening, will stay all night. Those brave Kentuckians, when the Indians showed themselves, threw down their guns and cleared themselves without firing at them.

Saturday, 3rd—This morning Capt. Langham with 150 men returned back after the flour; left camp about half-past 6 o'clock. Col. Gaines returned this evening with a party; it is reported that they found three dead men, one scalped, two not, and found one dead Indian. One of our men killed and had scalped him. Capt. Langham came in this evening with his party; found but very little flour, it is supposed the Indians have destroyed it.

July 4th, 1813—This morning at sunrise we fired thirteen guns in honor of the 4th of July, 1776. At 1 o'clock we fired eighteen, the National Salute; they were all fired from two brass twelve-pounders. After the firing was over, the officers all repaired to a large bower prepared by Lieut. Hawkins near the lower magazine and partook of a fine dinner. By the report of Gen. Clay, there were eighty-six officers commissioned and staff. There were eighteen toasts drank. I was taken with severe chills which passed off with fever and perspiration.

Monday, July 5th—This day the effects of the late Major Stoddard were sold. I have been indisposed all this day.

Tuesday, 6th—This day I am very sick, taking physic. Nothing particular new in the camp; tremendous heavy thunder with very heavy rain both last night and the night before last.

Wednesday, 7th—This day I am very much better of my disposition, having eaten something. The picket guard saw several Indians in the woods, as they say. One man fired on them; a party was sent in pursuit of them but returned without seeing them.

Thursday, 8th—Lieut. Larwill, his brother William, and Lieut. Henderson arrived here; the mail came with them.

Saturday, 10th—This day very pleasant. The picket guard saw several Indians a short distance from the garrison. A party was sent in pursuit of them but returned without discoveries.

Sunday, 11th—I crossed the river with Lieut. Larwill, Lieut. Henderson, Q.M. Thompson, and twenty of my men; made no discoveries. Spies that went down the river last night returned this evening making no discoveries.

Monday 12th—This morning I vomited, being very unwell. Am better this evening. The sick are fast recruiting in my company, only seven reported sick this morning.

Tuesday, 13th—Capt. Gratiot and Lieut. Larwill have surveyed the camp and country around it. My sick report this morning, five only.

Wednesday, 14th—I am very unwell but keep about. Somewhat rainy by showers, it sets in to be a steady rain about sundown.

Thursday, 15th—The mail arrived this evening. The spies returned from down the river; state they saw six Indians at a distance.

Saturday, 17th—Mr. Oliver arrived here with packhorses laden with corn.

Sunday, 18th—Rainy in the morning. The men are becoming more healthy. Capt. Martin of the spy boat sailed down the river to gain intelligence, if possible, of the British and Indians.

Monday 19th—Captain Shaw with his company left this camp for the Portage Blockhouse. Capt. Martin returned this evening with the spy boat. He sailed down as far as Cedar Point. He made no discoveries; he states he heard several cannon this morning in the direction of Malden.

Tuesday, 20th—This day rainy by showers. Lieut. Peters returned to camp this afternoon. He left here on Saturday in company with the mail and several others; he was on foot, the others on horseback. He fell rather behind his company and was surprised by two Indians who had harassed him through the woods for two days. He got rid of them yesterday but states that he saw as many as forty-five Indians on the large prairies, mounted on horses driving cattle. This season has been very cold and wet, has been a vast deal of thunder, rain, and heavy wind. At 9 o'clock this evening it is reported in camp that two sails were seen down the river about sundown. It is expected the British and the Indians are coming to pay us another visit. Capt. Martin with his company of spy rangers left camp on a trip up the river; to return tomorrow.

Wednesday, 21st—This morning our camp besieged by Indians and British. The Indians attacked our picket guard as they left the garrison this morning between break of day and sunrise; killed and took six or seven prisoners. The British are landing their forces down at the old British garrison. They appear to have a very large force, but the principal part are Indians by their appearance and leather tents. It is expected that Dixon has come on with the Indians from the other side of the Mississippi. We expect they intend to storm us if possible. We are all engaged in putting ourselves in the best possible state of defense. Our cannons are all in good order. At 10 o'clock this morning the men are throwing up traverses in different parts of the garrison, are securing the magazine, and what are not at work are at the pickets giving battle to the Indians.

I have given them several shots with the 18- and 12-pounders. The first shot I made at them put one to death, another shot in the course of the day killed one; it threw his gun as much as fifteen feet into the air. This one was seen carried off by two men.

Mr. Oliver with one other started this evening to meet Gen. Harrison. An express, Capt. McCune with two others, started in one hour after on the same business. Lieut. Mountjoy came into camp this day from Portage Blockhouse with eighteen men. They made their escape very strangely through the Indians; they were followed for two miles and fired upon by them several times, but did no harm.

Thursday, July 22nd—The whole garrison on the watch last night, only one-third asleep at a time; we expected an attack in the latter part of the night, but they have not troubled us nor this morning at 8 o'clock. By close examination we find they are planting batteries on the other side of the river and expect they are on this side in several places. If that should be the case they would give us a good deal of trouble, but they will not take this fort. It appears also that they are repairing the old British fort, but we are not certain of that as yet. It is expected they are as much as 6,000 strong, but not more than 1,000 whites, the rest are different tribes of Indians. Gen. Clay called all the officers together at 10 o'clock this day; he delivered his sentiments very fully in respect to the siege; also communicated to the officers that there was to be no surrender of this garrison to the British and their Indian allies. The Indians are saluting us with their hellhound yells and rifle shots this evening at 9 o'clock.

Friday, 23rd—The Indians are at their old business on the right angle of the garrison, firing on the men on the picket. We have one man slightly wounded within the garrison and one wounded in the thigh when at the river after water. Not one killed or badly wounded while in the garrison. About 11 o'clock Lieut. Col. Gaines with about 100 men sallied out from the garrison to reconnoiter the woods around the camp and to fetch in the dead that were killed on the 21st belonging to the picket guard. They found two very much mangled, they saw but four Indians who fired on our men. The colonel and party went twice around the fort and was covered by Col. Mill's regiment. They all returned into the fort about 10 o'clock. The Indians made their appearance very soon after that and are keeping up a heavy fire at our pickets at this time, 2 o'clock. About 300 mounted Indians have passed up the river since 1 o'clock on the other side of the river, crossed onto this side about two miles above this; we expect to have warm work this night.

Saturday, 24th—The enemy did not disturb us last night any farther than to keep us on diligent watch—we see nor hear anything of them this morning as yet, but expect to see them as soon as the fog clears off. About 9 o'clock we discovered the enemy at the old British fort in columns and their boats crossing over to this side to give battle this evening. They are all around the garrison, showing themselves in different places. They have fired but very little at us this day; the Indians are plenty to be seen at a distance.

Sunday, 25th—This morning all the men in the garrison were under arms at half past 2 o'clock; each man had not less than two nor over three muskets by his side, well charged, at the pickets. They have had no use for them this day. The Indians came to the edge of the woods and fire once in awhile. One of the soldiers shot a buck in the river this day. Our camp is in very good order for defense, our men in fine spirits. There appears to be by the smoke a large part of them in camp about two miles up the river in the woods. They have been firing into our camp five days and have not killed one man yet. Watchword this night "Musket."

Monday, 26th—The enemy have not troubled us last night or this morning more than usual. Capt. McCune and the Frenchmen sent from this camp to see Gen. Harrison arrived here about 7 o'clock with intelligence from the general at Lower Sandusky. State that he is collecting a large force there and that Gov. Meigs is raising the militia of this state which will be on in a few days. Also, our fleet will be ready to take part on the lake in a very short time.

About 4 o'clock this afternoon a very heavy firing took place at about one-half mile in the rear of our camp. It appeared like an engagement with the Indians; they keep up the heavy firing accompanied with their horrid savage yells. The supposed object was to draw out our troops from the garrison, thinking we had a reinforcement coming in and was attacked, and would sally out to their assistance. But we were too well aware of their intention to be taken in by their British and savage intrigue. Their object, no doubt, was to draw out a party of our men into the bush in the rear of our camp while the rest of their troops were on the flanks of our camps out of sight, watching to make an assault on our pickets while our men were engaged in the bush.

Just as this sham battle stopped, there came up the heaviest thunder shower that ever I experienced. I am positive I never in all my life saw it rain harder than it did for nearly one hour; our camp was completely inundated. The men have all discharged their pieces and loaded them fit for action. This is the sixth day of siege and not a man killed except what were killed at the picket guard the first day. One of two things was their intention this day by their sham battle—they either meant to fall on the back of our men and cut them off, or wait until they had got into the woods and make an assault on the garrison. At 11 o'clock this evening Capt. McCune, one Frenchman, and one other man started on express to Lower Sandusky to General Harrison.

Tuesday, 27th—The seventh day of the second siege at this place by the British and their Indian allies. Very few of them are to be seen this morning; their tents appear to be more numerous down at the old British garrison this morning than they have been for three days before. It is expected the heavy fall of rain last evening drove them out of the woods. Their operations are unknown; not more than from ten to fifteen Indians have been seen this day, and these principally on horseback. If they ever attempt to storm this garrison it will be this night, unless they think to starve us out, but that will be impossible in two months. We have plenty of flour, pork, and salt to last as long as they can conveniently stay. The watchword this evening is "Sword." Our men all in high spirits awaiting the attack. At 10 o'clock word passed through the garrison that two men had deserted; the watchword changed to "Madison." The suspicion was without foundation, there had not anybody left camp.

Wednesday, 28th—Eighth day of the siege. This morning very pleasant. The enemy very scarce, nothing to be seen or heard of them about our camp. Some few tents, men, and horses to be seen down at the old garrison on the bottom. This afternoon we discovered three small vessels and boats sailing down the river. Some of them appeared to be filled with men; also we saw a large number of mounted Indians crossing about two miles above this fort and passing down on the other side. Once in a while I gave them a shot from the 18-pound gun in the Big Battery and twelve from Blockhouse No. 1. These guns put them in quick motion. Gen. Clay sent out two spies, Abbot and Cheeks, this evening to view their camps. Their camps down the river were very large as they reported.

Thursday, 29th—The spies returned into camp this morning a little after daylight. They report they saw about twenty Indians in the camp below this fort; they state they had two very large encampments below. They also state that there were some Indians above this fort in the woods, how many they could not tell. By the appearance of their camp they have a very large force of Indians. Gen. Clay sent an express last night to Gen. Harrison. Our people this day are cleaning up the camp and ventured to the river to wash. Capt. Martin has not returned with his spies; it is very much feared that he has been cut off by the Indians. The spies report that the Indians had a great number of horses with them by the appearance of the encampment.

Very disagreeable affair took place last night in this garrison. The officer of the day and Lieut. John Henderson of my company of artillery got drunk, passed around the lines and abused several of the sentinels so much that they have entered a formal complaint against Lieut. Henderson to have him arrested, which will be done this evening.

The same two spies were sent out to reconnoiter the Indian camps; they came in before 2 o'clock, report they did not see any Indians but heard the rowing of a boat or boats and heard an Indian dog bark at them. The watchword "Kentucky."

Friday, 30th—This morning every officer and soldier in the garrison on the watch at 2 o'clock expecting if the enemy ever intended to make an assault on this garrison, it would be this morning. They have not shown themselves. The general sent out 200 men this morning about 9 o'clock to examine the grounds occupied by the Indians and British during the siege which commenced on the 21st and was raised on the 28th. The movements of the enemy have been very extraordinary; both coming and going out of this place they have taken off about thirty head of working oxen and some few packhorses. By the appearance of their encampment, they must have been as much as 6,000 strong, both Indians and British. By every appearance, they expected to decoy us out of the garrison into the woods where they had their Indians concentrated and cut us off by small detachments until they weakened our force by the Indian slaughter so much as to carry our pickets. Poor fellows! They have been sadly disappointed; the general took good care of their traps. It is generally believed here that the Indians have pressed the British to make this last move on Fort Meigs, and they (the British) were obliged so to do to save their own selves. They have gratified the Indians by coming; how far it will go in pacifying them is more than I can tell. The British will either have to compliment them with very heavy annuities or will have to suffer being plundered by them; that is without any doubt. Poor allies. If they cannot plunder the enemy, will plunder them that employ them. An express was sent this evening up to Fort Defiance in order to ascertain where the savages have been in that neighborhood during the last siege. The watchword this evening "Ohio is the boy."

Our camp is in perfect silence this evening. The men on duty as usual by order of the general, he not being fully satisfied that the enemy has abandoned the siege. Caution is one of the greatest traits of military glory that a general can be possessed of. The commanding officer cannot be too cautious of his enemy; they will come like a thief in the night when they are least expected.

Saturday, July 31, 1813—This morning the general sent out spies, some up and some down the river. They returned this evening; report that they saw no Indians, nor did they see any fresh signs. Out picket guard on the right wing of the camp, but about 300 yards from the pickets and in the woods, fired four shots; state that they saw two Indians. I am inclined to believe that they were mistaken; by the report of the spies, they surely must be. I am very unwell this evening with fevers and chills. The watchword this night is "Tennessee."

Epilogue

Fort Meigs stood only for a little more than two years. Its contributions to the war effort, though, were lasting. Following the first siege, the continued American occupation of the rapids during the spring and summer of 1813 had forced British officials to divert scarce resources from the timely completion of an expanded naval squadron on Lake Erie and prevented Procter from taking offensive action against Perry's force, still under construction in Erie, Pennsylvania. In the wake of the second siege, Procter's ability to mount any type of offensive action against his enemies ground to a halt completely. The American victory in July also significantly eroded Great Britain's alliance with the region's Native peoples. Although many bands near Detroit continued to support their traditional ally, the British–Indian alliance that had been a touchstone in the region's military, economic, and diplomatic affairs for generations had begun to unravel. Within months, it would disintegrate entirely.

Lastly, the battles at Fort Meigs allowed Harrison to successfully exploit the strategic advantage won by Perry. Because of Perry's success, the military efforts directed by Harrison, employing troops and materials acquired from Fort Meigs, led eventually to the full repatriation of Detroit and, with the exception of

Mackinac Island, the remainder of the Michigan Territory. Harrison's actions also brought about an American victory at Moraviantown in October 1813, and with it, the unchallenged occupation of the Detroit Theater at the war's conclusion.

Those successes had been extracted at great cost. There is no comprehensive list of all the troops who served at Fort Meigs. We know most of them only in the aggregate. They have become one of many, listed namelessly on periodic reports that enumerate the troop strength at the garrison or other similar documentation. Only infrequently can we discover the names of specific individuals. Sometimes soldiers are named within the rare surviving company muster roll; others are mentioned in passing within personal correspondence; occasionally a few are singled out in diaries or journals. Even for those whom we can identify by name, we usually can learn little else about their lives or circumstances. They emerge from the documents like fleeting apparitions, remain visible briefly, and just as quickly are gone.

Thousands of individuals passed through the gates and served at the post during the war: some for months, some for weeks, others for only days. Most are unnamed; all shared duty in conditions that were brutally difficult, dangerous, and exhausting. All struggled within these circumstances. Many eventually succumbed.

Fort Meigs today is the site of three cemeteries populated by those who died during their time at the post. We have no idea how many are buried there or who they are. They rest in graves unmarked and known only to God. The legacy of Fort Meigs resides within the bounds of these cemeteries and with the memory of those who survived. The legacy of Fort Meigs is one of perseverance, fortitude, and sacrifice. The men and women who occupied Fort Meigs during the War of 1812 endured hardship and adversity to usher the nation through a period of enormous uncertainty. For this, they have earned our gratitude. We stand in their debt.

Notes

PREFACE

1. [Daniel Lewis Cushing], *Fort Meigs and the War of 1812: Orderly Book of Cushing's Company, 2nd U.S. Artillery, April 1813–February 1813 and Personal Diary of Captain Daniel Cushing, October 1812–July 1813*, ed. Harlow Lindley (Columbus: Ohio Historical Society, 1975), 53–55. For a general study, see Dianne Graves, *In the Midst of Alarms: The Untold Story of Women and the War of 1812* (Montreal: Robin Brass Studio, 2007).
2. [Cushing], *Fort Meigs and the War of 1812*, 86, 108–9. See also "Eleazer D. Wood Account Return, July 24, 1813," War of 1812 Collection, Center for Archival Collections, Jerome Library, Bowling Green State University, Bowling Green, OH. For a general study, see Gerald T. Althoff, *Amongst My Best Men: African Americans in the War of 1812* (Put-In-Bay, OH: The Perry Group, 1993).
3. Joseph H. Larwill, "Journal of Joseph H. Larwill Relating to Occurrences Transpired in the Service of the U States Commencing April 5, 1812," MS, Burton Historical Collection, Detroit Public Library, Detroit, MI, n.p.

INTRODUCTION

1. For this and the following four paragraphs, see Donald R. Hickey, *The War of 1812: A Forgotten Conflict* (Urbana: University of Illinois Press, 1989), 5–29; see also *The Causes of the War of 1812: National Honor or National Interest?*, ed. Bradford Perkins (New York: Holt, Rinehart and Winston, 1962), and Reginald Horsman, *The Causes of the War of 1812* (Philadelphia: University of Pennsylvania Press, 1962).
2. For more information about Native violence in north-central Ohio, see L. B. Gurley, *Memoir of Rev. William Gurley, Late of Milan, Ohio, a Local Minister of the Methodist Episcopal Church* (Cincinnati: R. P. Thompson, 1856), 231–41.
3. David C. Skaggs, *William Henry Harrison and the Conquest of the Ohio Country: Frontier Fighting in the War of 1812* (Baltimore, MD: Johns Hopkins University Press, 2014), and Robert M. Owens, *Mr. Jefferson's Hammer: William Henry Harrison and the Origins of American Indian Policy* (Norman: University of Oklahoma Press, 2011). For Tenskwatawa, see R. David Edmunds, *The Shawnee Prophet* (Lincoln: University of Nebraska Press, 1983). See also Reginald Horsman, "Western War Aims, 1811–1812," *Indiana Magazine of History* 53 (1957): 9–18.
4. Adam Jortner, *The Gods of Prophetstown: The Battle of Tippecanoe and the Holy War for the American Frontier* (New York: Oxford University Press, 2011); Alfred Pirtle, *The Battle of Tippecanoe* (Louisville, KY: John P. Morton & Co., 1900). See also Patrick Bottiger, *The Borderland of Fear: Vincennes, Prophetstown, and the Invasion of the Miami Homeland* (Lincoln: University of Nebraska Press, 2016).
5. See David C. Skaggs and Gerald T. Altoff, *A Signal Victory: The Lake Erie Campaign, 1812–1813* (Annapolis: Naval Institute Press, 1997), 5–32; for Hull's campaign from Detroit, see Anthony J. Yanik, *The Fall and Recapture of Detroit in the War of 1812: In Defense of William Hull* (Detroit: Wayne State University Press, 2011).
6. For general works dealing with the War of 1812 in the West, see David Kirkpatrick, *The War of 1812 in the West: From Fort Detroit to New Orleans* (Yardley, PA: Westholme Publishing, 2019), and the dated but reliable Alec R. Gilpin, *The War of 1812 in the Old Northwest* (East Lansing: Michigan State University Press, 1958). Canadian participation is explored by Sandy Antal, *A Wampum Denied: Procter's War of 1812* (Ottawa: Carleton University Press, 1997). Native American involvement is detailed in John Sugden, *Tecumseh: A Life* (New York: Henry Holt and Company, 1997), and Robert S. Allen, *His Majesty's Indian Allies: British Indian Policy in Defence of Canada, 1774–1815* (Toronto: Dundurn Press, 1992); see also Larry L. Nelson, "The Maumee River Campaign, 1812–1813," in *The Battle of Lake Erie and Its Aftermath: A Reassessment*, ed. David Curtis

Skaggs (Kent, OH: Kent State University Press, 2013), 11–31, and Dennis Carter-Edwards, "The War of 1812 along the Detroit Frontier: A Canadian Perspective," *Michigan Historical Review* 13 (1987): 25–50.

7. George Brown, *Recollections of Itinerant Life: Including Early Reminiscences* (Cincinnati: R. W. Carroll & Co., 1866), 49–50.
8. For general studies of Fort Meigs, see Larry L. Nelson, *Fort Meigs: 1812 Battleground* (Columbus: Ohio Historical Society, 1999); Emanuel Hallaman, "The Invasions of Ohio in 1813 During the War of 1812" (MA thesis, Ohio State University, 1956).

CHAPTER ONE. THE FOOT OF THE MAUMEE RAPIDS

1. Samuel Williams, *Two Campaigns in the War of 1812–13* (Cincinnati: Robert Clarke & Co., 1871), v–vii, 9–35; see also [Samuel Williams], *The Samuel Williams Memoir*, ed. Patricia Fife Medert (Chillicothe, OH: Ross County Historical Society, 2000). For Tiffin, see William Edward Gilmore, *Life of Edward Tiffin, First Governor of Ohio* (Chillicothe, OH: Horney & Son, 1897).
2. The paper was known as *The Weekly Register* from 1811 until 1814, when it became *Niles' Weekly Register*. It retained that title until 1837, when it became *Niles' National Register*, the name used until its demise in 1849. See Norval Luxon, *Niles Weekly Register: News Magazine of the Nineteenth Century* (Baton Rouge: Louisiana State University Press, 1947).
3. Fort Miamis was a British outpost built in 1794 near the head of navigation on the Maumee River. The fort had been erected to oppose Anthony Wayne's advance down the Maumee Valley prior to the Battle of Fallen Timbers. British forces left the post in 1796. American troops occupied the garrison briefly, but had abandoned the facility by 1799 or early 1800. The post was in ruins by the outbreak of the War of 1812. See Clever F. Bald, "Fort Miamis, Outpost of Empire," *Northwest Ohio Quarterly* 16 (1944): 75–111.
4. A "pole," also known as a "perch" or a "rod," was equal to 16½ feet. See Andro Linklater, *Measuring America: How an Untamed Wilderness Shaped the United States and Fulfilled the Promise of Democracy* (New York: Walker and Company, 2002), 10.
5. Fort Malden in Amherstburg, Upper Canada (opposite Detroit in present-day Ontario), was the main British military installation in the Detroit Theater and the seat of British military power within the region.
6. A Subscriber [Samuel Williams], "Interesting Topography of Ohio," *Weekly Register*, July 9, 1813.

CHAPTER TWO. FORTIFYING THE RAPIDS, BUILDING FORT MEIGS

1. For Wood and Gratiot, see George W. Cullum, *Campaigns of the War of 1812–1815 against Great Britain, Sketched and Criticized; With Brief Biographies of the American Engineers* (New York: James Miller, 1879), 91–140 and 342–52.
2. "Sergeant Greenbury Keen Journal, 1812," MS, Ohio History Connection, Columbus, OH; [Daniel Lewis Cushing], *Fort Meigs and the War of 1812: Orderly Book of Cushing's Company, 2nd U.S. Artillery, April 1813–February 1813 and Personal Diary of Captain Daniel Cushing, October 1812–July 1813*, ed. Harlow Lindley (Columbus: Ohio Historical Society, 1975), 98. Early nineteenth-century artillery was designated by the weight of the solid shot that it fired. Six-pound cannon fired a solid iron ball, about the size of a modern baseball, weighing six pounds. Fort Meigs was protected by six-, twelve-, and eighteen-pounders. During the first siege, British troops employed artillery as large as twenty-four pounds against the Americans.
3. [Cushing], *Fort Meigs and the War of 1812*, 98; "Alex. Meek to My Worthy Friend, Feby 8, 1813," in *Document Transcriptions of the War of 1812 in the Northwest*, vol. 10, *Western Reserve Historical Society War of 1812 Collection*, ed. Richard C. Knopf (Columbus: Ohio Historical Society, 1962), 1: 175–76.
4. Artificers were skilled tradesmen such as blacksmiths, farriers, carpenters, armorers, and wagon and wheel wrights who provided the army with the ability to fabricate, maintain, and repair the materials and equipment needed while on campaign. [Cushing], *Fort Meigs and the War of 1812*, 98. For the fort's construction and modification over time, see Larry L. Nelson, "The Mapping of Fort Meigs," *Northwest Ohio Quarterly* 58 (1986): 123–42.
5. "Journal of the Northwestern Campaign of 1812–13, under Major-General William H. Harrison by Eleazer D. Wood," MS, State Historical Society of Wisconsin, Madison, WI; Cullum, *Campaigns of the War of 1812–1815*, 362–404; [Eleazer Derby Wood], *Journal of the Northwestern Campaign of 1812–1813 under Major-General Wm. H. Harrison by Eleazar* [sic] *D. Wood*, ed. Robert B. Boehm and Randall L. Buchman (Defiance, OH: Defiance College Press, 1975).
6. Brig. Gen. Joel Leftwich commanded a large force of Virginia Militia at the post. Harrison placed Leftwich in command of Fort Meigs during his absence. The six-month term of enlistment for the Virginia troops expired in early spring, and Leftwich and his men left Fort Meigs and returned home in early April. See Stuart Butler, *Patriots and Heroic Soldiers: Gen. Joel Leftwich and the Virginia Brigade in the War of 1812* (Berwyn Heights, MD: Heritage Books, 2008).

7. Dragoons were mounted troops, the equivalent of mid- to late-nineteenth-century cavalry.
8. Cullum, *Campaigns of the War of 1812–1815*, 369–84.

CHAPTER THREE. A RAID AGAINST THE INDIANS

1. Lee A. Wallace Jr., "The Petersburg Volunteers—1812–1813," *The Virginia Magazine of History and Biography* 82 (1974): 458–85.
2. Alfred M. Lorrain, *The Helm, the Sword, and the Cross: A Life Narrative* (Cincinnati: Poe & Hitchcock, 1862). For examples of Lorrain's early writings about the war, see A. M. Lorraine, "The Captured Bugle," *Ladies Repository, and Gatherings of the West 1* (1841): 278–79, and A. M. Lorraine, "The Sequel," *Ladies Repository, and Gatherings of the West* 5 (1845): 107–13.
3. Joseph H. Larwill, "Journal of Joseph H. Larwill relating to occurrences transpired in the service of the U States commencing April 5, 1812," MS, Burton Historical Collection, Detroit Public Library, Detroit, MI; Ben Douglas, *History of Wayne County, Ohio from the Days of the Pioneers and the First Settlers to the Present Day* (Indianapolis: R. Douglas, 1878), 284.
4. Henry Howe, *Historical Collections of Ohio* (Cincinnati: Bradley & Anthony, 1848), 525–26.
5. Lorrain, *The Helm, the Sword, and the Cross*, 125–27.
6. Larwill, "Journal."

CHAPTER FOUR. AN EXPEDITION AGAINST THE *QUEEN CHARLOTTE*

1. Unlike cannon, long-barreled guns that fired solid shot directly at their targets, short-barreled howitzers and mortars lobbed exploding shells high into the air, like pop flies hit at a softball game, where they detonated above their victims. These guns were designated by the diameter of the shell that they threw. "Armament of the British squadron, Lieutenant Francis Purvis of the *Detroit* to the court, Barclay Court Martial, 9 September 1814," reproduced in Frederick C. Drake, "Artillery and Its Influence on Naval Tactics: Reflections on the Battle of Lake Erie," in *War on the Great Lakes: Essays Commemorating the 175th Anniversary of the Battle of Lake Erie*, ed. William Jeffrey Welsh and David

Curtis Skaggs (Kent, OH: Kent State University Press, 1991), 17–29. For Fort Meigs's armament, see [Daniel Lewis Cushing], *Fort Meigs and the War of 1812: Orderly Book of Cushing's Company, 2nd U.S. Artillery, April 1813–February 1813 and Personal Diary of Captain Daniel Cushing, October 1812–July 1813*, ed. Harlow Lindley (Columbus: Ohio Historical Society, 1975), 102.

2. George W. Cullum, *Campaigns of the War of 1812–1815 against Great Britain, Sketched and Criticized; With Brief Biographies of the American Engineers* (New York: James Miller, 1879), 75–76.
3. A marquee was a large, circular walled tent used by officers.
4. Joseph H. Larwill, "Journal of Joseph H. Larwill relating to occurrences transpired in the Service of the U States commencing April 5, 1812," Burton Historical Collection, Detroit Public Library, Detroit, MI, n.p.

CHAPTER FIVE. LIFE IN CAMP, SPRING 1813

1. There are few secondary studies that focus on the daily lives of ordinary soldiers during their service in the War of 1812. See Eugene D. Watkins, "Cousin Jonathan: The Common United States Soldier in the War of 1812" (Ph.D. diss., University of Toledo, Toledo, OH, 2007), and Paul Le Roy, *Papers on the War of 1812 in the Northwest, no. 2: Some Social Aspects of the Life of Soldiers and the Organization of the Soldiers in the War of 1812* (Columbus: Anthony Wayne Park Board and The Ohio State Museum, 1958). See also Richard Holmes, *Redcoat: The British Soldier in the Age of Horse and Musket* (New York: W.W. Norton & Company, 2001). For Keen's observations, see "Sergeant Greenbury Keen Journal, 1812," MS, Ohio History Connection, Columbus, OH.
2. For this and the following paragraph, see Joseph H. Larwill, "Journal of Joseph H. Larwill relating to occurrences transpired in the service of the U States commencing April 5, 1812," MS, Burton Historical Collection, Detroit Public Library, Detroit, MI; [Daniel Lewis Cushing], *Fort Meigs and the War of 1812: Orderly Book of Cushing's Company, 2nd U.S. Artillery, April 1813–February 1813 and Personal Diary of Captain Daniel Cushing, October 1812–July 1813*, ed. Harlow Lindley (Columbus: Ohio Historical Society, 1975), 105–6.
3. For this and the following five paragraphs, see George W. Cullum, *Campaigns of the War of 1812–1815 against Great Britain, Sketched and Criticized; With Brief Biographies of the American Engineers* (New York: James Miller, 1879), 362–402, passim, and [Daniel Lewis Cushing], *Fort Meigs and the War of 1812*, 85–139, passim.
4. [Cushing], *Fort Meigs and the War of 1812*, 9.

5. "Statement of Charles Gratiot, March 1846 in Support of the Pension Application of Joseph Louis Dusseau," War of 1812 Pension File no. 25038, National Archives and Records Administration, Washington, DC.
6. Rev. A. M. Lorrain, "Rural Oration," *The Ladies Repository; A Monthly Periodical Devoted to Literature, Art, and Religion* (1851) 11: 257–61.
7. [Cushing], *Fort Meigs and the War of 1812*, 86; "Enrollment of Indians in the Military Service of the United States with the Army under the Command of General Harrison Operating in the Valley of the Maumee in the War of 1812, July 20–Aug. 21, 1813," Toledo–Lucas County Public Library, Local History and Genealogy Collections.
8. J. Sutton Wall, "Sketch of Colonel Joel Ferree's Regiment in the War of 1812," *Western Pennsylvania History* 11 (1928): 55–61.
9. "Diary of Samuel B. Walker, April-September 1813," MS, Loveland Historical Society, Loveland, OH, n.p.
10. Ibid.
11. In addition to the examples presented below, see "Samuel Bayles Book of Orders, April 23–August 12, 1813," MS, Rare Book and Special Collections, Thompson Library, The Ohio State University, Columbus, and "Order Book of Captain Peter Dudley's Company of Kentucky Militia," MS, Kentucky Historical Society, Frankfort, Kentucky. See also "Prologue to Victory: General Orders Fort Meigs to Put-In-Bay April–September 1813," *Register of the Kentucky Historical Society* 60 (1962): 9–35.
12. [James Mills], "A Regimental Book for the 1st Detachment of Ohio Militia containing Orders Received and Issued by Colonel James Mills of Butler County and State of Ohio, February 6 to August 4, 1813," typescript, Ohio History Connection, Columbus, and Cincinnati Historical Society, Cincinnati.
13. [Cushing], *Fort Meigs and the War of 1812*, 3–82, and [Daniel Lewis Cushing], *Captain Cushing in the War of 1812*, ed. Harlow Lindley (Columbus: Ohio State Archaeological and Historical Society, 1944); see also "Daniel Cushing, Capt., Orderly Book," Toledo–Lucas County Public Library Local History & Genealogical Collections, Sm. Coll. 14, War of 1812 Papers.
14. "Sergeant Greenbury Keen Journal, 1812." See also *To the Rapids: A Journal of a Tour of Duty in the Northwestern Army under the Command of Maj. General William H. Harrison*, ed. Sally Young, Robert Reid, and Ronald Reid (Columbus, 1990). "Picture of a Soldier's Life," *The Weekly Register*, May 8, 1813.
15. William Duane, *A Handbook for Infantry: Containing the First Principles of Military Discipline Founded upon Rational Method* (Philadelphia: Printed by the Author, 1813).
16. A Roram hat was a woolen hat with a fur face.

17. A roundabout was a lightweight, long-sleeved, short-waisted jacket. A surtout coat was a loose-fitting frockcoat.
18. [Mills], "A Regimental Book for the 1st Detachment," passim.
19. See also *Captain John Barrickman's Diary-Account and General Record Book in the War of 1812*, ed. June Barekman (Chicago: Genealogical Services Publications, n.d.), 13.
20. "Sergeant Greenbury Keen Journal, 1812."
21. [Cushing], *Fort Meigs and the War of 1812*, passim.
22. "Picture of a Soldier's Life," *The Weekly Register*, May 8, 1813.

CHAPTER SIX. FIRST SIEGE, APRIL 27–MAY 5, 1813

1. For general accounts of the first siege, see Alec R. Gilpin, *The War of 1812 in the Old Northwest* (East Lansing: Michigan State University Press, 1958), 173–93; Sandy Antal, *A Wampum Denied: Procter's War of 1812* (Ottawa: Carleton University Press, 1997), 217–40; Benson Lossing, *Pictorial Field Book of the War of 1812* (New York: Harper & Brothers, 1868), 473–93. See also Larry L. Nelson, *Fort Meigs: War of 1812 Battleground* (Columbus: Ohio Historical Society, 1999).
2. For this and the next two paragraphs, see "Embarkation Return of the Western Army, Commanded by Brig. General Procter on an Expedition to the Miamies, Amherstburg, 23rd April 1813," in *Michigan Pioneer and Historical Collections*, 40 vols. [hereafter cited as *MPHC*] (Lansing: Michigan Pioneer Historical Society, 1877–1929), 15: 276. See also *Select British Documents of the Canadian War of 1812, in 3 vols.*, ed. William Wood (Toronto: The Champlain Society, 1920), 2: 38.
3. [Daniel Lewis Cushing], *Fort Meigs and the War of 1812: Orderly Book of Cushing's Company, 2nd U.S. Artillery, April 1813–February 1813 and Personal Diary of Captain Daniel Cushing, October 1812–July 1813*, ed. Harlow Lindley (Columbus: Ohio Historical Society, 1975), 115–19; "Major Chambers to Secretary Freer, 13th May 1813" in *MPHC* 15: 289–91. For Harrison's remarks to Armstrong, see "William Henry Harrison to John Armstrong, February 24, 1813," *Messages and Letters of William Henry Harrison*, 2 vols., ed. Logan Esarey (Indianapolis: Indian Historical Commission, 1922), 2: 368–69.
4. George W. Cullum, *Campaigns of the War of 1812–1815 against Great Britain, Sketched and Criticized; With Brief Biographies of the American Engineers* (New York: James Miller, 1879), 386–90; [Cushing], *Fort Meigs and the War of 1812*, 116. For a description of the bombproofs based upon archaeological excavations conducted at the site in 1975 see *Field Reports in Archaeology, Fort Meigs*, ed. Randall L. Buchman (Defiance: Department of

History, Defiance College, 1975), 8–11.

5. "Diary of Samuel B. Walker, April-September 1813," MS, Loveland Historical Society, Loveland, OH, n.p.

6. For this and the next three paragraphs, see [Cushing], *Fort Meigs and the War of 1812*, 116–19, Cullum, *Campaigns of the War of 1812–1815*, 386–94 and "Minutes of the Principal Occurrences Which Have Taken Place during the Siege of Fort Meigs, from the 25th of April to the 9th of May; Taken Down by a Volunteer in the Fort," *Ohio Fredonian*, June 7, 1813. See also James Cochrane, "The War in Canada, 1812–1814," MS, Welch 41st Regimental Museum, Cardiff, Wales.

7. Cullum, *Campaigns of the War of 1812–1815*, 392–93.

8. For this and the next four paragraphs, see Larry L. Nelson, "Dudley's Defeat and the Relief of Fort Meigs during the War of 1812," *Register of the Kentucky Historical Society* 104 (2006): 5–42; Lieutenant Joseph Rogers Underwood, "Dudley's Defeat and Running the Gauntlet," typescript, MS 58, MSS Division, Kentucky Library, Western Kentucky University, Bowling Green.

9. For Clay's landing, see "Hawkins to Crittenden, August 1813," Green Clay Papers, MIC 163, Ohio History Connection, Columbus, OH; "James Young to Eliza Tunstal, May 10, 1813," James Young Love & Thomas Love Papers, MSS AL 897, Filson Historical Society, Louisville, Kentucky; see also Bill Pickard, "I'll Never be Noticed on a Galloping Horse: A War of 1812 Double Horse Burial at Fort Meigs," *Northwest Ohio History* 83 (2015): 20–32. For Miller's assault, see John Livingston, "Colonel William Christy," in *Portraits of Eminent Americans Now Living* (New York: R. Craighead, 1854), 241–49, and "Daniel Cushing to Snow Baker," in [Cushing], *Fort Meigs and the War of 1812*, 143–46.

10. "Exchange of Prisoners," in *MPHC* 15:285, "Return of Offices, Non-commissioned Officers & Privates taken from the Enemy of 5th May 1813 at the Battle of the Miamie," in *MPHC* 15: 278; see also Wood, *Select British Documents*, 39.

11. "Return of Killed, Wounded, Missing, and Prisoners of the Army under the Command of Brig. General Procter at the Battle at the Miamis 5th May 1813," in *MPHC* 15: 277; "Harrison to the Secretary of War, May 13th, 1813," in Esarey, *Messages and Letters*, 2: 442–47. The unnamed Kentucky officer's comments are found in "Historical Sketch of the Siege of Fort Meigs, Communicated by an Officer of the Kentucky Militia," *Analectic Magazine* 13 (1819): 508–17.

12. "General Orders, April 29th," in [Cushing], *Fort Meigs and the War of 1812*, 14–15.

13. *Memoir of Alexander Bourne, 1786–1849, of Indian Neck Wareham, Massachusetts and Chillicothe, Ohio*, ed. Nicholas Benton (New York: Middlesex House Press, 2000); Neil Salsich, ed., "The Siege of Fort Meigs, Year 1813: An Eyewitness Account by Alexander

Bourne," *Northwest Ohio Quarterly* 17 (1945): 139–54 and 18 (1946): 39–48.

14. "Major Chambers to Secretary Freer, 13th May 1813," in *MPHC* 15: 289–91.
15. [John Richardson], "A Canadian Campaign by a British Officer," *New Monthly Magazine and Literary Journal* 17 (1826): 541–48; 19 (1827): 162–70, 248–54, 448–57, 538–51. See also Major [John] Richardson, *War of 1812, First Series, Containing a Full and Detailed Narrative of the Operations of the Right Division of the Canadian Army* (Brockville, ON, 1842), and *Richardson's War of 1812, with Notes and a Life of the Author*, ed. Alexander Casselman (Toronto: Historical Publishing, 1902). For Richardson's literary career, see David R. Beasley, *The Canadian Don Quixote: The Life and Works of Major John Richardson, Canada's First Novelist* (Buffalo, NY: Davus Publishing, 2004).
16. Shadrach Byfield, *A Narrative of a Light Company Soldier's Service in the 41st Regiment during the Late American War* (Bradford, England: John Bubb, 1840).
17. "Statement of Militia Captains, 6th May 1813," and "Brig. Gen. Procter to Sir George Prevost, May 14th, 1813," in *MPHC* 15: 280 and 293–96.
18. Black Hawk, *Life of Ma-Ka-Tai-Me-She-Kia-Kiak or Black Hawk, Dictated by Himself* (Boston: Russell, Odiorn, & Metcalf, 1834); see also Daniel E. Harrison, "'They had won their battle, too': An Odawa Narrative of the War of 1812," in *Border Crossings: The Detroit River Region in the War of 1812*, ed. Denver Brunsman, Joel Stone, and Douglas D. Fisher (Detroit: Detroit Historical Society, 2012), 124–35; Carl Benn, *Native Memoirs from the War of 1812: Black Hawk and William Apess* (Baltimore: Johns Hopkins Press, 2014); *A Mohawk Memoir from the War of 1812, John Norton—Teyoninhokarawen*, ed. Carl Benn (Toronto: University of Toronto Press, 2019), and *The Journal of Major John Norton*, ed. Carl F. Klinck and James J. Talman (Toronto: The Champlain Society, 1970), 21–22.
19. [Cushing], "General Orders, April 29th," 14–15.
20. Cullum, *Campaigns of the War of 1812–1815*, 385–402.
21. Alfred M. Lorrain, *The Helm, the Sword, and the Cross: A Life Narrative* (Cincinnati: Poe & Hitchcock, 1862), 127–41.
22. A carcass was a powerful incendiary artillery shell fired from a mortar or howitzer.
23. Matthew Elliott. Mathew Elliot was an agent for the British Indian Department, the Crown agency responsible for maintaining Britain's diplomatic, economic, and military alliances with the region's Native peoples. See Reginald Horsman, *Matthew Elliott: Indian Agent* (Detroit: Wayne State University Press, 1964), especially 206–9.
24. Salsich, "The Siege of Fort Meigs, Year 1813," 17 (1945): 139–54 and 18 (1946): 39–48.
25. "Major Chambers to Secretary Freer, 13th May 1813," in *MPHC* 15: 289–92.
26. Donald F. Melhorn Jr., "A Splendid Man": Richardson, Fort Meigs, and the Story of Metoss," *Northwest Ohio History* 69 (1998): 133–60.

27. Dickson was a fur trader and interpreter for the British Indian Department.
28. [John Richardson], "A Canadian Campaign by a British Officer," *New Monthly Magazine and Literary Journal* 19 (1827): 161–70.
29. Byfield, *A Narrative of a Light Soldier's Service*, 67–71.
30. "Statement of Militia Captains, 6th May 1813," in *MPHC* 15: 280.
31. "Brig. Gen. Procter to Sir George Prevost, May 14th, 1813," in *MPHC* 15: 293–96.
32. Black Hawk, *Life of Black Hawk*, 40–43.

CHAPTER SEVEN. DUDLEY'S DEFEAT

1. Larry L. Nelson, "Dudley's Defeat and the Relief of Fort Meigs during the War of 1812," *Register of the Kentucky Historical Society* 104 (2006): 5–42; John Trowbridge, "Doomed to Their Fate: Kentuckians at Dudley's Defeat, 5 May 1813," *Kentucky Ancestors* 40 (2005): 150–68 and 191–204. The total American casualties at the French Town battle were 397 killed and 547 captured. See Ralph Naveaux, *Invaded on all Sides* (Marceline, MO: Walsworth Publishing, 2008), and Dennis M. Au, *War on the Raisin* (Monroe, MI: Monroe Historical Commission, 1981).
2. "Address and Resolution Respecting the Militia of Kentucky in the North Western Army," January 29, 1813" and "To the Militia of Kentucky in the N.W. Army, Encouragement of Volunteers in Kentucky," in *Document Transcriptions of the War of 1812 in the Northwest*, vol. 5, *The National Intelligencer Reports the War of 1812 in the Northwest*, ed. Richard C. Knopf (Columbus: Ohio Historical Society, 1961), pt. 2, 20–21; "Isaac Shelby to William Henry Harrison, January 30, 1813," "Shelby to Harrison, March 20, 1813," Shelby to Harrison, April 4, 1813," in *Messages and Letters of William Henry Harrison*, 2 vols., ed. Logan Esarey (Indianapolis: Indian Historical Commission, 1922), 2: 342–46, 392–95, 414–15.
3. The movements of Clay's brigade can be traced through the Green Clay Papers, William L. Clements Library, University of Michigan, Ann Arbor, and Clay's "General Orders," typescript, Filson Historical Society, Louisville, Kentucky. See also "Prologue to Victory: General Orders, Fort Meigs to Put-In-Bay, April-September 1813" [G. Glenn Clift, ed.], *Register of the Kentucky Historical Society* 60 (1962): 9–35.
4. See Nelson, "Dudley's Defeat," 15–20.
5. George W. Cullum, *Campaigns of the War of 1812–1815 against Great Britain, Sketched and Criticized; With Brief Biographies of the American Engineers* (New York: James Miller, 1879), 392–93.

6. "David Trimble to Micajah Harrison, June 7, 1813," David Trimble Collection, Ross County Historical Society, Chillicothe, OH.
7. Green Clay to William Henry Harrison, May 9, 1813, in *Document Transcriptions of the War of 1812 in the Northwest*, vol. 7, *Letters to the Secretary of War, 1813*, ed. Richard C. Knopf (Columbus: Ohio Historical Society, 1961), pt. 2: 97–98.
8. Lieutenant Joseph Rogers Underwood, "Dudley's Defeat and Running the Gauntlet," typescript, MS 58, MSS Division, Kentucky Library, Western Kentucky University, Bowling Green, Kentucky.
9. Capt. Leslie Combs, *Dudley's Defeat Opposite Fort Meigs May 5th, 1813* (Cincinnati: William Dodge, 1869); "Leslie Combs to Green Clay, May 6th, 1815," 6YY20, Lyman C. Draper Collection, State Historical Society of Wisconsin. See also *Narrative of the Life of General Leslie Combs* (New York: American Whig Review Office, 1852), 13–16.
10. "Asa K. Lewis to Brig. Genl. Green Clay," Ayer Manuscript Collection MSS 512, Newberry Library, Chicago.
11. Thomas Christian, *Campaign on the Ohio Frontier: Sortie at Fort Meigs, May 1813* (Cleveland: Western Reserve & Northern Ohio Historical Society, 1873); see also [Thomas Christian], "Campaign of 1813 on the Ohio River" *Register of the Kentucky Historical Society* 67 (1969): 260–68.
12. "Shawnee Chiefs to Harrison, 19 May 1813" enclosed in "John Wingate to Harrison 15 June 1813," in *The Papers of William Henry Harrison, 1800–1815*, 10 microfilm reels, ed. Douglas E. Clanin et al. (Indianapolis: Indiana Historical Society, 1993–1999) 8: 399–407.
13. Combs, *Dudley's Defeat.*
14. "Asa K. Lewis to Brig. Genl. Green Clay,"
15. A roundabout was a short-waisted, long sleeved jacket with a tall collar.
16. Thomas Christian, *Campaign on the Ohio Frontier: Sortie at Fort Meigs, May 1813* (Cleveland: Western Reserve & Northern Ohio Historical Society, 1873).
17. "Shawnee Chiefs to Harrison, 19 May 1813."

CHAPTER EIGHT. LIFE IN CAMP, SUMMER 1813

1. For this and the following paragraph, see [Daniel Lewis Cushing], *Fort Meigs and the War of 1812: Orderly Book of Cushing's Company, 2nd U.S. Artillery, April 1813–February 1813 and Personal Diary of Captain Daniel Cushing, October 1812–July 1813*, ed. Harlow Lindley (Columbus: Ohio Historical Society, 1975), 119–34, passim; "Harrison to the Secretary

of War, May 13th, 1813," in *Messages and Letters of William Henry Harrison*, 3 vols., ed. Logan Esarey (Indianapolis: Indian Historical Commission, 1922), 2: 422–27.

2. "Harrison to Poague, May 5th, 1813," "John Wingate to Harrison, May 28, 1813," "Harrison to R. M. Johnson, June 11, 1813," "Harrison to the Secretary of War, June 24, 1813," in *Messages and Letters*, 2: 448–49, 463–64, 468–70, 478–79; [Cushing], *Fort Meigs and the War of 1812*, 123,124, 126.
3. For this and the following paragraph, see [Cushing], *Fort Meigs and the War of 1812*, 26–48, passim.
4. Ibid., 4–36.
5. Ibid., 28–29.
6. "Harrison to the Secretary of War," June 11, 1813," *Messages and Letters*, 470–72; "A. Campbell to Thomas Worthington, June 13, 1813," in *Document Transcriptions of the War of 1812 in the Northwest*, vol. 3, *Thomas Worthington and the War of 1812*, ed. Richard C. Knopf (Columbus: Anthony Wayne Parkway Board and Ohio State Museum, 1957), 196; John C. Fredrikson, "The Pittsburgh Blues and the War of 1812: The Memoir of Private Nathaniel Vernon," *Pennsylvania History* 56 (1989): 196–212; Elder John Rogers, ed., *Autobiography of Elder Samuel Rogers* (Cincinnati: Standard Publishing Co., 1880), 18–19.
7. "Anderson to the Secretary of War, August 10, 1813," *Document Transcriptions of the War of 1812 in the Northwest*, vol. 7, *Letters to the Secretary of War, 1813*, ed. Richard C. Knopf (Columbus: Ohio Historical Society, 1961) 3: 58–59.
8. "Order Book of Peter Dudley's Company, Kentucky Militia," Kentucky Historical Society, Frankfort.
9. "Police of Fort Meigs, July 17, 1813" and "Guard Report of 18th July, 1813," Burton Collection, Detroit Public Library. Samuel R. Brown, *Views of the Campaigns of the North-Western Army* (Troy, NY: Francis Adancourt, 1814); Samuel R. Brown, *Views of Lake Erie* (Troy, NY: Francis Adancourt, 1814); Samuel L. Brown, *An Authentic History of the Second War for Independence* (Auburn, NY: J. G. Hathaway, 1815).
10. "Diary of Samuel B. Walker, April–September 1813," MS, Loveland Historical Society, Loveland, OH, n.p.
11. [James Mills], "A Regimental Book for the 1st Detachment of Ohio Militia containing Orders Received and Issued by Colonel James Mills of Butler County and State of Ohio, February 6 to August 4, 1813," typescript, Ohio History Connection, Columbus, and Cincinnati Historical Society, Cincinnati; "Fourth of July in Camp," *National Intelligencer*, July 29, 1813. The *National Intelligencer* was published in Washington, DC, under a variety of similar titles from 1800 to 1870. See William E. Ames, *A History of the National Intelligencer* (Chapel Hill: University of North Carolina Press, 1972).

12. "Order Book of Capt. Peter Dudley's Company."
13. "Police of Fort Meigs, July 17, 1813."
14. Brown, *Views of the Campaigns of the North-Western Army*, 113–19.
15. [Mills], "A Regimental Book for the 1st Detachment."
16. "Fourth of July in Camp."

CHAPTER NINE. SECOND SIEGE, JULY 20–28, 1813

1. Larry L. Nelson, "A Mysterious and Ambiguous Display of Tactics: The Second Siege of Fort Meigs, July 21–28, 1813" *Ohio History* 120 (2013): 5–28; Sandy Antal, *A Wampum Denied: Procter's War of 1812* (Ottawa: Carleton University Press, 1997), 241–73; David C. Skaggs and Gerald T. Altoff, *A Signal Victory: The Lake Erie Campaign, 1812–1813* (Annapolis: Naval Institute Press, 1997), 58–88.
2. "Procter to Unaddressed, June 15, 1813," "Procter to McDonall, July 4, 1813," and "Procter to Prevost, July 4, 1813," in *Michigan Pioneer and Historical Collections*, 40 vols. (Lansing: Michigan Pioneer Historical Society, 1877–1929) [hereafter cited as *MPHC*] 15: 317–18, 330–31, 331–32.
3. "Procter to Myers, May 23, 1813," "Brig. Gen. Vincent to Unaddressed, June 2, 1813," "Procter to Prevost, June 4, 1813," and "To Procter without signature, July 11, 1813," in *MPHC*, 15: 301–2, 308–9, 319, 336–37.
4. "Procter to Unaddressed, June 15, 1813," "Procter to McDonall, July 4, 1813," and "Proctor to Prevost, July 4, 1813," in *MPHC* 15: 317–18, 330–31, 331–32.
5. "Procter to McDonall, June 10, 1813," "Procter to unaddressed, June 15th, 1813," and "Procter to Prevost, July 4th, 181," in *MPHC* 15: 17–18, 330–31, 31–32.
6. "Mr. Dickson to Secretary Freer, June 23, 1813," "Captain Roberts to Secretary Freer, June 23rd, 1813," Capt. Roberts to Secretary Freer, June 25th, 1813," and "Procter to McDonall, June 29, 1813," in *MPHC* 15: 321–22, 322–23, 325–26. See also L. A. Tohill, "Robert Dickson, British Fur Trader on the Upper Mississippi," *North Dakota Historical Quarterly* 2 (1928–29): 2–29, 83–128, 182–203.
7. "Major General De Rottenburg to unaddressed, August 1, 1813," in *MPHC* 15: 345.
8. For this and the following four paragraphs, see [Daniel Lewis Cushing], *Fort Meigs and the War of 1812: Orderly Book of Cushing's Company, 2nd U.S. Artillery, April 1813–February 1813 and Personal Diary of Captain Daniel Cushing, October 1812–July 1813*, ed. Harlow Lindley (Columbus: Ohio Historical Society, 1975), 134–39.
9. [Cushing], *Fort Meigs and the War of 1812*, 136–37; Bruce Bowlus, "A Signal Victory: The

Battle for Fort Stephenson, August 1–2, 1813," *Northwest Ohio History* 63 (1991): 43–57.

10. "An Interesting Journal of the Second Siege of Fort Meigs, by an Officer of Respectability at that Place," *Weekly Register*, September 14, 1813; Major [John] Richardson, *War of 1812, First Series: Containing a Full and Detailed Narrative of the Operations of the Right Division of the Canadian Army* (Brockville, ON, 1842).
11. "An Interesting Journal of the Second Siege of Fort Meigs."
12. Richardson, *War of 1812, First Series*, 104–5.

CHAPTER TEN. REDUCTION AND ABANDONMENT

1. David Curtis Skaggs, "Gaining Naval Dominance on Lake Erie," in *The Battle of Lake Erie and Its Aftermath: A Reassessment*, ed. David Curtis Skaggs (Kent: Kent State University Press, 2013), 32–43, and Dennis Carter Edwards, "The Battle of Lake Erie and Its Consequences: Denouement of the British Right Division and Abandonment of the Western District to American Troops, 1813–1815," in *War on the Great Lakes: Essays Commemorating the 175th Anniversary of the Battle of Lake Erie*, ed. William Jeffrey Welsh and David Curtis Skaggs (Kent, OH: Kent State University Press, 1991), 41–55.
2. "Harrison to the Secretary of War, July 6, 1813," "Harrison to Governor Shelby, 20th July, 1813," in *Messages and Letters of William Henry Harrison*, 2 vols., ed. Logan Esarey (Indianapolis: Indiana Historical Commission, 1922), 2: 483–84 and 493–94.
3. "Harrison to Clay, August 15, 1813," William Henry Harrison Papers and Documents, M0364, Indiana Historical Society, Indianapolis; "Clay to Harrison, August 19, 1813," and "Orders to Green Clay, August 20, 1813," in *The Papers of William Henry Harrison, 1800–1815*, 10 microfilm reels, ed. Douglas Clanin et al. (Indianapolis: Indiana Historical Society, 1993–1999), 9: 1–5 and 9: 10.
4. "Harrison to the Secretary of War, August 22, 1813," in Esarey, *Messages and Letters*, 2: 525–26. See also David Curtis Skaggs, "Invading Canada: Joint Operations Across Lake Erie," in Skaggs, *The Battle of Lake Erie and Its Aftermath*, 62–80; David C. Skaggs, "River Raisin Redeemed: William Henry Harrison, Oliver Hazard Perry, and the Midwestern Campaign, 1813," *Northwest Ohio History* 77 (2010): 67–84.
5. "Extract of a Letter from a Volunteer in Captain Dudley's company, to his friend at this place, dated "Camp Meigs, Sept. 1," (Worthington) *Western Intelligencer*, December 29, 1813, Joseph H. Larwill, "Journal of Joseph H. Larwill relating to occurrences transpired in the service of the U States commencing April 5, 1812," MS, Burton Historical Collection, Detroit Public Library, Detroit, MI.

6. "Duncan McArthur to wife, September 12th, 1813," Duncan McArthur Papers, MSS 31831, Manuscript Division, Library of Congress. See also Duncan McArthur Papers, MIC 47, Ohio History Connection, Columbus, OH.
7. "Diary of Capt. James Bonner, Penn. Vol., War of 1812, from October 3rd 1813 to 22d April, 1814—Upper Sandusky and Fort Meigs," *Western Reserve Historical Society Tract no. 49* (Cleveland: Western Reserve Historical Society, 1879), 100–1; "Urbana, Ohio Oct. 11," (Richmond, Virginia) *Enquirer*, November 11, 1814.
8. "Extract of a Letter from a Volunteer in Captain Dudley's company, to his friend at this place"; "Harrison to McArthur, September 15, 1813," McArthur Papers, Library of Congress; Robert Breckenridge McAfee Papers, 1813–1859, Filson Historical Society; see also [Robert McAfee], "The McAfee Papers: Book and Journal or Robt. B. McAfee's Mounted Company in Col. Richard M. Johnson's Regiment, from May 19th, 1813, Including Order &c.," *Register of the Kentucky Historical Society* 26 (1928): 4–23, 107–36, and 237–48. Robert B. McAfee, *History of the Late War in the Western Country* (Lexington, KY: Worsley & Smith, 1816).
9. "Selections from the Gano Papers," *Quarterly Publication of the Historical and Philosophical Society of Ohio* 18 (1923): 17–18 and 35–36.
10. Nicholas Benton, ed., *Memoir of Alexander Bourne, 1786–1849, of Indian Neck Wareham, Massachusetts and Chillicothe, Ohio* (New York: Middlesex House Press, 2000).
11. "Extract of a Letter from a Volunteer in Captain Dudley's Company."
12. "Harrison to McArthur, September 15, 1813."
13. "The McAfee Papers," 115–17.
14. "Col. John Delong to Maj. Gen. John S. Gano, December 30, 1813, Selections from the Gano Papers," *Quarterly Publication of the Historical and Philosophical Society of Ohio* 18 (1923): 17–18.
15. "General Orders, Head Quarters Ohio Militia, Lower Sandusky, February 2nd, 1814, Selections from the Gano Papers," *Quarterly Publication of the Historical and Philosophical Society of Ohio* 18 (1923): 35–36.
16. Benton, *Memoir of Alexander Bourne*, 62.

CHAPTER ELEVEN. CUSHING'S DIARY

1. Daniel Cushing Collection, MSS 5945, Daniel Cushing Papers, MSS 4678, and Daniel Cushing Correspondence, MSS 3447, Ohio History Connection, Columbus, OH. [Daniel Cushing] *Orderly Book of Cushing's Company, 2nd U.S. Artillery, April 1813–February 1814*

and Personal Diary of Captain Daniel Cushing, October 1812–July 1813, ed. Harlow Lindley (Columbus: Ohio Historical Society, 1975), 141–46, and P. L Rainwater, "The Siege of Fort Meigs," *The Mississippi Valley Historical Review* 19 (1932): 261–64.

2. [Daniel Lewis Cushing], "Captain Cushing in the War of 1812," ed. Harlow Lindley, *Ohio Historical Collections*, vol. 11 (Columbus: Ohio State Archaeological and Historical Society, 1944). For Lindley's career, see R. E. Banta, *Indiana Authors and Their Books, 1816–1916* (Crawfordsville, IN: Wabash College, 1949), 192.
3. [Daniel Lewis Cushing], *Fort Meigs and the War of 1812: Orderly Book of Cushing's Company, 2nd U.S. Artillery, April 1813–February 1813 and Personal Diary of Captain Daniel Cushing, October 1812–July 1813*, ed. Harlow Lindley (Columbus: Ohio Historical Society, 1975).
4. [Cassius Marcellus Clay], *Oration of Cassius Marcellus Clay before the Maumee Valley Historical and Monumental Association, of Toledo, Ohio, at Put-in-Bay Island, Lake Erie, on the 10th of September, 1891, The Anniversary of the Capture of the British Fleet by Oliver Hazard Perry* (Philadelphia: J. B. Lippincott, 1891), 7.
5. "James Taylor Eubank Letterbook," Kentucky Historical Society. See also "Letterbook of James Taylor Eubank, *Register of the Kentucky Historical Society* 19 (1921): 54–62.
6. "Copy of Daniel Cushing, Captain 2nd U. S. Artillery at the Sieges of Fort Meigs, 1813," War of 1812 Papers, Genealogical and Local History Collections, Sm. Coll. 14, Toledo–Lucas County Public Library.
7. A pintle was a large spike attached to the cannon's limber. The limber was a two-wheeled cart that allowed the gun to be towed, containing its ammunition and the tools used to fire and maintain the piece.
8. Cushing is referring to the encampment's artillery park. When encamped, the army placed the artillery and its crews together in a central location or "park," where they could be quickly deployed in case of attack.
9. The Reverend Joseph Badger, identified as "Mr. Baggin" in the 1908 transcription. Badger was an early missionary in the Connecticut Western Reserve and served as chaplain in Harrison's army. See Joseph Badger, *Memoir of Joseph Badger* (New York: C. S. Francis, 1854), and Bryon R. Long, "Joseph Badger, the First Missionary of the Western Reserve," *Ohio Archaeological and Historical Quarterly* 1 (1917): 1–42.
10. This and the entry for April 27 are taken from the James Taylor Eubank Letterbook; see "James Taylor Eubank Letterbook," Kentucky Historical Society.
11. Roche de Bout is a large limestone outcropping in the Maumee River opposite present-day Waterville, OH.

Bibliography

MANUSCRIPT REPOSITORIES

Burton Historical Collection, Detroit Public Library: Green Clay Papers; "Journal of Joseph H. Larwill relating to occurrences transpired in the service of the U States commencing April 5, 1812."

Center for Archival Collections, Jerome Library, Bowling Green State University: War of 1812 Papers.

Cincinnati Historical Society: [James Mills], "A Regimental Book for the 1st Detachment of Ohio Militia containing Orders Received and Issued by Colonel James Mills of Butler County and State of Ohio, February 6 to August 4, 1813," typescript.

Filson Historical Society: James Young Love & Thomas Love Papers; Robert Breckenridge McAfee Papers, 1813–1859.

Kentucky Library, Western Kentucky University: "Lieutenant Joseph Rogers Underwood, Dudley's Defeat and Running the Gauntlet," typescript.

Library of Congress, Washington, DC: Duncan McArthur Papers.

Loveland Historical Society, Loveland, Ohio: "Diary of Samuel B. Walker, April-September 1813."

Martin F. Schimdt Research Library, Kentucky Historical Society: James Taylor Eubank Letterbook; "Order Book of Captain Peter Dudley's Company of Kentucky Militia"; Robert McAfee Papers.

Newberry Library, Chicago: Ayer Manuscript Collection.

National Archives and Records Administration, Washington, DC: War of 1812 Pension Records.

Ohio History Connection:

[James Mills], "A Regimental Book for the 1st Detachment of Ohio Militia containing Orders Received and Issued by Colonel James Mills of Butler County and State of Ohio, February 6 to August 4, 1813," typescript; Daniel Cushing Collection; Daniel Cushing Papers; Daniel Cushing Correspondence; Duncan McArthur Papers; Green Clay Papers; Sergeant Greenbury Keen Journal, 1812.

Rare Book and Special Collections, Thompson Library, The Ohio State University: "Samuel Bayles Book of Orders, April 23–August 12, 1813."

Ross County (Ohio) Historical Society, Chillicothe, Ohio: David Trimble Collection.

State Historical Society of Wisconsin: "Journal of the Northwestern Campaign of 1812–13, under Major-General William H. Harrison, by Eleazer D. Wood"; Lyman C. Draper Collection.

Toledo–Lucas County Public Library, Genealogical and Local History Collection: War of 1812 Papers; "Enrollment of Indians in the Military Service of the United States with the Army under the Command of General Harrison Operating in the Valley of the Maumee in the War of 1812, July 20–Aug. 21, 1813."

Welch 41st Regimental Museum, Cardiff, Wales: James Cochran, "The War in Canada, 1812–1814."

William L. Clements Library, University of Michigan, Ann Arbor: Green Clay Papers.

PUBLICATIONS

Althoff, Gerald T., *Amongst My Best Men: African Americans in the War of 1812*, Put-In- Bay, OH: The Perry Group, 1993.

Allen, Robert S., *His Majesty's Indian Allies: British Indian Policy in Defence of Canada, 1774–1815*, Toronto: Dundurn Press, 1992.

Antal, Sandy, *A Wampum Denied: Procter's War of 1812*, Ottawa: Carleton University Press, 1997.

Au, Dennis M., *War on the Raisin*, Monroe, MI: Monroe Historical Commission, 1981.

Badger, Joseph, *Memoir of Joseph Badger*, New York: C. S. Francis, 1854.

Bald, Clever F., "Fort Miamis, Outpost of Empire," *Northwest Ohio Quarterly* 16 (1944): 75–111.

Banta, R. E., *Indiana Authors and Their Books, 1816–1916*, Crawfordsville, IN: Wabash College, 1949.

Barekman, June, ed., *Captain John Barrickman's Diary-Account and General Record Book in the War of 1812*, Chicago: Genealogical Services Publications, n.d.

Benn, Carl, *Native Memoirs from the War of 1812: Black Hawk and William Apess*, Baltimore: Johns Hopkins Press, 2014.

Benn, Carl, ed., *A Mohawk Memoir from the War of 1812, John Norton—Teyoninhokarawen*, Toronto: University of Toronto Press, 2019.

Benton, Nicholas, ed., *Memoir of Alexander Bourne, 1786–1849, of Indian Neck Wareham, Massachusetts and Chillicothe, Ohio*, New York: Middlesex House Press, 2000.

Black Hawk, *Life of Ma-Ka-Tai-Me-She-Kia-Kiak or Black Hawk, Dictated by Himself*, Boston: Russell, Odiorn, & Metcalf, 1834

Bonner, James, "Diary of Capt. James Bonner, Penn. Vol., War of 1812, from October 3rd 1813 to 22nd April, 1814—Upper Sandusky and Fort Meigs," *Western Reserve Historical Society Tract no. 49*, Cleveland: Western Reserve Historical Society, 1879.

Bottiger, Patrick, *The Borderland of Fear: Vincennes, Prophetstown, and the Invasion of the Miami Homeland*, Lincoln: University of Nebraska Press, 2016.

Bowlus, Bruce, "A Signal Victory: The Battle for Fort Stephenson, August 1–2, 1813," *Northwest Ohio History* 63 (1991): 43–57.

Brown, George, *Recollections of Itinerant Life: Including Early Reminiscences*, Cincinnati: R. W. Carroll & Co., 1866

Brunsman, Denver, Joel Stone, and Douglas D. Fisher, eds., *Border Crossings: The Detroit River Region in the War of 1812*, Detroit: Detroit Historical Society, 2012.

Buchman, Randall L., ed., *Field Reports in Archaeology, Fort Meigs*, Defiance, OH: Department of History, Defiance College, 1975.

Butler, Stuart, *Patriots and Heroic Soldiers: Gen. Joel Leftwich and the Virginia Brigade in the War of 1812*, Berwyn Heights, MD: Heritage Books, 2008.

Byfield, Shadrach, *A Narrative of a Light Company Soldier's Service in the 41st Regiment during the Late American War*, Bradford, England: John Bubb, 1840.

Carter-Edwards, Dennis, "The War of 1812 along the Detroit Frontier: A Canadian Perspective," *Michigan Historical Review* 13 (1987): 25–50.

Carter-Edwards, Dennis, "The Battle of Lake Erie and Its Consequences: Denouement of the British Right Division and Abandonment of the Western District to American Troops, 1813–1815," in *War on the Great Lakes: Essays Commemorating the 175th Anniversary of the*

Battle of Lake Erie, ed. William Jeffrey Welsh and David Curtis Skaggs, Kent, OH: Kent State University Press, 1991, 41–55.

Casselman, Alexander, ed., *Richardson's War of 1812, with Notes and a Life of the Author*, Toronto: Historical Publishing, 1902.

Christian, Thomas, *Campaign on the Ohio Frontier: Sortie at Fort Meigs, May 1813*, Cleveland: Western Reserve & Northern Ohio Historical Society, 1873.

[Christian, Thomas], "Campaign of 1813 on the Ohio River," *Register of the Kentucky Historical Society* 67 (1969): 260–68.

Clanin, Douglas E., et al., eds., *The Papers of William Henry Harrison, 1800–1815*, 10 microfilm reels, Indianapolis: Indiana Historical Society, 1993–1999.

Clay, Cassius Marcellus, *Oration of Cassius Marcellus Clay before the Maumee Valley Historical and Monumental Association of Toledo, Ohio, at Put-in-Bay Island, Lake Erie, on the 10th of September, 1891, the Anniversary of the Capture of the British Fleet by Oliver Hazard Perry*, Philadelphia: J. B. Lippincott, 1891.

Combs, Capt. Leslie, *Dudley's Defeat Opposite Fort Meigs May 5th, 1813*, Cincinnati: William Dodge, 1869.

Cullum, George W., *Campaigns of the War of 1812–1815 against Great Britain, Sketched and Criticized; With Brief Biographies of the American Engineers*, New York: James Miller, 1879.

Cushing, Daniel Lewis, *Fort Meigs and the War of 1812: Orderly Book of Cushing's Company, 2nd U.S. Artillery, April 1813–February 1813 and Personal Diary of Captain Daniel Cushing, October 1812–July 1813*, ed. Harlow Lindley, Columbus: Ohio Historical Society, 1975.

Douglas, Ben, *History of Wayne County, Ohio from the Days of the Pioneers and the First Settlers to the Present Day*, Indianapolis: R. Douglas, 1878.

Drake, Frederick C., "Artillery and Its Influence on Naval Tactics: Reflections on the Battle of Lake Erie" in *War on the Great Lakes: Essays Commemorating the 175th Anniversary of the Battle of Lake Erie*, ed. William Jeffrey Welsh and David Curtis Skaggs, Kent, OH: Kent State University Press, 1991, 17–29.

Duane, William, *A Handbook for Infantry: Containing the First Principles of Military Discipline Founded upon Rational Method*, Philadelphia: Printed by the Author, 1813.

Edmunds, R. David, *The Shawnee Prophet*, Lincoln: University of Nebraska Press, 1983.

Esarey, Logan, ed., *Messages and Letters of William Henry Harrison*, 2 vols., Indianapolis: Indian Historical Commission, 1922.

Fredrikson, John C., "The Pittsburgh Blues and the War of 1812: The Memoir of Private Nathaniel Vernon," *Pennsylvania History* 56 (1989): 196–212.

Gilmore, William Edward, *Life of Edward Tiffin, First Governor of Ohio*, Chillicothe, OH: Horney & Son, 1897.

Gilpin, Alec R., *The War of 1812 in the Old Northwest*, East Lansing: Michigan State University Press, 1958.

Graves, Dianne, *In the Midst of Alarms: The Untold Story of Women and the War of 1812*, Montreal: Robin Brass Studio, 2007.

Gurley, L. B., *Memoir of Rev. William Gurley, Late of Milan, Ohio, a Local Minister of the Methodist Episcopal Church*, Cincinnati: R. P. Thompson, 1856.

Hallaman, Emanuel, "The British Invasions of Ohio in 1813 during the War of 1812," MA Thesis, The Ohio State University, 1956.

Harrison, Daniel E., "'They had won their battle, too': An Odawa Narrative of the War of 1812," in *Border Crossings: The Detroit River Region in the War of 1812*, ed. Denver Brunsman, Joel Stone, and Douglas D. Fisher, Detroit: Detroit Historical Society, 2012, 124–35.

Hickey, Donald R., *The War of 1812: A Forgotten Conflict*, Urbana: University of Illinois Press, 1989.

"Historical Sketch of the Siege of Fort Meigs, Communicated by an Officer of the Kentucky Militia," *Analectic Magazine* 13 (1819): 508–17.

Holmes, Richard, *Redcoat: The British Soldier in the Age of Horse and Musket*, New York: W.W. Norton & Company, 2001.

Horsman, Reginald, *The Causes of the War of 1812*, Philadelphia: University of Pennsylvania Press, 1962.

Horsman, Reginald, *Matthew Elliott: Indian Agent*, Detroit: Wayne State University Press, 1964.

Horsman, Reginald, "Western War Aims, 1811–1812," *Indiana Magazine of History* 53 (1957): 9–18.

Howe, Henry, *Historical Collections of Ohio*, Cincinnati: Bradley & Anthony, 1848.

Jortner, Adam, *The Gods of Prophetstown: The Battle of Tippecanoe and the Holy War for the American Frontier*, New York: Oxford University Press, 2011.

[Keen, Greenbury], *To the Rapids: A Journal of a Tour of Duty in the Northwestern Army under the Command of Maj. General William H. Harrison*, Sally Young, Robert Reid, Ronald Reid, eds., Columbus, 1990.

Kirkpatrick, David, *The War of 1812 in the West: From Fort Detroit to New Orleans*, Yardley, PA: Westholme Publishing, 2019.

Klinck, Carl F., and James J. Talman, eds., *The Journal of Major John Norton*, Toronto: The Champlain Society, 1970.

Knopf, Richard C., ed., *Document Transcriptions of the War of 1812 in the Northwest*, 10 vols., Columbus: Ohio Historical Society, 1957–1962.

Le Roy, Paul, *Papers on the War of 1812 in the Northwest, no. 2: Some Social Aspects of the Life of Soldiers and the Organization of the Soldiers in the War of 1812*, Columbus: Anthony

Wayne Park Board and The Ohio State Museum, 1958.

"Letterbook of James Taylor Eubank," *Register of the Kentucky Historical Society* 19 (1921): 54–62.

Linklater, Andro, *Measuring America: How an Untamed Wilderness Shaped the United States and Fulfilled the Promise of Democracy*, New York: Walker and Company, 2002.

Livingston, John, "Colonel William Christy," in *Portraits of Eminent Americans Now Living*, New York: R. Craighead, 1854, 241–49.

Long, Bryon R., "Joseph Badger, the First Missionary of the Western Reserve," *Ohio Archaeological and Historical Quarterly* 1 (1917): 1–42.

Lorrain, Alfred M., *The Helm, the Sword, and the Cross: A Life Narrative*, Cincinnati: Poe & Hitchcock, 1862.

Lorrain, Rev. A. M., "Rural Oration," *The Ladies Repository; A Monthly Periodical Devoted to Literature, Art, and Religion* 11 (1851): 257–61.

Lorraine, A. M., "The Captured Bugle," *Ladies Repository, and Gatherings of the West* 1 (1841): 278–79.

Lorraine, A. M., "The Sequel," *Ladies Repository, and Gatherings of the West* 5 (1845): 107–13.

Lossing, Benson, *Pictorial Field Book of the War of 1812*, New York: Harper & Brothers, 1868.

Luxon, Norval, *Niles Weekly Register: News Magazine of the Nineteenth Century*, Baton Rouge: Louisiana State University Press, 1947.

[McAfee, Robert], "The McAfee Papers: Book and Journal of Robt. B. McAfee's Mounted Company in Col. Richard M. Johnson's Regiment, from May 19th, 1813, Including Orders &c.," *Register of the Kentucky Historical Society* 26 (1928): 4–23, 107–36, and 237–48.

McAfee, Robert B., *History of the Late War in the Western Country*, Lexington, KY: Worsley & Smith, 1816.

Melhorn, Donald F., Jr., "'A Splendid Man': Richardson, Fort Meigs, and the Story of Metoss," *Northwest Ohio History* 69 (1998): 133–60.

Michigan Pioneer and Historical Collections, 40 vols., Lansing: Michigan Pioneer Historical Society, 1877–1929.

Narrative of the Life of General Leslie Combs, New York: American Whig Review Office, 1852.

Naveaux, Ralph, *Invaded on All Sides*, Marceline, MO: Walsworth Publishing Co., 2008.

Nelson, Larry L., "Dudley's Defeat and the Relief of Fort Meigs during the War of 1812," *Register of the Kentucky Historical Society* 104 (2006): 5–42.

Nelson, Larry L., *Fort Meigs: 1812 Battleground*, Columbus: Ohio Historical Society, 1999.

Nelson, Larry L., "The Mapping of Fort Meigs," *Northwest Ohio Quarterly* 58 (1986): 123–42.

Nelson, Larry L., "The Maumee River Campaign, 1812–1813," in *The Battle of Lake Erie and Its Aftermath: A Reassessment*, ed. David Curtis Skaggs, Kent, OH: Kent State University

Press, 2013, 11–31.

Nelson, Larry L., "A Mysterious and Ambiguous Display of Tactics: The Second Siege of Fort Meigs, July 21–28, 1813," *Ohio History* 120 (2013): 5–28.

Owens, Robert M., *Mr. Jefferson's Hammer: William Henry Harrison and the Origins of American Indian Policy*, Norman: University of Oklahoma Press, 2011.

Perkins, Bradford, ed., *The Causes of the War of 1812: National Honor or National Interest?* New York: Holt, Rinehart and Winston, 1962.

Pickard, Bill, "I'll Never Be Noticed on a Galloping Horse: A War of 1812 Double Horse Burial at Fort Meigs," *Northwest Ohio History* 83 (2015): 20–32.

Pirtle, Alfred, *The Battle of Tippecanoe*, Louisville, KY: John P. Morton & Co., 1900.

"Prologue to Victory: General Orders Fort Meigs to Put-In-Bay April-September 1813," *Register of the Kentucky Historical Society* 60 (1962): 9–35.

Rainwater, P. L., "The Siege of Fort Meigs," *The Mississippi Valley Historical Review* 19 (1932): 261–64.

[Richardson, John], "A Canadian Campaign by a British Officer," *New Monthly Magazine and Literary Journal* 17 (1826): 541–48; 19 (1827): 162–70, 248–54, 448–57, 538–51.

Richardson, Major [John], *War of 1812, First Series, Containing a Full and Detailed Narrative of the Operations of the Right Division of the Canadian Army*, Brockville, ON, 1842.

Salsich, Neil, ed., "The Siege of Fort Meigs, Year 1813: An Eyewitness Account by Alexander Bourne," *Northwest Ohio Quarterly* 17 (1945): 139–54 and 18 (1946): 39–48.

"Selections from the Gano Papers," *Quarterly Publication of the Historical and Philosophical Society of Ohio* 16 (1921): 25–80; 17 (1922): 77–104; 18 (1923): 5–36.

Skaggs, David Curtis, ed., *The Battle of Lake Erie and Its Aftermath: A Reassessment*, Kent, OH: Kent State University Press, 2013.

Skaggs, David Curtis, "Gaining Naval Dominance on Lake Erie," in *The Battle of Lake Erie and its Aftermath: A Reassessment*, ed. David Curtis Skaggs, Kent, OH: Kent State University Press, 2013, 32–43.

Skaggs, David Curtis, "Invading Canada: Joint Operations across Lake Erie," in *The Battle of Lake Erie and Its Aftermath: A Reassessment*, ed. David Curtis Skaggs, Kent: Kent State University Press, 2013, 62–80.

Skaggs, David C., "River Raisin Redeemed: William Henry Harrison, Oliver Hazard Perry, and the Midwestern Campaign, 1813," *Northwest Ohio History* 77 (2010): 67–84.

Skaggs, David C., *William, Henry Harrison and the Conquest of the Ohio Country: Frontier Fighting in the War of 1812*, Baltimore: Johns Hopkins University Press, 2014.

Skaggs, David C., and Gerald T. Altoff, *A Signal Victory: The Lake Erie Campaign, 1812–1813*, Annapolis: Naval Institute Press, 1997.

Sugden, John, *Tecumseh: A Life*, New York: Henry Holt and Company, 1997.

Tohill, L. A., "Robert Dickson, British Fur Trader on the Upper Mississippi," *North Dakota Historical Quarterly* 2 (1928–29): 2–29, 83–128, 182–203.

Trowbridge, John, "Doomed to Their Fate: Kentuckians at Dudley's Defeat, 5 May 1813," *Kentucky Ancestors* 40 (2005): 150–68 and 191–204.

Wall, J. Sutton, "Sketch of Colonel Joel Ferree's Regiment in the War of 1812," *Western Pennsylvania History* 11 (1928): 55–61.

Wallace, Lee A., Jr., "The Petersburg Volunteers—1812–1813," *Virginia Magazine of History and Biography* 82 (1974): 458–85.

Watkins, Eugene D., "Cousin Jonathan: The Common United States Soldier in the War of 1812," Ph.D. diss., University of Toledo, Toledo, OH, 2007.

Welsh, William Jeffrey, and David Curtis Skaggs, eds., *War on the Great Lakes: Essays Commemorating the 175th Anniversary of the Battle of Lake Erie*, Kent, OH: Kent State University Press, 1991.

Williams, Samuel, *Two Campaigns in the War of 1812–13*, Cincinnati: Robert Clarke & Co., 1871.

Williams, Samuel, *The Samuel Williams Memoir*, ed. Patricia Fife Medert, Chillicothe, OH: Ross County Historical Society, 2000.

Wood, Eleazer Derby, *Journal of the Northwestern Campaign of 1812–1813 under Major-General Wm. H. Harrison by Eleazar [*sic*] D. Wood*, ed. Robert B. Boehm and Randall L. Buchman, Defiance, OH: Defiance College Press, 1975.

Wood, William, ed., *Select British Documents of the Canadian War of 1812*, 3 vols., Toronto: The Champlain Society, 1920.

Yanik, Anthony J., *The Fall and Recapture of Detroit in the War of 1812: In Defense of William Hull*, Detroit: Wayne State University Press, 2011.

Index

C

N

O

Y